Prisons, Punishment and the Pursuit of Security

Critical Criminological Perspectives

The Palgrave *Critical Criminological Perspectives* book series aims to showcase the importance of critical criminological thinking when examining problems of crime, social harm and criminal and social justice. Critical perspectives have been instrumental in creating new research agendas and areas of criminological interest. By challenging state defined concepts of crime and rejecting positive analyses of criminality, critical criminological approaches continually push the boundaries and scope of criminology, creating new areas of focus and developing new ways of thinking about, and responding to, issues of social concern at local, national and global levels. Recent years have witnessed a flourishing of critical criminological narratives and this series seeks to capture the original and innovative ways that these discourses are engaging with contemporary issues of crime and justice.

Series editors:
Professor Reece Walters
Faculty of Law, Queensland University of Technology, Australia

Dr. Deborah Drake
Department of Social Policy and Criminology, The Open University, UK

Deborah Drake
PRISONS, PUNISHMENT AND THE PURSUIT OF SECURITY

Maggi O'Neill and Lizzie Seal (*editors*)
TRANSGRESSIVE IMAGINATIONS
Crime, Deviance and Culture

Critical Criminological Perspectives
Series Standing Order ISBN 9780–230–36045–7   hardback
(*outside North America only*)

You can receive future titles in this series as they are published by placing a standing order. Please contact your bookseller or, in case of difficulty, write to us at the address below with your name and address, the title of the series and the ISBN quoted above.

Customer Services Department, Macmillan Distribution Ltd, Houndmills, Basingstoke, Hampshire RG21 6XS, England

Prisons, Punishment and the Pursuit of Security

Deborah H. Drake
Lecturer in Criminology,
Department of Social Policy and Criminology,
The Open University, UK

First published 2012 by
PALGRAVE MACMILLAN

Palgrave Macmillan in the UK is an imprint of Macmillan Publishers Limited, registered in England, company number 785998, of Houndmills, Basingstoke, Hampshire RG21 6XS.

Palgrave Macmillan in the US is a division of St Martin's Press LLC, 175 Fifth Avenue, New York, NY 10010.

Palgrave Macmillan is the global academic imprint of the above companies and has companies and representatives throughout the world.

Palgrave® and Macmillan® are registered trademarks in the United States, the United Kingdom, Europe and other countries.

ISBN 978–0–230–28293–3

This book is printed on paper suitable for recycling and made from fully managed and sustained forest sources. Logging, pulping and manufacturing processes are expected to conform to the environmental regulations of the country of origin.

A catalogue record for this book is available from the British Library.

Library of Congress Cataloging-in-Publication Data
Drake, Deborah.
Prisons, punishment and the pursuit of security / Deborah Drake.
p. cm.
ISBN 978–0–230–28293–3
1. Prisons—England. 2. Justice, Administration of—England.
3. Prisons—United States. 4. Justice, Administration of—
United States. I. Title.
HV8424.A62012 .D73 2012
365'.942–dc23   2012010269

10   9   8   7   6   5   4   3   2   1
21 20 19 18 17 16 15 14 13 12

Printed and bound in the United States of America

Contents

List of Tables and Figures

Tables

Figures

Acknowledgements

I am immeasurably grateful to my colleagues in the Department of Social Policy and Criminology at the Open University. It is just the right environment for nurturing critical scholarship and I feel privileged to work with you all. In particular, I want to thank those who provided encouragement throughout the writing process and took over some of my other work so that I could concentrate on finishing this book: Abigail Rowe, Louise Westmarland, Allan Cochrane, Ross Fergusson, Damon Briggs, Kate Smith, Katy Simmons, Ali Andrew, Hilary Canneaux, Adam Nightingale, Gerry Mooney, Sarah Neal and Graham Pike. I also want to thank Donna Collins for her expert administrative support and her constant willingness to help with whatever I land on her desk.

In terms of the research on which this book draws I am grateful to Professor Alison Liebling who supervised my PhD research. I thank her for sharing her expertise and knowledge on prison research. Her experience of empirically based research in difficult settings is an invaluable resource that I benefitted from in numerous ways. Thanks also to Linda Durie for her wonderful support and assistance with the transcripts and to Mary Gower and Stuart Stone at the Radzinowicz Library for their expertise and constant encouragement.

I am grateful also to the Directorate of High Security, which commissioned the Prisoners' Experiences and Quality of Life in Dispersal Prisons project, and to the steering group that consulted on it. I would also like to thank the nine members of staff who worked on this project with me. I hope your experiences of the research process were rewarding. It is unfortunate that there was no way to continue what we started.

I also extend my immense gratitude to the prisoners, discipline and civilian staff, governors and senior managers who contributed to this research in both direct and indirect ways. I am grateful to senior managers in the Directorate of High Security for grating access to undertake the research and I would like to thank every individual who gave up their time for an interview, informal chat or to help facilitate the research in other ways. I can appreciate how difficult it must have been for my liaison officers and other members of staff to try to accommodate a civilian (female) outsider on top of already very demanding and difficult working lives. I am in your debt. Likewise, I am grateful for the welcoming openness that was extended to me by the men in custody who assisted with this research. Thank you for allowing me to hang around your domestic spaces, for speaking to me frankly about your circumstances and for sharing your considerable wisdom with me. I tried to remain mindful and respectful of the fact that I was sometimes occupying what were generally 'private' places. I hope that my presence was not experienced as intrusive or voyeuristic. This book is for you. I hope you think it was worth it.

I want to thank all those who provided comment on early drafts, read full drafts, and engaged in discussion and debate with me as I was thinking through the ideas in this book. Thanks to Janet Newman, John Clarke, Ian Loader and Caroline Lanskey for early feedback and discussions on particular chapters and ideas. I am most indebted to those who read the full manuscript or substantial sections of it: Reece Walters, Joel Harvey, Beccah Gibson, Joe Sim, Anne Brunton, John Muncie and Rod Earle. Your comments were incredibly helpful. Any errors, half-baked arguments or examples of faulty reasoning that still remain are, of course, my responsibility alone.

Thanks very much to Philippa Grand at Palgrave for accepting the proposal for this book and to the anonymous reviewers for your helpful comments. Thanks also to the editors, Andrew James and Ellie Shillito, who helped with the process. I am extremely grateful to Janet MacMillan for guiding me through the copy-editing process and for being so careful and considerate in her comments and corrections.

Finally, I want to thank my family and closest friends for their continued support and encouragement, which also often included feeding me and looking after me in other ways as I worked my way through both the research and the writing process: Frank and Florence, Dan and Jeannie, Donna and Ken, Joel and Dan, Beccah and Rob, Tara, Helen, Mary, Stuart, Anne, Abi and Andy.

1
Demythologising the Prison and its Uses

Introduction

As of this year, 2011, there are 10.1 million human beings living in custodial settings, either as detainees or as sentenced prisoners (Walmsley, 2011). The number of people imprisoned is growing on five continents. The increased reliance on the prison attests to its popularity as a sanction and is indicative of its pre-eminence as a much favoured crime control tool. Prisons persist, in part, as a result of the belief in society that they play a key role in assuring higher levels of human security and social order. Thus, the prison is a well-entrenched feature of national crime control strategies and is poised to play an ever greater role in global crime control agendas and security strategies. This book problematises the persistent use of the prison and its role in the pursuit of higher levels of human security.

Drawing on research[1] undertaken in men's[2] long-term, maximum-security prisons in England,[3] this book examines three interconnected problems: the tendency of the prison to obscure other social problems and conceal its own failings, the pursuit of greater levels of human security through repressive and violent means, and the persistence of the belief that human beings can be inherently or incorrigibly bad or evil. In this introductory chapter I will briefly present each of these problems in turn, and in doing so will set out the aims of the book.

The (purported) purposes and (hidden) functions of the prison

[I]t is necessary to strip from the social institution of punishment its ideological veils and juristic appearance and to describe it in its real

1

relationships … Punishment is neither a simple consequence of crime, nor the reverse side of the crime. (Rusche and Kirchheimer, 1968, p. 5)

Prisons, we are given to understand, play an integral role in keeping us safe from those among us who have proven their dangerousness or who otherwise have transgressed property laws or other laws that have been deemed important for maintaining social order, safety and security. Prisons are also widely believed to serve five other purposes (or some combination thereof): rehabilitation, incapacitation, deterrence (from future offending), general prevention (deterrence from committing crime in the first place) and the delivery of justice. The difficulty is that there is, to date, no persuasive or definitive evidence that prisons effectively fulfil any of these purposes. Indeed there is evidence to the contrary (see especially, Gilligan, 2000; Mathiesen, 2000; Kupers, 2006). And yet the use of prisons persists.

This book begins from the premise that there a number of obstacles that prevent us from recognising the failure of prisons to contribute to safer, more secure societies or to solve problems of crime or interpersonal violence. It aims to more closely examine these obstacles and illustrate how they distort public perceptions and inhibit opportunities to think more critically and carefully about problems of public safety, crime and disorder, and security. It has been established by Thomas Mathiesen (2000) that the trouble with prisons is that they serve a variety of functions in society that have little to do with punishment or their other purported purposes. In *Prison on Trial*, Mathiesen (2000, p. 142) argues:

[T]he prison physically helps to bifurcate society between the 'productive' and the 'unproductive'; it sets up a structure which, quite observably, places the prisoners in a powerless situation; it also sets up a structure which places members of one class in such a situation that the attention we might pay to the members of another is diverted; and it uses a variety of physical – but not only physical – methods to stigmatize members of the former class. But the functions are ideological: they make prisons appear meaningful and legitimate.

Prisons, then, serve particular ideological functions that make their existence difficult to challenge. Mathiesen (2000, pp. 141–3) outlines four such functions and it is worth summarising them here in order to clearly establish the starting point for this book.

According to Mathiesen, the prison, firstly, serves an *expurgatory function* where it houses a proportion of the unproductive, surplus population that is produced in (particularly, but not only) capitalist market economies. Secondly, it serves a *power-draining function* where prisoners remain 'unproductive non-contributors to the system containing them' (ibid., p. 141). Thirdly, the prison serves a *diverting function* where the danger and harm posed and caused by prisoners or perpetrators of state-defined crimes is overemphasised in order to obscure the danger and harm posed and caused by those individuals and classes with power in society. Fourthly, prisons fulfil a *symbolic function*, to stigmatise those they hold, whilst allowing the rest of us to set ourselves apart from 'them' and the social ills that led them into prison. These four ideological functions, Mathiesen (ibid., p. 140) argues, render the prison a meaningful and legitimate sanction. However, he adds, there is a further function of the prison, which is its *action function*, and which it holds as the most observable type of sanction in society. The prison stands as the strongest form of evidence we have that something is being done about crime and disorder. As Mathiesen (ibid., p. 143) states: 'No other sanction fulfils this function as well.'

As a result of the hidden functions of the prison that obscure their failure to achieve their purported purposes, prisons have come to play a paradoxical role in the relationship between crime, state responses and public reactions to it and the problem of insecurity. So, for example, when one member of society harms another our response is to activate the criminal justice process, which dictates that the perpetrator must be caught, tried and imprisoned. This process, we are told, is the most effective means we have for achieving our collective safety and security. The state, which has responded with the full force of the law and perhaps even 'harsh justice' or law-and-order measures, has done everything within its power to ensure social order is restored and maintained. The paradox, however, arises when the problem of crime persists, when ex-prisoners reoffend or when social barometers reveal that fear of crime amongst the general public is on the rise. The continued failure of the prison calls into question the means by which security is pursued more generally and intersects with the other two problems with which this book is concerned, namely: the rise of ideologies of security which favour repressive, coercive measures and the tendency to construct people who pose a threat as other or incorrigibly bad. These two subsequent problems will be considered in turn.

The quest for security

Penal systems carry deep meanings. They convey information on central features of the states they represent. Nothing told more about

> Nazi Germany, about the USSR or about Maoist China than their penal apparatus – from their police practice, via courts to prisons, camps and Gulags. In concrete cases, we can evaluate states according to their penal systems. (Christie, 2004, p. 101)

As this quotation by Nils Christie suggests, there is much to be learned about current state practices and strategies by examining the internal life of prisons and the strategies of penal systems. During the course of the research on which this book draws, the concept of security came to the fore as a dominant construct with significant power to shape penal policy, practice and thought. These developments in prisons coincide with the rise in the prominence of security currently taking place in wider social contexts.

The quest for security is not novel or new. However, across many countries around the world, the concept of security – particularly when it is used to refer to matters of national and international security – is undergoing a transformation in its meaning, use and application, which necessarily has implications for the *ways* it is sought (Aradau and van Munster, 2007; Zedner, 2009; Hallsworth and Lea, 2011).

The ascension and growing prominence of the concept of security has undoubtedly been gradual in the political realm (Zedner, 2009). However, its ascension was accelerated, and its conceptual power bolstered, by the events of 9/11 and subsequent acts of political violence and, importantly, by the way those events were responded to. Of particular influence in its ascension was the declaration by the United States of a 'war on terror'. With respect to this response and the terminology used, Elisabeth Young-Bruehl (2006, p. 62) has stated: '… as impersonal a phrase as "war on drugs" and far more dangerous; when no enemies are named, the door is open to limitless war outside all rules of war.' On the range of actions that have accompanied the declaration of this war, Claudia Aradau and Rens van Munster (2007, p. 90) have argued:

> [T]he 'war on terror' is a … complex discursive and institutional formation … configured by practices that are neither exclusively nor predominantly military, a specific imbrication of continuity and discontinuity. From Guantanamo Bay to biometrics and increased surveillance, or from extraordinary rendition to the categorization of terrorist suspects as enemy combatants, the 'war on terror' has regimented a whole series of practices that do not fall under the description of war.

If the so-called war on terror and its nebulous, apparently globalised reach define the present political moment then security (and the pursuit of it) is surely the ideological diktat that shapes how this war is fought and justifies the means it employs to 'win' it (though its winnable-ness must, most assuredly, be questioned). The ability of the state to guarantee security is politically contested (Lazarus, 2007). Nevertheless, in many nation states its pursuit (particularly with respect to national security) has become an overriding concern of politicians and state agencies of power (though it should also be recognised that the degree to which the pursuit of security influences particular political agendas differs between nation states). In this pursuit, the concept of security is often cast as both a means and an end. As Lucia Zedner (2009, p. 12) argues:

> In the name of security, things that would ordinarily be politically untenable become thinkable … The pursuit of security signals an urgency and importance that stifles debate as to priorities, resources, and countervailing interests. To invoke security is a move to foreclose debate as to the wisdom of a policy or the necessity of a measure.

The power of a concept to foreclose debate and to render that which was previously unthinkable *thinkable* must surely warrant our considerable attention (as members of society, academics, politicians), not least because of its power to influence and silently embed itself as a taken-for-granted element of political and public life. Some of the measures justified in the pursuit of security may be seen as consistent with elements of totalitarianism. The number and range of security measures that have been undertaken as part of the war on terror have challenged existing laws and rights to privacy and thereby suggest a totalitarian denial of the legal protections that are seen to undermine the ideology associated with maintaining security.

Hannah Arendt was long concerned with what she saw as 'the most essential political criterion for judging the events of our time: will it lead to totalitarian rule or will it not?' (Arendt, 1948, p. 763, see also Arendt, 1968). Arendt eventually came to argue that while totalitarianism would no longer take on its mid-twentieth century forms, its elements would continue to remain with us (Young-Bruehl, 2006, p. 46). Totalitarian elements, in subtle forms, may (and do) exist in political regimes that are not wholly totalitarian (including in so-called democratic ones). Whilst there is little danger of a fully totalitarian political regime taking hold in existing democratic nations, for example, there is cause for collective public concern when existing laws that protect liberty, privacy and human rights are challenged by a state. These tactics, which may be seen as elements of totalitarian rule, need to be noticed and named as such in order to better understand the public realm in which we are living and the transformations – and their potential meanings – that are occurring.

As this book shows, this rise of the prominence of security in wider society has coincided with its rise in prominence within the penal realm. These developments carry implications for the way security is conceived and pursued both in society and in prisons, but they also signal some troubling trends with respect to the methods used to pursue security and the ideologies that justify them. As this book will illustrate, prisons provide a useful, though concentrated, illustration of the power of the concept of security and hold for us some warnings about the ideologies that increasingly accompany its pursuit.

It should also be recognised that prisons have another inherent connection to the concept of security – the belief that through the use of the prison we will gain higher levels of public security and personal safety. This idea relates back to the first problem with which this book is concerned, the multiple functions and purported purposes that prisons serve. It is also intertwined with the third problem considered in this book, the persistent belief that problems of crime and insecurity result from threatening, dangerous others and their individual pathologies. In essence, this belief is underpinned by the view that those who commit crime or pose other threats to safety and security are somehow, fundamentally, different from those who do not. This book questions these assumptions and argues, instead, for the superficiality of evil.

The superficiality of evil

This book is based on qualitative, ethnographic research in all five men's long-term, maximum-security prisons in England. Further details of the methods used in this research and the population on which it is based can be found in the Appendix. However, it is of relevance to state at the outset that the population of long-term, maximum-security prisons in England are frequently described in official and media discourses as some of the 'most difficult and dangerous prisoners in the country' (HMCIP, 2002, p. 9). Many are labelled variously as 'dangerous villains', 'incorrigibly bad' or as 'evil monsters'. The final problem with which this book is concerned is the construction of dangerous others and the persistence of the concept of evil.

The sad truth of the matter is that most evil is done by people who never make up their minds to be or do evil or good. (Arendt, 1971a, p. 180)

As will become evident, the thinking of Hannah Arendt informs this book in numerous ways. Arendt wanted to draw attention to the types of thinking that can lead to human beings being treated as less than human. This is one of the underlying concerns of this book too, and as a result, it intermittently follows trajectories of thinking that are similar to those examined by Arendt. Arendt drew attention to the problem of evil and its superficiality or, in her words, its banality. The idea of the superficiality of evil is encapsulated in the quotation above, and is a little understood and rarely considered aspect of human affairs. It is a problem that concerns the troubling reality that people sometimes commit terrible and unthinkable acts of harm, cruelty and violence against other people. Arendt, covering Adolf Eichmann's 1961 trial for his role in committing crimes against the Jewish people, crimes against humanity and war crimes during the period of the Nazi regime, was struck by Eichmann's normality. In the epilogue of her book *Eichmann in Jerusalem: A Report on the Banality of Evil* (2006, p. 276) she wrote:

The trouble with Eichmann was precisely that so many were like him, and that the many were neither perverted nor sadistic, that they were, and still are, terribly and terrifyingly normal. From the viewpoint of our legal institutions and of our moral standards of judgment, this normality was much more terrifying than all the atrocities put together.

Arendt's impression of Eichmann was not well received by many. The idea that the perpetrators of such colossal and extreme acts of violence could be 'normal' or ordinary is something that is regarded as generally unacceptable. Nevertheless, Christie has drawn similar conclusions about guards he interviewed who had tortured and killed in the *Nacht and Nebel* (Night and Fog) camps in the north of Norway. Christie also mentions his conversations with Professor Batawia (a professor of forensic psychiatry) in Warsaw who carried out long conversations with the commander of one of the large concentration camps and came away with comparable impressions. Christie (2004, p. 88) writes:

We compared notes ... We found that we had two common experiences. First neither of us had met any monsters from the camps. Bad news for those hoping to find beasts behind the atrocities; by and large they were not there. Second, neither the Polish, nor the Norwegian society was particularly interested in getting acquainted with our results. Batawia was flatly forbidden to publish; my small articles were ignored. It was not until a new generation had grown up that I was asked to publish the whole report as a book (in Christie 1952/74).

Similarly – and the reason for drawing attention to Arendt's and Christie's observations – my own research, which included over 200 in-depth interviews with long-term prisoners, some of whom had committed extremely serious, violent acts of harm against other people, revealed no 'monsters'. The trouble with human beings is that they sometimes commit terrible acts of violence against one another – for a whole variety of reasons. We continue to fail to fully understand this problem due to the persistent belief in the idea that people who do such things are somehow inherently bad.

It should be recognised that acts of individual, interpersonal violence are a different order of harm from those committed by states. However, the persistent idea that any form of human harm is solely the result of individual pathology, and that it is not influenced by social conditions and structures, limits our thinking in dangerous ways both in terms of the violence caused by individuals and by violent states. As Zygmunt Bauman (1989) puts forward, social interaction is a powerful force for legitimising acts of inhumanity. He argues (ibid., p. 166): 'Cruelty is social in its origin much more than it is characterological.' If this is the case, then it is of vital importance that we begin to acknowledge the types of thinking that are foreclosed when we construct individuals as aberrant or as other and to consider more carefully the social conditions and structures that influence the occurrence of violence. Violent states and violent state practices are legitimated by and propagate ideologies that justify the dehumanisation of individuals or particular groups. These ideologies may produce social conditions and structures that sustain and encourage further violence and harm. Moreover, by locating the problem of violence solely within individuals, our attentions are drawn away from social, political and economic conditions and power structures in social life (including those drawn along the lines of gender, 'race' and sexuality) and the vulnerabilities and inequalities they create. Our attentions are also drawn away from noticing or defining other types of activities as violent, such as, for example, corporate negligence (Tombs and Whyte, 2003a). Furthermore, it is important to think more carefully about the way societies decide to respond when violent acts occur (or, conversely, do not respond in the case of some forms of violence). The way we decide to 'treat' those who have committed certain types of violence has implications both for the person being subjected to 'treatment' (e.g., criminal sanctions, punishment, use of the death penalty) and for social life more generally. The responses societies make in the face of violence may make it more likely for it to recur, whilst also sustaining social conditions, structures and state practices that foster it.

This book argues that part of the reason that violence is viewed more often as an individual pathology and not as originating in social conditions is due to the persistence of a belief in the concept of evil. It is suggested that, in part, the idea that some people are evil remains salient in the public consciousness because such constructions are reinforced in popular culture and mass media (Greer and Jewkes, 2005). However, these constructions are perhaps also fuelled by a seemingly instinctive aversion to the idea that human beings hold the capacity to commit terrible acts of violence against one another – either interpersonally or on a large scale. Perhaps it is easier to view people who commit seemingly unthinkable acts as other or, in any case, different from 'us' (Greer and Jewkes, 2005, p. 21). The pain that is felt when particularly serious crimes or atrocities occur brings out in us all an aversion to the persons or person who caused them and when in such pain we instinctively call for condemnation and vengeance. Such pain may close off (either permanently or temporarily) our capacity for understanding and for thinking carefully about how we might react. Further, the avoidance of the idea that sometimes normal and ordinary people commit unspeakable acts of violence or are complicit in activities that result in serious harm to other people leaves important dimensions of human affairs gapingly underconsidered.

What is important about Arendt, Christie's and my own observations and why they need to be more carefully considered is that they present evidence against an essentialised view of evil (see also Waldram, 2009a). That is, if the individuals who committed acts that are amongst the most violent in human history (in the case of Eichmann and the other Nazis) were not essentially evil, then there was capacity for them to be otherwise and the possibility that the conditions in which they committed the atrocities could have been avoided. On the subject of evil, Arendt (1978, p. 251) wrote:

It is indeed my opinion now that evil is never 'radical', that it is only extreme, and that it possesses neither depth nor any demonic dimension. It can overgrow and lay waste the whole world precisely because it spreads like a fungus on the surface. It is 'thought-defying' ...

because thought tries to reach some depth, to go to roots, and the moment it concerns itself with evil, it is frustrated because there is nothing. That is its 'banality'.

The banality of evil, particularly as seen by Arendt in Eichmann, helps to elucidate the potential superficiality of evil or, more tangibly, the separation of evil and thoughtless deeds and actions from thoroughly or inherently evil people. It is one of the contentions of this book that if there are only essentially evil acts and superficially (i.e., not essentially) evil people then the ways we respond to such acts, and the people who commit them, need further thinking about. By separating terrible acts from the individuals who may commit them, we reopen the problem of how to respond to such acts and what to do about those ordinary and normal people who perpetrate them. In doing so, we are able to think more deeply about the question of punishment, but also about our own actions as a society (and within criminal justice systems) and their potential consequences. Criminology – and the majority of the disciplines on which it draws – has spent remarkably little time grappling with this problem. Part of the reason there has been so little academic consideration of this topic is because the question of what we should do when acts of terrible harm are perpetrated has been continually obscured by the multiple purposes and functions served by criminal justice, punishment and the prison. As this book argues, each of these social institutions is imbued with dominant subjectivities (Hudson, 2006) and serves a variety of other functions that draw attention away from their failure to respond effectively to the harms human beings sometimes inflict on one another. Such obstacles highlight the importance of critical thought and the need to persistently challenge that which is taken for granted and to identify the parameters and purposes of dominant ideologies. These tasks form the underpinning strands of this book.

Puncturing the myths: the importance of exposing ideologies

Exposing the ideologies that shape different features of social and political life is an important aspect of challenging the taken for granted. On the term 'ideology' Jeffrey Reiman and Paul Leighton (2010, p. 191) write: 'When ideas, however, unintentionally, distort reality in a way that justifies the prevailing distribution of power and wealth, hides society's injustices, and thus secures uncritical allegiance to the existing social order, we have what Marx called ideology.' Whilst the term is sometimes diluted to refer simply to a worldview or value system, Reiman and Leighton (2010, p. 192) argue that: 'This moral neutralization of the concept of "ideology" dulls an instrument that thinkers such as Marx and others have sharpened into an effective tool for cutting through the illusions that dog our political life.' Whilst Reiman and Leighton's defence of a strictly Marxist definition of the term is persuasive, the insistence that in order to be designated an ideology an idea must justify prevailing distributions of power and wealth seems to leave out ideologies that justify other prevalent ideas that are not necessarily or obviously linked to these prevailing influences. Although Karl Mannheim's (1936) total conception of ideology is exactly the definition of ideology that Reiman and Leighton argue against (i.e., a worldview or *Weltanschauung*), his general definition of ideology may hold more explanatory power: 'an idea or ideas "incongruent with reality", which have the effect of protecting a contradictory reality, and supporting the status quo' (Goodwin, 2007, p. 21). This definition gives the term greater plasticity which allows for its application to other systems of ideas, for example, those which might be based on principles explicitly opposed to prevailing capitalist distributions of power and wealth, such as socialist ideologies or (some) welfarist ideologies; or, likewise, ideologies that are based more heavily on unequal distributions of power (though, of course, power and wealth can be closely tied), such as racist or patriarchal ideologies. Moreover, the status quo that may be supported by an ideology need not be a dominant, hegemonic one, but could be an existing state of affairs amongst a particular social group or faction within society. A version of Mannheim's more malleable definition of ideology, therefore, is the one that will be used and applied in this book. Ideology will be used to describe ideas or systems of ideas that form a recognisable *version* of reality that then supports a status quo and justifies particular ways of responding to this constructed reality.

Identifying competing and differing ideologies can provide a valuable way to examine the social and political world. By delineating the principles that fit within a particular ideology we are able to trace how it links to other or more dominant ideologies, and think about how contingent and varying ideological frameworks converge and configure to shape social institutions, political life and social value systems. It can also bring out into the open realities about our social world that tend to remain hidden. Moreover, the exercise of identifying ideologies can draw out the hegemonic tenets of society, and in doing so, allow us to call into question the sets of values, attitudes and underlying moral assumptions on which they are based. The field of critical criminology has been particularly adept in this regard. Indeed, it is perhaps best characterised by its tendency to continually challenge that which is taken for granted and to question the immutability of social life. On being critical, Jock Young (2002, p. 271), quoting Zygmunt Bauman, has argued:

> Zygmunt Bauman in recent interviews ponders on the nature of critical theory: 'What I understand by that term is the kind of theorising which accepts that, first, "things are not necessarily what they seem to be" and second that "the world may be different from what it is" ...'. And Bauman is fiercely dismissive of those who would view human culture as a thing of inertia, the place of habit, routine, absence of reflection – a sort of stabilising 'preservative' of humanity ... (Bauman and Tester, 2001, p. 33) ... It is my belief that critical criminology is more relevant today than ever ... it is striking how the problems faced in the 1970s [when critical criminology was being developed] are built larger today and how the concerns are more a harbinger of the present than a moment of the past.

The key ideas in the above quotation that are of relevance here are the recognition that the social world can change (or be changed), that it might be different to what it is and that critical criminology has something to offer in this regard. Although imagining alternatives and ways of changing it can be difficult prospects, as Young (2002) suggests we must continually challenge and think about the meanings and hidden realities of our social world if we are to better understand it and change it.

To some extent our social problems persist because the dominant ideologies that shape our social and political lives hide them from view and prevent us from gaining a deeper understanding of human affairs. These problems, then, remain unquestioned and perhaps even become unquestionable. This book draws attention to the penal realm, an area of social life that few people have had the opportunity to examine or fully reflect on. It uses this opportunity to think about some difficult and persistent problems of social life and to address some of the gaps in our thinking about these problems. Christie (2000, p. 202) has stated that: 'Those of us who work close to penal systems have special responsibilities, but not as experts.' He makes it clear that as criminologists we are not the experts, we are *commentators* whose responsibility it is to challenge, to question and, as Christie puts it, 'to puncture the myths' (ibid.). This book attempts to fulfil these responsibilities by questioning, firstly, some of the preconceived ideas and taken-for-granted assumptions about prisons, prisoners and punishment and, secondly, the means and methods we are currently using to pursue greater levels of human security.

Overview of the chapters

Chapters 2 through 5 of this book focus more heavily on the problems of prisons than the final three chapters, which broaden out to consider the interconnections between prisons and punishment and wider social concerns. Chapter 2 examines the persistent and increasing use of the prison and some possible reasons for this trend. It suggests that the pressures and effects of globalisation are contributing to a growing global ideological hegemony of imprisonment that reinforces the symbolic functions of prisons and taken-for-granted assumptions about their use. It is argued that the use of the prison as a crime control tool and its role within the pursuit of security are becoming more difficult to resist and to question.

Chapter 3 argues that the use of the prison has always been accompanied by complexity in institutional penal affairs. It suggests that opportunities within nation states to question the extent to which prisons effectively serve any of their purported purposes have continually been obscured by their bulky machinery and day-to-day operational matters. This argument is elucidated by examining the formation and early evolution of long-term, maximum-security prisons in England. The chapter provides an in-depth illustration of the ways that the ideological functions of the prison and, in particular, the political economic dimensions of imprisonment become obscured by operational, security or administrative matters, as are the wider social problems prisons are apparently intended to solve. By examining the competing goals and contradictory logics on which the practice of imprisonment are based, this chapter also continues the examination of the ways in which prisons are designed to fail.

Chapters 4 and 5 delve deeper into the evolution of English maximum-security imprisonment, but in the contemporary context. Chapter 4 concentrates on the rise of the prominence of the concept of security in these prisons and the implications that this has had on penal policy and prison practice and on the way prisoners are constructed and managed. Chapter 5, by contrast, begins the examination of punishment. Drawing on the experiences of prisoners, this chapter bears witness to the severity of the punishment that is the loss of one's liberty. It aims to illustrate the meanings and effects of harsh justice from the perspectives of prisoners and calls into question the utility of punishment.

Whilst the prison might provide a concentrated version of the state it represents, it is nonetheless a useful barometer for tracing the methods and parameters of state power. Chapter 6, therefore, examines the way security is constituted in both the penal and the social realms. It highlights the insights that are gained through considerations of the prison in relation to the pursuit of security in society more generally. Further, it draws out the potential significance of the symbiotic relationship between the prison and the pursuit of security and the role the prison is poised to play under increasingly globalised economic conditions.

The ideologies of security, described in Chapter 6, include a tendency to construct as other those who are deemed to be threatening to either public safety or national security. Such notions connect easily to persistent beliefs amongst the general public that those who commit serious acts of violence or are otherwise threatening are inherently bad. Chapter 7 moves on to consider the persistence of these beliefs and the reasons that the failure of prisons and criminal justice systems remain obscured from public view. It also considers why it is that prisons and punishment may not be effective means for responding to problems of interpersonal harm and violence.

Chapter 8 reflects on the key issues that are covered within this volume and draws out the value of the critical standpoint in making the invisible visible. It identifies some of the moral stumbling blocks that have prevented us from thinking differently about problems of harm and the pursuit of human security. The book finally concludes by presenting some alternative goals of criminal justice and ways of thinking about how to pursue more humane and reasoned responses when faced with the problem of human violence or when other threats to human security and safety arise.

2
The Growing Hegemony of Imprisonment

Introduction

The exchange of ideas and ways of thinking about common social problems and how to manage them have never been more globally free flowing than in our present times (McLuhan, 1964). With respect to prisons there appears to be an increasing consensus that they are an acceptable means by which problems of crime can be tackled. A growing reliance on the prison has led some to argue that there has been a shift towards penal convergence, though not a complete homogenisation of punishment (Cavadino and Dignan, 2006, p. 438).

This chapter considers this convergence alongside a growing hegemony of imprisonment or, in other words, an increasing reliance on the use of the prison as a crime control tool. It suggests that the dominant ideological foundations of imprisonment fundamentally orient the purposes of the prison more heavily towards punishment than social welfare, and towards the harms associated with street crime, poverty or interpersonal violence rather than state or corporate crime. It is argued that differing political and economic orientations of nation states account for differences in the commitment to the use of prisons and commensurate levels of the 'consumption' of punishment (Simon, 2010). However, trends towards the increased usage of the prison may suggest growing pressure on governments to more fully commit to ideologies of imprisonment and direct the punitive machinery of prisons towards less eligible social groups or, increasingly, towards social members deemed as other. In insecure social, political and economic climates the temptation may be high to rely more heavily on the prison to manage the social problems associated with poverty, structural inequalities and uncertain economic conditions.

15

Likewise and at the same time, the growing hegemony of prisons reinforces their symbolic importance in the public consciousness. That is, prisons increasingly signify as a bulwark against public disorder, lack of safety, insecurity and social fragmentation. Due to these signifying and symbolic roles of prisons, it is argued that their legitimacy as crime control tools has become increasingly difficult to question even in those nations which have retained a high social welfare commitment in penal matters.

The trend towards penal convergence

The use of punishment varies between different societies and within societies at different times. The most widely used form of punishment – imprisonment – is applied to differing extents between (and often within, see Barker, 2009) legal jurisdictions. Examination of a selection of rates of imprisonment from North America, Europe and Australasia reveal divergent trends and rates of change with respect to the use of imprisonment. As Table 2.1 illustrates the highest user of the prison in 2011 is the United States at 743 per 100,000 of the population. Amongst the most parsimonious nations in Western democracies are Finland and Denmark.

Table 2.1   Selected imprisonment rates per 100,000 population in 2000 and 2011 and percentage change

Country	2000	2011	% Change
USA	680	743	+9.26
Russia	730	568	−22.19
New Zealand	150	199	+32.66
Spain	110	159	+44.54
England and Wales	125	153	+22.40
Australia	110	133	+20.90
Canada	110	117	+6.36
France	90	97	+7.77
Netherlands	90	94	+4.44
Switzerland	85	79	−7.05
Sweden	60	78	+30.00
Germany	95	85	−10.52
Denmark	65	74	+13.84
Finland	45	59	+31.11

Source: Walmsley, 2000, 2011.

Whilst there are clear differences in the 'consumption' of punishment (Simon, 2010), there is a general trend towards an increased reliance on the use of the prison. These trends cannot be straightforwardly accounted for by commensurate increases in crime rates (see Lappi-Seppälä, 2008). Thus the increasing reliance on the prison has, for some time, attracted attention within criminology (e.g., Hallsworth, 2000; Pratt et al., 2005).

Up until the 1970s, the use of punishment (imprisonment and the death penalty, in particular) appeared to be receding, especially in the Western world. Loïc Wacquant (2005), for example, has noted that penal scholars in the early 1970s were arguing that the use of the prison was in decline and saw 'imprisonment not merely as a stagnant institution but as a practice in irreversible if gradual decline, destined to occupy a secondary place in the diversifying arsenal of contemporary instruments of punishment' (ibid., p. 4). Trends towards a decline in the use of the prison, it might be argued, were, in part, associated with the recognition amongst academics and penal policymakers that prisons had little effect on crime rates, and indeed could increase the likelihood of recidivism (Cayley, 1998). Put simply, prison did not 'work' to solve the problem of crime or increase public safety and there seemed to be a growing recognition that it needed to be used sparingly and other alternatives needed to be found. However, the trend towards a decline in imprisonment was abruptly reversed in the latter decades of the twentieth century when many countries began relying more heavily on the use of the prison (Hinds, 2005). This trend has been identified as a 'punitive turn' (Hallsworth, 2000) or a 'new punitiveness' (Pratt et al., 2005). Further, tendencies towards the use of the prison seem to be spreading on a global level and therefore they demand urgent analysis and careful theoretical consideration.

Estella Baker and Julian Roberts (2005) have suggested that globalisation (defined as the creation and proliferation of transnational and global relationships and their processes) is a main contributor to the international spread of punitive policies. They (ibid., p. 136) argue that this spreading occurs in three ways: '[through the] homogenisation or harmonisation of problems and responses across a diversity of jurisdictions; acceleration of penal policy transfer across jurisdictions; promotion of short-term punitive responses at the expense of longer-term, evidence-based policies.' They state, further, that with increased global relationships comes mounting pressure to comply with particular policies and statutory approaches. In the context of crime control these pressures result in 'simplistic penal policies that have considerable mass appeal and a level of "portability" from one jurisdiction to another' (ibid., p. 132). With respect to the use of imprisonment, in particular, I suggest that within an increasingly globalised context, the hegemony of imprisonment and the ideological assumptions on which it is usually based are becoming more prevalent. As a result, it is not necessarily a question of a 'new' punitiveness but, as Joe Sim (2009, p. 15) has argued, a 'continuity of punishment' that is further intensifying the already punitive dimensions of practices of imprisonment.

Questioning the 'newness' of punitiveness

> For those who have ruthlessly (and, in many ways, hopelessly) governed the society in the last three decades, the iconic and symbolic presence of the prison is paramount. (Sim, 2009, p. 9)

Whilst there is undeniable evidence that many countries around the world have increased their prison populations, certainly over the last two decades (see Lappi-Seppälä, 2008; Drake, 2009; Walmsley, 2011), the question of whether imprisonment rates are the best indicator of punitiveness or penal severity remains unanswered. Likewise, it has been argued persuasively by Sim (2009) (with particular focus on British prisons but holding some relevance for other penal systems as well) that the discontinuity thesis of the new punitiveness may underemphasise some of the continuities that have remained a feature of the delivery of punishment since (at least) the nineteenth century (see also Jewkes and Johnston, 2006). He argues that the punitive dimension of imprisonment continually overshadows other supposed purposes of imprisonment, especially the capacity of the prison to rehabilitate. Sim (2009, p. 5) argues that 'if the discourse of social welfare was so important to prison regimes up until the 1970s, as official accounts and new penologists claim, why was this discourse not institutionalised in the everyday practices of the prison system?' Furthermore, he suggests that the so-called failure of the rehabilitative ideal in British prisons 'misses a fundamental point. Rehabilitation polices never worked because, in the majority of penal institutions, they were *never* actually put into practice' (ibid., pp. 5–6). The punitive and coercive underpinnings of practices of imprisonment have often made it difficult, if not impossible, to fulfil more positive purposes. The use of the prison as a means of crime control is an inherently punitive practice. In this respect, as Sim argues, there is no 'newness' in the idea of punitiveness. However, the renewed commitment to the prison (and its punitive underpinnings) and its increased use across jurisdictions, especially those that have previously been parsimonious in their use of the prison, is an area that requires further exploration.

Political economy and social determinants of prison use

Michael Cavadino and James Dignan (2006) have argued that account-ing for variations in imprisonment rates has proven a difficult task. Likewise, finding an explanation for increases in prison use also remains elusive. Much research has illustrated that correlations between crime rates and imprisonment rates are exceptionally weak (Young and Brown, 1993, pp. 23–33; Beckett and Western, 2001, pp. 49–50; Greenberg, 2001: p. 82). Therefore variations in imprisonment rates in different nations cannot be explained empirically by their differing crime rates. Stronger correlations, however, have been found between penalisation and particular political economic configurations (Cavadino and Dignan, 2006; Downes and Hansen, 2006; Lacey, 2008; Lappi-Seppälä, 2008; Pratt, 2008a, 2008b; Snacken, 2010). For example, countries that have higher levels of welfare investment have correspondingly lower levels of imprisonment. Similarly, correlations have been found between impris-onment rates and democratic political structures (Lappi-Seppälä, 2007, 2008; and see Chapter 6 of this volume) and political decision-making on issues of crime and punishment (Snacken et al., 1995; Snacken, 2007, 2010).

Drawing on longitudinal data, American sociologist John Sutton (2000) has robustly identified strong correlations between social and political factors and crime rates. His research (ibid., pp. 376–7) has found that independent of changes in crime rates, prison numbers decline when employment rates increase, that declines in welfare spending are associated with growths in imprisonment rates, that right-wing governments and conservative politics are associated with increased prisoner numbers and, moreover, that there is an 'interac-tion between right-party rule and unemployment growth', thereby suggesting that 'politics not only matters, it trumps economics'. These findings seem to suggest that the parsimonious or excessive use of the prison is reliant on the extent to which political sensibili-ties support an ideology of imprisonment or, conversely, the extent to which ideologies of imprisonment support political sensibilities (or political economic agendas). This suggestion, then, requires some consideration of what the essential components of an ideology of imprisonment might be. Examining the political economy and social determinants of prison use alongside the common features within ideologies of imprisonment, therefore, may offer some useful insights for understanding the reasons behind increasing trends towards the use of the prison.

The ideological architecture of imprisonment

Country-specific sets of cultural values, public sensibilities and historical influences shape the particular configurations of criminal justice and penal policies in different legal jurisdictions. Therefore the commitment to social welfare concerns in a broader social context and to rehabilitative or punitive ideals within prisons can differ substantially between political and penal systems and in prisons themselves. Further, there is increasing recognition that considerable variation can exist within countries in relation to penal and criminal justice policy and practice (Hannah-Moffat and Maurutto, 2003; Barker, 2009). Therefore efforts to explain the seemingly global trend towards the increased use of the prison should aim to find the common drivers for the use of the prison and the relevance these might hold for different political and cultural contexts.

If the concept of imprisonment is stripped down to its fundamental features, the elements that underpin systems of imprisonment are brought into clearer view. Such an exercise makes it more possible to identify the basic features and central tenets that support ideologies of imprisonment. As a starting point in this task it is useful to briefly consider the ideological foundations of British prisons as an exemplar.

Contemporary British prisons retain a residue of Victorian (late nineteenth, early twentieth century) ideals and sensibilities, including the notion of exile, the importance of punishment, the principle of less eligibility/austerity and the belief that prisoners require moral, spiritual or other personal (i.e., character) reshaping or reform (Sieh, 1989; Coyle, 2005). These ideas about the purpose of and the values that shape the practice of imprisonment form the components of what can be described as the ideological 'architecture' of British prisons. I refer to it as 'architecture' because these central tenets have endured in British prisons despite changing penal policies, administrative practices or the development of new penal knowledges. Although there have been historical moments when some of these components seemed to fade into the background, while others came to the fore, they have each remained ever-present, exacting influence in both implicit and explicit ways throughout the history of the modern British prison. I will consider each of these components briefly in turn.

The use of the prison as a direct punishment imposed by the court was an extension of the practice of exile. Instead of transporting prisoners to the colonies, which had ended in 1867, criminals were 'to be punished for their crimes by being exiled behind the high walls of the prison' (Coyle, 2005, p. 27). The two most fundamental features of early prisons, then, were punishment and the segregation or exclusion of those who committed some form of harm against persons, society or property. But the relationship between the causation of harm, one's removal from society and his or her punishment within a prison was not as straightforward as it seems.

British prisons have had a long association with social and economic exclusion, class structure and a 'fear of the dangerous classes'. John Pratt (1997, p. 14) has argued that the early Victorians feared the dangerous classes due to the perception that they 'possessed a power of destruction: destruction not simply of property but order, tradition and law itself; and without these central pillars of support, modern society was thought to be in danger of collapse'. Sophie Holmes and Keith Soothill (2007, p. 592) argue that by the end of the nineteenth century, due to a weakening of solidarity amongst the working classes, 'the threat posed society by the dangerous classes shifted to a perceived threat to individuals by dangerous criminals' who were mostly engaged in petty crimes, especially property crime. At the same time, the so-called dangerous groups in society largely began to merge into different segments of the working classes: the skilled and unskilled and the deserving and undeserving poor (ibid., citing Pratt, 1997). Much of the initial use of imprisonment, then, was directed towards those segments of the impoverished classes who were unskilled and seen as undeserving and who engaged in property or other acquisitive crimes (and to a lesser extent interpersonal crimes). Importantly, prisons and the orientation of the criminal law were designed to focus more heavily on the activities of the poor because they were founded on ideals that served the interests of those with wealth and power (Kropotkin, 1992). Recall Mathiesen's (2000, p. 142) argument that prisons reinforce aspects of social 'structure which place members of one class in such a situation that the attention we might pay to the members of another is diverted'. Prisons, criminal justice and the law, then, were established to focus almost exclusively on harms or crimes of the poor and only exceptionally on crimes of the powerful (and especially not crimes of the state). Moreover, as Barbara Hudson (2006, p. 30) has argued, the law in most Western societies:

> reflects the subjectivities of the dominant white, affluent, adult, male. This dominant subjectivity is both subject and object of law: it is object in that it is he whose behaviour law has in mind when it constructs its proscriptions and remedies; and it is this subject who constructs the law. Through its discourse and its practices, criminal justice continually invokes and reproduces the male, white subjectivity of law.

Duplicity and contradiction in law and criminal justice will be discussed more fully in Chapter 7, but it is important to note at this point that the values, ideals and subjectivities on which the law and the prison were based have played an important role in establishing and reinforcing ideas about the types of harms or crimes that are punishable, who should be singled out, excluded and punished and about how that punishment should be constituted.

Due to the relationship between the prison and class structure, the principle of less eligibility, in particular, has played a crucial role in shaping ideas about what prison experiences ought to involve, the way those experiences should deliver punishment and in setting appropriate limits on what prison conditions should include. Ahmed White (2008, p. 793) has argued that the principle of less eligibility includes: 'a dynamic, interactive view of the relationship between prison conditions and political economy, one centred on the fundamental idea that the social meaning of punishment is relative to the life conditions of the lower class.' Put simply, this principle demands that the conditions inside prison should not be better than the lowest significant social class in free society (Sieh, 1989). That is, 'prisoners, because of their proved wrongful behaviour, are the least eligible of all citizens for social benefits' (Clear and Cole, 1986, p. 315). This principle forms one of the central ideological foundations of British prisons and has played (and continues to play) a significant role in maintaining their punitive edge. It is linked to the idea of prisons as a deterrent and as a form of punishment. Austere prison conditions, therefore, were viewed as appropriate both to deter and to punish the less eligible.

The Victorian legacy to the prison also includes, finally, a role for the prison as a place for reform or conversion towards normative ideals. The idea that prisons should be places of reform or rehabilitation have origins rooted in both British upper-middle-class sensibilities and Christian values (McGowen, 1995, p. 85). These sensibilities and values begin from a premise that those who commit crime are undisciplined or feral. From this paternalistic view, criminals need to be provided with opportunities to reform their errant ways, become educated or learn the value of hard work and, through austere but decent prison experiences, become more civilised. Such ideas were developed significantly through the penal reform efforts of the nineteenth century led by such figures as John Howard and other wealthy Christian philanthropists (Ignatieff, 1978). Part of the purpose of imprisonment, then, was thought to be the task of reforming (fundamentally changing) the character of criminals to make them conform to normative ideals or to otherwise better prepare them (through education or training) to become full contributors to social and economic life.

The ideological architecture described above was, in part, reified and made tangible in British prisons in the work of the Gladstone Committee, which was charged with reforming the British penal system in the late nineteenth century. This inquiry, led by Herbert Gladstone MP, included a broad consideration of the conditions of imprisonment, which had been prompted by concern over prison accommodation, labour and the treatment and classification of prisoners. Significantly, the Gladstone Report (1895) set out 'deterrence' and 'reformation' as the two primary aims of imprisonment. Prison conditions, therefore, needed to be unpleasant enough so as to deter crime and future criminality (thus, remaining consistent with the principle of less eligibility and the emphasis on austerity). However, at the same time, prison experiences needed to provide opportunities for prisoners to change their errant ways, learn how to work or gain education and become law-abiding, participating citizens (i.e., provide opportunities for reform). These aims, which it may be argued are contradictory and incompatible (see Thomas, 1972), have enduringly shaped approaches to prison practice in Britain, albeit in uneven and desultory ways.

The extent to which the ideological underpinnings of imprisonment in Britain resonate and manifest in prison environments and penal systems elsewhere will inevitably vary. However, the enduring influence of British colonial rule, it may be argued, is at least partly implicated in establishing some core values that shape common practices and uses of imprisonment in many countries (Sieh, 1989). Although there is a high degree of cultural contingence in legal and penal systems around the world and across Commonwealth and former Commonwealth countries, many penal systems share some of the same underpinning values as those found in the British system. Moreover, it might be argued that by virtue of the fact that the use of the prison persists, and seems to be proliferating, certain components of an ideology of imprisonment must resonate across jurisdictions. If this is indeed the case, it is necessary to attempt to identify the essential characteristics of imprisonment that are common across jurisdictions.

Common features within ideologies of imprisonment

When stripped down to their most essential components, ideologies and practices of imprisonment tend to include three elements – in varying measures. First and foremost, and by definition, the use of imprisonment requires the belief that the wilful exclusion, segregation or exile of certain members of society is an appropriate response when particular, socially censured acts are committed. Second, but no less essentially, the use of imprisonment also includes varying commitments to punishment and, to a lesser extent, to rehabilitation. Examples of differing commitments to both punishment and rehabilitation can be found in different contemporary penal systems (for example, many states within the US are concerned with ensuring prisons deliver punishment, whilst Sweden has traditionally shown a firmer commitment to rehabilitation). However, punishment more often holds greater weight and prominence across penal systems than rehabilitation. The punishment dimension of prison experiences can easily and quickly overwhelm the more positive goals. As already suggested, simultaneous commitments to rehabilitation and punishment within a single penal system are incompatible and, as a result, punitive concerns invariably undermine or overwhelm rehabilitative efforts.

It might be argued, then, that the increasing dominance of the prison as a crime control tool must be indicative of, firstly, firmer commitment to the exclusion or segregation of those who have committed acts that warrant societal censure. By relying more heavily on the prison even states with largely inclusive social policies are tacitly supporting exclusionary methods as a means of managing social problems. With respect to the use of the prison as an exclusionary device, prisons become places where states symbolically censure and actively segregate those social members who are not fully participating in law-abiding society (by committing acquisitive crimes, for example) or are engaging in activities that attract social derision (for example, perpetrating serious harms against other members of society). The choice of imprisonment over other sanctions suggests a weakening of state commitments to understanding and solving the social causes of crime and opting instead for a simple symbolic response – a response that locates the cause of crime more definitively within individuals.

Secondly, increased reliance on the prison must also indicate either an increased desire or drive to punish or an increased belief in the merits of rehabilitation or some combination of the two. Some nation states, such as those that have adopted a law-and-order political rhetoric, clearly have a firmer commitment to punishment. Here the principles of less eligibility and austerity continue to form key components of the way imprisonment is practised. There are, of course, variations between law-and-order approaches, with British political discourse arguing in favour of decent but austere prison conditions, whilst some American practices have sought to implement other forms of harsh justice (e.g., chain gangs, boot camps, etc.). But common to these approaches is the belief that prisoners are less eligible subjects (or sometimes objects) who are undeserving of social benefits and, therefore, conditions of imprisonment should only provide the bare minimum in terms of material provision.

Whilst some commitment to punishment may also be present within penal systems that have traditionally aimed to use the prison more sparingly, this commitment is often tempered in official discourses by the view that the punishment of imprisonment is extracted through the loss of one's liberty. In such systems, prison conditions, then, should not add further hardship (such values are evident in many Scandinavian penal systems, see Sieh, 1989; Pratt, 2008a, 2008b). In addition, some of the more parsimonious nations have tended to argue that prisons should only be used as a last resort because the removal of people from society inevitably causes social disruption and further personal damage. Such principles are incongruous with an increasing reliance on the prison (Table 2.1 reveals percentage change increases in some nations that have hitherto tended towards policies of penal parsimony, e.g., Sweden, Denmark). The increased use of imprisonment, then, may be suggestive of a cultural shift taking place where the belief in and the desire for punishment may be increasing in those nations which have previously subordinated the punishment function of the prison to social welfarist concerns. Public calls for the use of the prison may be increasing whilst, at the same time, there may be an increasing tendency for governments to rely more heavily on the symbolic function of the prison to exemplify that something is being done to assure greater levels of social security.

Finally, the idea that prisons should provide opportunities for rehabilitation and reform also varies considerably between (and within) penal systems. Many of the more parsimonious nations or those which have remained fairly stable in their use of the prison (such as Canada) retain commitments to rehabilitative strategies despite the recognition of the inherently punishing nature of imprisonment (e.g., see the official rhetoric of the Correctional Service of Canada or the Kriminalvården, the Prison and Probation Service of Sweden). Some commitment to rehabilitation can also still be found in nations that have in the main embraced law-and-order political rhetoric, including Britain and some states in the US. Indeed, many penal systems around the world continue to include a wide range of activities, programmes and skills training for prisoners. However, as Sim (2009) has argued in reference to British prisons, there is some question about the extent to which rehabilitative work can take place within the overwhelmingly punitive environment of prisons. Further, the commitment to the reform or rehabilitative function of prisons has often, in practice, been lacking. In the British context, rehabilitative ideals have tended to be viewed as optional within the ideology of imprisonment, whilst the other components of imprisonment feature more prominently (exclusion, deterrence/punishment, less eligibility and austerity). The success of rehabilitative strategies, therefore, has been difficult to evidence. The increased reliance on the prison cannot be attributed to the success stories of those jurisdictions that have continued to employ rehabilitative strategies. Moreover, if punishment is indeed becoming a more explicit feature of all penal systems then the capacity for rehabilitative success will be further hindered both by the requirement to create more 'punishing' prison environments and the growing problem of increased prisoner numbers.

If there is an increasingly dominant ideology of imprisonment (albeit with varying degrees of explicit commitment to punishment and rehabilitation), then there is a need to understand how and why this is occurring, given the variations in approaches to and practices of imprisonment that continue to persist. It may be suggested that there is a growing global consensus that prisons are an accepted – and, importantly, an *expected* – means by which problems of crime can and should be tackled. Therefore there may be a growing tendency and temptation for many nation states to use the prison more heavily in attempts to manage ongoing problems of street or acquisitive crime. Moreover, occurrences of violent crime or other particularly serious crimes seem to ensure a firm commitment to the prison. The various ideological functions that prisons serve (outlined in the work of Mathiesen, discussed in Chapter 1) inevitably become intertwined with the public's real fears about the threat of serious harm. Therefore the symbolic role of prisons becomes particularly salient in times of persistent uncertainty. It may be that currently there are growing justifications for the symbolic use of the prison that are difficult for individual nation states to ignore.

Exploring global justifications of imprisonment

Loïc Wacquant (2001, 2009) has argued that the increased reliance on the prison in the United States and elsewhere is 'due to the increasingly frequent, indeed routine, use of imprisonment as an instrument for managing social insecurity' (2001, p. 404). Wacquant attributes this social insecurity to what he sees as a transformation from a Keynesian to a Darwinian state (Wacquant, 2001, 2006, 2009). The Keynesian state, Wacquant argues, is associated with social solidarity, inclusiveness and economic redistribution. The Darwinian state, by contrast, is founded on neo-liberal individualism and free market capitalism (Wacquant, 2001, 2009). Wacquant (2001, p. 404) focuses his analysis on the material and economic conditions of, particularly American, neo-liberal political ideology, but argues that there are also discernable tendencies in other economically advanced countries, including Western Europe and Australia. He suggests that the configuration of the labour market, which has resulted from free market capitalism, has become increasingly flexible, insecure and individualised. The combination of 'precarious employment' (Wacquant, 1999, p. 215) and an increased emphasis on ideas of individualism, which hold people responsible for their own social and economic circumstances, jointly contribute to general and growing levels of social insecurity (Wacquant, 2006, pp. 26–34). Like other theorists who have postulated a link between political economy and punishment, Wacquant argues that such economic conditions lead to surplus labour. However, Wacquant (2009) centralises the role of the prison in the political economic structure and heralds the formation of a penal state where excluded, surplus and non-participating populations are imprisoned. The prison, therefore, is used as a means of managing social insecurity through punishing the poor.

Whilst Wacquant's account of the growing prominence of the prison is extremely persuasive, there are some potential omissions that need further consideration. It is incontestable that the criminal law and prisons are more heavily oriented towards the types of crimes (street, property, other acquisitive crimes or drug-related harms) more likely to be committed by people at the lower end of the social spectrum against the more affluent (often male) segments of society. The prison was designed primarily, as Wacquant (and, inter alia, Christie, 2000; Mathiesen, 2000; Reiman and Leighton, 2010) has argued, to absorb unemployed, surplus populations. However, it should also be recognised that despite the fact that prisons play a key role in political economic structures and in justifying the prevailing distributions of wealth and power, they are also the places in which the state holds those among us who have perpetrated very serious acts of interpersonal harm against other people. Therefore there is a blurring between the role of prisons in political economic structures and their role in public safety. There is a complex relationship between social structures, socio-economic factors and violent interpersonal crime (see, for example, Hsieh and Pugh, 1993). However, the fact that Western criminal justice systems and uses of the prison were conceived by powerful (male) elites with certain crimes (largely property) and certain populations (working class, men) in mind means that they are particularly poorly suited to respond to other types of harm. As Hudson (2006, p. 30) has argued, Western criminal justice systems were not designed to protect women or members of minority ethnic groups from harms they may suffer as a result of their gender (e.g., rape or domestic violence) or ethnicity (e.g., hate crime). And yet, as these sorts of harms have begun to be more recognised and processed through criminal justice systems (though still not very effectively) the prison has been relied upon to absorb these populations as well. This distinction is important because in the public consciousness prisons increasingly serve an important function in society: they securely contain individuals who have committed acts of interpersonal harm. This fact can easily become lost in analyses of the prison that focus too heavily on the political economic dimensions of imprisonment. Nonetheless, the role of prisons in maintaining public safety is an important part of why prisons continue to persist, despite their failures. It is also a significant dimension to consider when contemplating the increased use of the prison within individual nation states (i.e., when high profile or particularly violent crimes occur, public calls for punishment may increase). Likewise, the idea of prisons as a bulwark against public disorder, insecurity and 'dangerous others' can perform a powerful symbolic function that resonates within public consciousness. At the same time, it distracts us (academics, the public, governments) from thinking more carefully about what to do when human beings cause harm to one another – either at interpersonal levels (such as in the case of paedophilic harms, domestic violence, murder) or larger-scale harms (corporate manslaughter, state violence, genocide).

Another area of Wacquant's analysis that needs further consideration relates to his emphasis on neo-liberalism. As already noted, with respect to the issue of political economy, Wacquant's analyses single out some important observations about the role of prisons in both state-building and in political economic structures. However, by locating his analyses within a particular theory of political economic practice – namely, neo-liberalism – he limits the generalisability of his theorisations. Nicola Lacey (2010, pp. 780–1) has questioned the extent of neo-liberalism's global influence. One of the key counterpoints Lacey (ibid., p. 782) presents is the recognition that pressure towards felixibilisation in labour markets is not as deeply felt in all economies, particularly those which are more highly coordinated, as in northern Europe and Scandinavia. She argues that these countries have been 'less influenced by "neo-liberalism" than have liberal market economies, such as the USA or the UK' (ibid.). Moreover, Lacey highlights the importance and complexity of state institutions and, in turn, the actors who shape and are shaped by them. She observes (ibid., p. 781) that 'states are, of course, complex entities at institutional levels'. She concludes (ibid., p. 790) by arguing that one of the omissions in Wacquant's analysis that urgently requires explanation is 'the question of why some countries do, and some do not, produce decisive penal severity amid a relatively widespread diffusion of law and order, and penal populist rhetoric'. As Lacey indicates, the best way of answering such questions is through transnational, comparative research. Such an endeavour is beyond the scope of this book, but I would argue there is also some merit in building on and exploring further one of the other linkages made by Wacquant: the connection between the use of imprisonment and the management of social insecurity.

Prisons and insecurity

Wacquant's observation of the use of prisons as instruments to manage insecurity is an important one that requires further, in-depth consideration. As discussed above, Baker and Roberts (2005) have suggested that globalisation may facilitate tendencies towards convergence both in the homogenisation of problems and responses to them. The rise in the prominence of the problem of security (both in a subjective and an objective sense) is, arguably, a global phenomenon. Likewise, particular strategies for pursuing it seem to be converging and proliferating. These ideas will be examined in greater depth throughout later chapters in this book (particularly Chapter 6). However, at this point I wish to put forward the idea that the increased reliance on the prison may be indicative of an increasing tendency within individual nation states to symbolically manage the perennial, elusive, and apparently growing, concern with social insecurity.

The gradually increasing use of the prison in five continents (Walmsley, 2011) may suggest that the prison is already playing a significant role in symbolically tackling the problem of insecurity. It might be argued that the central tenets of the ideology of imprisonment (described above as exclusion, punishment and rehabilitation) hold some resonance across many cultures and political divides, even if in different measures. As a result, the use of the prison as a means to symbolically manage public insecurities may be a convenient tactic for governments to take. The symbolic role of the prison in popular culture and in the public consciousness may provide an impetus for nudging individual states towards heavier prison usage to manage subjective feelings of insecurity amongst their respective populations. If there is a growing global hegemony of an ideology of imprisonment, then this convergence of thinking may be reinforcing already established beliefs in the role of the prison within individual nation states. The symbolic function of the prison and the taken-for-granted assumptions about what prisons are for, therefore, may be facilitating a gradual drift towards increased prison use around the world. The global legitimisation of imprisonment, it might be argued, may increase public expectations for the use of this sanction, thus making it more tempting and more likely that governments will give in to these expectations. The increased use of the prison is taking place in spite of acknowledged continued failings of the prison as a means for either controlling crime or curing other social problems (e.g., improving social mobility or social cohesion) and its contradictory and incompatible goals of punishment and rehabilitation. The power of its symbolic and taken-for-granted place within crime control agendas may simply be too strong to continue to resist, particularly in times of increasing uncertainty and insecurity. That is, use of the prison may correlate with subjective feelings of safety and well-being amongst populations, which inevitably vary with a range of other social, economic and political factors (these ideas are explored further in Chapter 6).

One way of examining how prisons come to be associated with the pursuit of security (and conversely how the pursuit of security has begun to infiltrate the inner world of prisons) is to take a bottom-up, analytical approach beginning at the institutional and policy levels. Further, tendencies towards harsher penal measures, the commensurate diminishing of social welfarist concerns and the connection of these trends to the pursuit of security may also be best observed at institutional and policy levels. One of the crucial shifts that Wacquant spends less time on in his analyses is the shift in American penal ideology away from rehabilitative purposes of imprisonment towards a law-and-order ideology (Cavadino and Dignan, 2002, pp. 24–6). Indeed, identification of the ways in which such shifts take place within individual nation states might offer some useful insights into the particular drivers or gradual processes that have preceded them. Although examinations of this nature within a single jurisdiction will inevitably only draw out highly contingent institutional or state-specific features, they may offer insight into the *ways* such transitions take place. Such explorations will also assist in identifying the processes by which wider trends and ideologies are manifest at institutional levels. Chapters 3 to 5 undertake such examinations by considering the early development and evolution of men's long-term, maximum-security prisons in England. These prisons provide an in-depth illustration of the difficulties associated with the contradictory purposes of prisons (particularly, punishment and rehabilitation) and the gradual changes that have taken place at institutional levels, which have contributed to the intensification of the focus on punishment and the decline of social welfarist concerns. In addition, because these are long-term prisons they also provide an opportunity to take into account the way prisons do sometimes serve the purposes that the public expects them to, namely: to hold securely those who have committed serious acts of harm against other people.

Conclusion

Despite the lack of evidence that the prison successfully fulfils its supposed purposes, there persists a strong social and political attachment to it as a crime control tool and as a symbol of societal censure. Rather than abating, however, the use of the prison appears to be gaining in popularity across many nation states, with imprisonment rates increasing fairly steadily, particularly in North America, the United Kingdom, Australasia and other Western European countries from 1970 onwards. There would appear to be a growing consensus that prisons are an acceptable means by which problems of crime can be tackled. As increasingly taken-for-granted social institutions, it may be argued that they come to signify and symbolise other social and political concerns, particularly those associated with public safety and national and global security. The punishment function of the prison and its orientation towards marginal, less eligible groups or dangerous others is becoming magnified in increasingly uncertain social and economic conditions. This magnification is intensified further by a growing tendency towards the use of the prison for symbolic purposes that are justified by an increasingly global hegemony of imprisonment, which has been bolstered both by law-and-order politics and exclusionary political rhetorics.

With the acceptance of the prison as the preferred means of crime control the question of how best to manage problems associated with social breakdown, disorder or transgression automatically invite responses which focus, firstly, on how to punish or otherwise treat those deemed criminal and, secondly, on how to make prisons work better to achieve this task. As will be illustrated in the examination of English long-term, maximum-security prisons, in Chapters 3 through 5, experiments with rehabilitation and less austere prison environments have been attempted at different times. However, the punitive foundations of imprisonment have frequently negated these attempts. The use of the prisons has always been accompanied by a complexity in institutional penal affairs. Therefore opportunities in nation states to question the extent to which prisons serve any of their purported purposes have continually been obscured by the bulky machinery of prisons and the running of day-to-day operational matters. Further, the continued failure of prisons has often resulted in calls for greater penal severity. As will be revealed, a firm public and political commitment to prisons and the various complexities that they bring with them seem to ensure that they remain a feature of criminal justice landscapes.

3
Establishing Long-Term, Maximum-Security Imprisonment in England

Introduction

This chapter examines the development of English long-term, maximum-security prison policy and its early practice. The story of the establishment of these prisons is of particular interest because their pedigree includes aspects of liberal Western European penal thinking, but with more punitive tendencies. Informed by considerations of policy and academic literature and interviews with long-serving prison service senior managers and staff, the chapter explores in detail what might be called the first era in the evolution of English long-term, maximum-security prisons, which took place between 1968 and 1994. This era saw a continual grappling with the tensions between implementing a liberal regime aimed at rehabilitating prisoners, minimising the negative effects of long-term imprisonment and attempts to establish security and control. By contrast, the second era (discussed in Chapter 4), from 1995 onwards, saw a gradual decline of liberal principles in favour of more austere and repressive prison regimes that were further bolstered by the growing importance of the concept of security.

Close examination of the development and evolution of English long-term, maximum-security prisons effectively illustrates the contradictions associated with the ideology of imprisonment, in particular, the tensions between delivering punishment and fulfilling rehabilitative ideals. A detailed look at English maximum-security imprisonment provides a unique opportunity to examine specific aspects of penal policymaking, implementation and transition that are often lost in broader or comparative penal analyses. Furthermore, these detailed examinations of penal policy and practice expose the way the bulky and intricate machinery of a penal system can obscure its ideological underpinnings and the wider purposes prisons serve. This chapter and the next exemplify the ways that political economic dimensions and other ideological functions of imprisonment become lost in operational, security or administrative matters, as do the wider social problems prisons are apparently intended to solve.

The bulky machinery of prisons and criminal justice

In the present Prison Service it's like you've got this empty room … there's nothing in the room at all [and] in the middle of the room there's this little engine and it's chugging away there. And people come in and say:

What's that?
That's the Prison Service engine!
What does it do?
Well, it chugs away.
Yeah, but it doesn't have any wheels; it's just bolted there in the middle of the room.
Yeah, but that's what it does. It goes. It consumes fuel and needs people to fix it and maintain it and everything else.
But what does it do?
Well, it runs!!
Yeah, but what else?
Well, that's what it does. It runs.

In a nutshell that's the Prison Service. It runs, it exists, so it can run to be there running. Oh, what's this bill here; oh, it's fuel for the Prison Service engine, you know? Hey, what about all these wage bills here? Those are for mechanics who service the Prison Service engine; they've got to be paid and they've got to go on courses to learn how the engine works. And this bloody great engine is just chugging away in this empty room, consuming things. But what does it *do*? Don't ask that question, you're a troublemaker, aren't you? I've met people like you before. You're being awkward. … because it's always run, it's been running for hundreds of years, it's one of Britain's proudest traditions. (prisoner)

The above somewhat facetious description of the British Prison Service was made by a prisoner, serving a whole-life tariff, who was interviewed during the research on which this book draws. Prisoners' perspectives on the experience of punishment will be considered in Chapter 5. However, the sentiment encapsulated within the above quotation reflects one of the main aims of this chapter, namely to elucidate the bulky machinery of prisons and the way it detracts from their failings and their other ideological functions. The bulky machinery to which I am referring is, primarily, found in the complex organisational structures and practical dilemmas that the running of a penal system inevitably produces. Less tangibly, however, this machinery also includes the policies and legal frameworks that the use of prisons requires and produces. Systems of imprisonment are encumbered by the attempt to operationalise the practical roles prisons are expected to fulfil (that is, at the very least to house those who commit certain censured acts, but more challengingly to reform people, to punish them and to ensure public safety). As will be shown, attempts to operationalise and fulfil these roles inevitably result in the implementation of various policies, legal considerations and penal experiments – each of which is accompanied by its own elaborate apparatus, requiring significant attention in its own right from policy-makers, governments and practitioners. The next section of this chapter begins to illustrate this complexity by examining the context, events and circumstances under which the decision to establish long-term, maximum-security prisons in England was made.

Ideological and historical underpinnings of English maximum-security prisons

The values of the liberal elite

In relation to the study of prisons and punishment it is useful to first acknowledge the values and apparent trends in thinking that became dominant amongst the ruling liberal elites who were influential in shaping penal policy and applying limits to prescriptions of punishment in Britain. Ian Loader (2006) has argued that crime policy in England and Wales in the middle decades of the twentieth century was largely shaped by liberal elites. He (ibid., p. 562) carefully investigates 'liberal elitism as a "structure of feeling" or sensibility … as a set of express and implied beliefs and values about the proper conduct of government towards crime and the public passions it arouses'. Drawing on reading and analysis of key texts and extended biographical interviews with former civil servants and other key figures concerned with crime and penal politics, Loader argues that the governing elite who were responsible for crime and penal policy held a ruling disposition that could be characterised (as one of his interviewees dubbed it) as 'Platonic guardianship', 'which *generated* policies and *conditioned* reactions to events' (ibid., p. 563).

Loader outlines three commitments of Platonic guardianship: the project of being civilised, building good thinking consensus, and managing public opinion. The approach of liberal elitism in pursuing effective crime and penal policy, according to Loader's research, included commitment to being decent, humane and constrained, and was articulated and legitimated to the public in these terms (ibid., p. 564). Further, there was a view that public demands for vengeance needed to be 'managed' in 'an effective and civilised manner' (ibid.). To meet such ends, attempts were made to 'build good thinking consensus' (ibid., p. 565), which involved developing crime and penal policy on the basis of and in deliberation with expert knowledge and opinion. As Loader's research makes clear, there was a relatively small group of elites, made up of politicians, senior administrators, penal reformers and academic criminologists, who worked to shape crime and penal policy and who were 'wedded to the belief that government ought to respond to crime (and public anger and anxiety about crime) in ways that above all, seek to preserve "civilised values"' (ibid., p. 563). As will begin to become evident in the next section of this chapter, these values and the influence they had on penal policymaking, in part influenced the context in which the decision to establish long-term, maximum-security prisons was made.

The abolition of the death penalty

The increased use of long-term imprisonment and the decision to establish maximum-security prisons in England was precipitated by the decision to suspend and then abolish the death penalty. Before delving into the details of the precise way in which this occurred, it is important to first sketch out some of the contextual background behind the decision for abolition.

The decision to abolish the death penalty was neither consensus-based nor the result of public pressure to do so. Indeed, the issue was considerably debated in the House of Lords and was not an altogether popular decision with the general public (Potter, 1993). This can be evidenced by the fact that in 1966, just one year after the moratorium on the death penalty began, Ian Brady and Myra Hindley were convicted of the Moors Murders (the victims were children) and public outcry called for a reinstatement of the death penalty (Thomas, 1972). The decision for abolition, then, was not necessarily a reconfiguration of social values in relation to punishment nor was it an indicator of growing public intolerance of harsh punishments (though there had been public protests against some executions in the late 1950s and early

1960s). The passing of the Death Penalty Act 1965, it may be argued, was made possible by a confluence of factors which converged at a particular historical moment (for a more detailed examination of abolition, see Potter, 1993). In addition, the final move towards abolition was not a wholesale shift in the sensibilities of the British public, but a decision taken on their behalf by ruling elites.

The group of liberal elites in favour of abolition (and, in particular, Labour MP Sydney Silverman who introduced the private member's bill to suspend the death penalty) were concerned with finding more humane ways of dealing with the violation of social norms (Potter, 1993). Although retribution was agreed (by those debating the issue) as a necessary and valid goal of punishment, it was suggested by proponents of abolition that there should also be the 'possibility of reformation' (Lord Ramsay, quoted in ibid., p. 201). Abolition was advocated for on the grounds that execution devalued human life and left no possibility for reclamation. Further, it was argued that after a period of imprisonment (albeit a lengthy period, though no specific guidelines were discussed in this regard) a person could be returned to society as 'reformed'. The beliefs in the reformative potential of imprisonment and of human beings and the need for retribution are important precursors to understanding the thinking that came to shape the policy of long-term imprisonment in England.

In a practical sense, the suspension of the death penalty began to exert new pressures on penal practice and organisation. That is not to say, however, that the increased use of long-term prison sentences was a result of the cessation of the *practice* of capital punishment, but it did seem to be associated with the abolition of its *possibility* as a punishment.

Numbers of long-term and especially life-sentenced prisoners began to rise dramatically after the moratorium on the death penalty began. In 1962 the life-sentenced prisoner population was around 350. By 1968 this number had risen to 550 and by 1977 it was 1,286. This was an increase of 233 per cent (King and Morgan, 1980, p. 79). This increase cannot be explained as a result of an accumulation of prisoners who would have previously been executed. From March 1957 (when the Homicide Act was passed, which differentiated between capital and non-capital murders) to December 1964 when the Abolition Bill was introduced, only 29 executions took place (Potter, 1993, p. 192). Further, it was not that there had been a dramatic increase in violent crime or murder. It is true that from 1965 onwards there were a higher number of people *convicted* for murder (Richards, 1999, p. 23). However, this was not indicative of an increase in homicide rates. The murder rate from at least the 1940s through to the end of the late 1970s remained relatively stable (see ibid., p. 11). The sudden increase in murder convictions, then, can be explained by the apparent reluctance of juries to convict people for murder or capital murder (after the 1957 Homicide Act) for fear of the possibility that those convicted could face the death penalty (Potter, 1993).

In addition to a rise in convictions, abolition also seemed to result in increased terms of imprisonment for life-sentenced prisoners[1] and the imposition of longer fixed-term sentences. After abolition, life sentences began to include mandatory minimum terms of imprisonment. Prior to this it was possible for a life-sentenced prisoner to be released early. In 1953 the Royal Commission on Capital Punishment reported that most life-sentenced prisoners who had been spared the death penalty[2] were released on licence after 10–13 years' imprisonment (Padfield, 2002, p. 16). Further, Nicola Padfield (ibid.) found that:

> In the period between 1900–1949 15 lifers served less than a year and 53 served only one to three years. One served 22 years, no one served longer than that ... By 1953, it was exceptional for anyone to serve more than 15 years and the usual sentences were much shorter.

It seems that the *possibility* of the death penalty – more so than its use – had been instrumental in tempering the use of long-term imprisonment as it appeared to encourage a modicum of compassionate leniency amongst jurors and in sentencing practices. There is a certain irony in the fact that the possibility of the most final of punishments resulted in less punitive sentencing. However, this does not suggest that the availability of harsher punishments would necessarily reduce their active use. It may indicate, by contrast, that if criminal justice processes include space for leniency then jurist and court decision-making may be more inclined towards generosity.

The fact of increasing numbers of prisoners serving long sentences began to pose practical problems for the prison system and, as will be discussed in the next section, was an indirect influence on the establishment of maximum-security prisons in England.

Establishing maximum-security prisons

The decision to create English maximum-security prisons was precipitated by gradual changes in sentencing and operational difficulties with the management of prisoners. Increases in sentence lengths and higher numbers of long-term prisoners, as discussed above, had given rise to questions about the particular needs and custodial arrangements for long-term prisoners. The problem of how to manage prisoners who may pose risks to security (that is, those who may escape) had begun to be seriously considered by penal policymakers in the early 1960s when plans for a maximum-security block were debated (King and Morgan, 1980, p. 70). There was a prevailing view amongst high-level prison managers, however, that security measures in prisons should not be excessive. Further, the concept of security was not strictly thought about in terms of tactical arrangements in prisons. The Chairman of the Prison Commission (Arthur W. Peterson) argued that prisons should offer a *sense of security* for prisoners as well as safety for both prisoners and staff. Further, there seemed to be concern that high levels of physical prison security would lead to repressive prison conditions, which were thought to be undesirable for the treatment and adjustment of prisoners. In a short paper in the *British Journal of Criminology* in 1961, which reported on the prison-building programme, Peterson (1961, pp. 308–9) argued:

> Modern methods of penal treatment are based on the principle that a man cannot be led to adjust himself to the demands of society by depriving him of every form of social experience while he is in prison. Freedom of association between inmates and a regime which provides opportunities for varied activities with some freedom of choice for the individual inmate provide the conditions within which his ability to change himself for the better can be tested and developed.

Due to this apparent 'minimum use of security principle', a maximum-security block was not built at this time (King and Morgan, 1980, p. 70), but questions about how to manage security risks persisted and became more pertinent when a number of high-profile prison escapes occurred in the mid-1960s. Further, the fact that a substantial proportion of these and a number of previously recorded prison escapes had been carried out by long-term prisoners meant that questions surrounding both long-term and maximum-security imprisonment arose simultaneously (Home Office, 1968, para. 44, p. 18).

The Mountbatten Report

Between August 1964 and December 1966 five high-profile escapes occurred from five separate prisons (Home Office, 1966). Among the escapees was George Blake, a former British spy convicted for being a double agent for the Soviet Union, who was serving an unprecedented 42-year prison sentence. In response to the escapes and out of concern about prison security more generally the then Home Secretary (Roy Jenkins) commissioned Lord Mountbatten to head an inquiry.

The Mountbatten Report (1966) represents an important policy moment in the history of penal matters in England and Wales. It is the document that established the use of security categories for prisons and prisoners, which continue to be used in England and Wales today.[3] Moreover, the Mountbatten Report marked the first time that prison security was examined in tactical terms. The report discusses a wide range of operational strategies that could be deployed to strategically enhance prison security (including the use of dog patrols, specialist security training, and radio links between prisons and local police). Although a retrospective analysis of the Mountbatten Report might suggest that, in many respects, it was measured and careful in its process and tone (particularly in comparison to the more vitriolic prison inquiry reports of the 1990s, see Chapter 4), it was perceived by some in penal policy quarters to represent a very different ideological position from that which prevailed. For example, Price (2000), examining the origins of security categorisation, cites Thomas (1972) who identified the 'lean to security after the report's publication as being "ideologically unthinkable" in previous decades, times still dominated by the inter-war ethos of treatment, training and reform' (Price, 2000, p. 6). Indeed, significant aspects of the report reveal moments of divergence from prevailing welfarist or liberal perspectives and foreshadow the conceptualisation of security as the raison d'être in prison administration that was to occur in the mid-1990s (see Liebling, 2002; and Chapter 4, this volume).

The concern over the management of long-term prisoners was, in part, associated with a belief that such prisoners were the most likely to pose operational threats to control and security. The Mountbatten Report presents the view that the increasing propensity towards security breaches (i.e., escapes) was associated with the imposition of long prison sentences. The report (Home Office, 1966, para. 205, p. 54) stated:

> A new factor has been introduced in recent years by the suspension of the death penalty and the unprecedentally [sic] long fixed sentences of imprisonment that have been imposed by the Courts. The whole philosophy of prison administration and treatment has depended on the fact that even a man sentenced to life imprisonment had a reasonable hope that if he mended his ways he would be allowed to return to free society. Although a man's behaviour under prison conditions is rightly not the only consideration in deciding when to release him, it is certainly relevant, and the hope of release

is a powerful disincentive to escape. Similarly, men with long fixed sentences are able to earn remission of which they will lose some or all if they make a successful or unsuccessful attempt to escape. This system of rewards and punishments does not apply to the very long sentences which have been imposed in recent years – or to a sentence which is in fact for life or most of it – and it is certainly unlikely to influence the behaviour of a man serving 42 years if he is weighing up the advantages of making an attempt at escape.

The above text sets the problem of long-term imprisonment against the apparent belief (at the time) that control and security relied, in part, on the incentive of eventual release. In this sense, concerns over the use of long-term imprisonment were partly associated with operational matters. However, it is also evident that there was a prevailing liberal philosophy that even prisoners sentenced to life imprisonment should have a reasonable hope of release. There is a consistency of thinking in the Mountbatten Report with sentiments expressed in debates surrounding the abolition of the death penalty, particularly the view that a prescribed punishment should not be final. Lord Ramsay had argued that although retribution was a valid aspect of punishment, it ought to include the 'possibility of reclamation ... the possibility of a person being alive, repentant, and different' (quoted in Potter, 1993, p. 201).

The more liberal underpinnings of aspects of the Mountbatten Report (in comparison to more recent prison inquiries, see Chapter 4) notwithstanding, the report and most of its recommendations were not well received by the Home Office. Although its recommendation to adopt security categorisations was unceremoniously accepted and implemented, its other major recommendation – which was to establish a single fortress-style maximum-security prison for prisoners in the highest security category – was met with concern by Home Office policymakers. Their concerns rested in the notion of concentrating high-risk prisoners in a single institution. Specifically, they feared that concentration would create the possibility of a mass breakout or rescue attempt, difficulties with staffing and problems with control and design (Price, 2000, p. 6). Due to the discomfort amongst decision-makers in the Home Office with the notion of concentration, the standing governmental advisory panel, known as the Advisory Council on the Penal System, were asked to undertake a second inquiry, which was tasked with considering the regime for long-term, maximum-security prisoners. For these purposes a subcommittee, chaired by Professor Leon Radzinowicz, a professor of criminology, was formed.

The Radzinowicz Report

Like the Mountbatten Report, the Radzinowicz Report (1968) provides a useful snapshot of the values, discourses and knowledges that converged to create the maximum-security prison system in England. Significantly, the report argued against the proposal of concentration recommended in the Mountbatten Report. It argued, instead, for a policy of dispersal. Thus began, as Price (2006, p. 6) has argued, a long-standing policy debate over concentration versus dispersal that obscured further considerations of security policy for some years to come. However, it is important to acknowledge here that the Mountbatten and Radzinowicz reports set out three, then current, assumptions about prison security that were to remain intact (at least amongst some policymakers and practitioners) for much of the succeeding two decades.

Firstly, it was believed that the painfulness of prison needed to be ameliorated in order to reduce risks to security. Secondly, it was thought that prison security (defined as the prevention of escapes) was facilitated by 'constructive' prison experiences and the humane treatment of prisoners (because these elements provided a disincentive to escape). And finally, threats to security (including loss of control within an establishment) were believed to occur when a prison regime was perceived by prisoners as too repressive. As will become evident below in this chapter, these assumptions were to lead to significant problems with order and control in maximum-security prisons due to the confounding of problems of security with problems of control in official policy (King and Morgan, 1980). Further, there was a lack of recognition in any of the policy documentation that it is difficult to create reformative or rehabilitative environments given the inherently punitive nature of imprisonment. The Radzinowicz Committee's considerations of the operational problems associated with the administration of prisons were forestalled and preempted by the committee's prevailing concerns over the decision to concentrate or disperse high-risk prisoners.

The Radzinowicz Report argued that the problem with concentration was the belief that security should not be pursued at the expense of a constructive regime – even for the most serious or violent prisoners. The report conveyed a clear sense of discomfort with the idea of increasing the 'co-efficient of security' to such an extent as to lead to a repressive prison regime. The report (Home Office, 1968, para. 48, p. 20) stated:

> Finally, and most importantly, we believe, on the basis of all the evidence we have received, that the strengthening of the security of the perimeter removes the very understandable fear in the minds of

many of our English witnesses[4] that the improvement of security will damage the general regime of the prison, lead to greater restrictions being placed on prisoners and thus hinder their treatment and even, perhaps, lead to riots or disturbances within the prison itself.

Ultimately, the Radzinowicz Report argued in favour of a policy of dispersal. This policy aimed to disperse prisoners who required higher conditions of security amongst 'three or four secure, long-term recidivist prisons where the majority would be absorbed into the general population of those prisons' (ibid., para. 209, p. 79). In the event, the policy favouring dispersal was agreed in July 1968 and seven prisons were selected to become part of the first dispersal system.[5]

It is important to note that the population of maximum-security prisons in England has always been a mixture of prisoners – a small number of whom have been convicted of serious harms (serial murder, political violence, espionage, repeated sexual offences) and a larger number of whom have been convicted of less serious harms (burglary, robbery, dangerous driving, arson). Although the majority of maximum-security prisoners in the current dispersal[6] system tend to be those who have been convicted of murder, attempted murder or manslaughter (around 39 per cent, see Figure A.3 in the Appendix), many of even these prisoners could have been allocated to lower-security prisons. This peculiarity of the dispersal prisoner population has had a number of consequences throughout the history of the dispersal system, as will be discussed throughout my examination of the evolution of the dispersal system.

Paternalistic liberalism

The values and principles on which maximum-security confinement in England were founded were, in many ways, consistent with the 'structure of feeling' described by Loader (2006, pp. 563–4) in relation to the notion of Platonic guardianship which he characterised as liberal elitism (described above). In the formation of the policies that sought to guide maximum-security imprisonment, however, it may be that the values that influenced policymakers would be more accurately characterised as paternalistic liberalism.

Despite their divergent recommendations, the Mountbatten and Radzinowicz reports encapsulate a set of values, knowledges and beliefs about prisons and prisoners that assist in understanding why long-term, maximum-security prisons in England took on the particular configuration and approach that they did. Philosophically speaking the rationale behind the original dispersal system was, in sum, based on a number of assumptions that were commensurate with a paternalistic liberalist sentiment that prevailed amongst 1960s liberal elite policymakers. On the one hand, there was a clear sense of penal optimism and belief in the human subject. The discourses used in the Mountbatten and Radzinowicz reports diverged considerably from those that are proliferating in the present-day making of penal policy. On the other hand, the paternalistic tone inherent in some of the arguments seemed to include both a 'politics of resentment' (Friedenberg, 1980, p. 281) and a commitment to maintaining a stratified economic and class structure. It should be remembered that whilst liberal social welfarist ideals included concern for improving the social conditions of the lower classes, they also included the view that they were somewhat 'uncivilised' and needed to be reformed through rehabilitation or other individualised interventions. Prisoners, in particular, were largely constructed as 'unfortunates' in need of paternalistic guidance or societal intervention. Such sentiments remain a problematic feature of present-day interventions and rehabilitative strategies and are magnified by theories of crime that favour a rational choice perspective (Clarke and Felson, 1993; Felson, 2002). Further, what is missing from present-day penal policy considerations, but was evident in 1960s policymaking, is the expressed belief that imprisonment should be used *as* and not *for* punishment.

In penal policy documents of the 1960s there was some indication that the loss of one's liberty was in itself viewed as a severe punishment. The Radzinowicz Report, in particular, put forward the position that no further hardship should be delivered to prisoners through the conditions of their confinement. Long prison sentences were seen as severe and harsh punishments. In this sense, both the Mountbatten and Radzinowicz reports were less concerned with the principle of less eligibility and the need for prison austerity and more concerned with providing a humane regime. As the retributive element of imprisonment was being served by a lengthy prison sentence, their recommendations focused more on protecting reformative concerns. In 1960s penal policy rhetoric, at least, the aim of prison regimes was to provide prisoners with opportunities for self-improvement, to express their autonomy and to prepare to lead law-abiding lives upon their release (Home Office, 1968). Further, there was recognition that the experience of imprisonment was one that necessarily resulted in negative side effects. This was described explicitly in the Radzinowicz Report, which identified the loss of family contact, restrictions on freedom of movement, lack of opportunities for decision-making, alienation and ostracism from wider society, living alongside other people who one may not choose to be in the company of under normal circumstances and being confined against one's will at the hands of the state (ibid.). In light of these unavoidable negative aspects of prison life, the Radzinowicz Report argued that much needed to be put in place in order to attempt to neutralise these effects. The viewpoint that imprisonment was a difficult and punishing experience was a dominant view amongst those who had the power to shape prison policy at the time that maximum-security or dispersal prisons were established. However, as will become evident below, translating these ideas into practice proved exceptionally difficult in the inherently punitive environment of prisons.

Dispersal prisons in practice 1968–94

In the newly formed dispersal system staff and managers struggled to translate the policy of 'a liberal regime within a secure perimeter' (Sparks et al., 1996, p. 6) into practice. Part of the difficulty was that none of the original dispersal prisons were purpose-built as maximum-security prisons[7] and four out of the seven were of a Victorian design. This necessarily limited the creation of the specific conditions and practices that might be more conducive to a humane or liberal regime. Further, there was no account taken of the extent of the punitive culture amongst the existing prison staff who would work in the new dispersal prisons. Whilst there cannot be said to be a homogenous occupational culture amongst prison officers, the nature of prison work inherently produces some tendencies towards punitivity and 'us versus them' constructions of staff–prisoner relationships (see Haney et al., 1973; Crawley, 2004; Scott, 2008). Therefore there were difficulties in establishing the liberal regime ethos in most of the dispersal prisons (Drake, 2006, 2008).

Despite the structural limitations and the difficulties of staff implementing the new regime, the new prisons did provide comparatively better material conditions in relation to lower-security prisons in England and other models of maximum-security confinement that have been adopted elsewhere (see King, 1999; Carlton, 2007; Shalev, 2009). For example, prisoners in all dispersal prisons were (and still are) accommodated in single cells. This was in contrast to most other British prisons at that time. Dispersal prisons also sought to provide a limited amount of space for (some) prisoners to cook their own food if they so chose, and generally spacious gymnasia, workshops and outside facilities. In addition, dispersal prisons were amongst the first to have in-cell sanitation installed.[8] In these ways dispersal prisoners, on the whole, did not suffer the difficulties associated with overcrowding, insufficient activities, slopping out[9] or food quality[10] that lower-category prisoners in Britain have sometimes experienced.

In the original dispersal system (and in contrast to current dispersal prisons) there was also a range of privileges that were (at times) afforded to prisoners and were not common in other prisons.[11] The main areas where prisoners' privileges could be elevated in dispersals from the 1970s through to the mid-1990s were visits, personal property allowances and relative freedom, though it should be noted that these privileges were not available in all dispersals throughout this period and periodically they were given and withdrawn within establishments. The essence of dispersal prison policy was the attempt to create prison experiences that allowed for a reasonable amount of freedom and autonomy for prisoners, a variety of constructive activities (i.e., workshops and education), and opportunities for maintaining family contact. In practice, however, the dispersal policy proved to be fraught by seemingly irresolvable problems of order, control and safety, as well as the persistence of punitive practices, which undermined attempts to create more humane and liberal prisoner experiences.

Problems of order and control

In practice, dispersal prisons showed that there were difficulties in finding a balance between a liberal regime, establishing order and maintaining control (for more detailed considerations of the control problems that troubled dispersal prisons throughout the 1970s, 1980s and early 1990s, see: King and Morgan, 1980, Ch. 3; Home Office, 1984; Sparks et al., 1996; Liebling, 2002; Drake, 2006, 2008). Although the new dispersal prisons appeared to be appropriately secure – there were no escapes from dispersal prisons in their first 19 years of operation – they were troubled by control problems almost immediately. There were disturbances at Parkhurst in 1969, Albany in 1971 and Gartree in 1972 (King and Morgan, 1980, p. 74). A series of fires and incidents, including the taking of hostages, occurred in Albany in 1973 and in 1976 a riot in Hull caused so much damage that Hull had to be removed from the dispersal system for almost a year (ibid., p. 75; Home Office, 1984, p. 58). Interviews with long-serving staff and senior managers conducted during the research on which this book draws (see Appendix for further details) retrospectively characterised the early years of the dispersal system as disorganised or uncoordinated. Dispersal prisons were also difficult places in which to negotiate order:

> There was a prevailing view that there should be dispersals, but if you got much further into the consciousness you'd be pushed to find any clear view about how they were controlled ... we'd say we ended up achieving peace by negotiation, really. We didn't feel particularly powerful, so there was a constant process of tempering with the prisoners who you knew and using shoddy compromising. We would say: 'we won't close your drug dealing operation down, because in the main you don't cause too many problems for us and you give us a bit of grass[12] information, so, it's okay for you to go on dealing.' Those sorts of things were never written down, but in a way, that's how business was done, and in a way, how people felt it *had* to be done to maintain peace and quiet in an estate that had had some horrendous, very dangerous, riots. (senior manager, Prison Service)

Many prison officers who worked in the early dispersal system retrospectively characterised these early years as 'unsafe', 'disorderly' and 'frightening'.

> Staff did not want to come to work. They would drive in to work, get sick in the car park, return home and call in sick. (long-serving prison officer)

Accounts such as this were commonplace amongst long-serving dispersal prison staff and seemed to be indicative of the crisis that was spreading across British prisons throughout the 1970s, 1980s and early 1990s (Fitzgerald and Sim, 1982; Home Office, 1984; King, 1985; Scraton et al., 1991; Sim, 1994).

Problems of control in dispersals and in other prisons necessarily instigated a multiplicity of working theories to explain the difficulties – each emanating from a different perspective or level of analysis. A comprehensive account of competing views on the problems of order, including those in the early dispersal system, can be found in Roy King and Rod Morgan's (1980) in-depth consideration of the work of the May Committee (an inquiry into the United Kingdom Prison Service). However, the official view that prevailed within the Prison Service and amongst those making penal policy was built, as Sim (1994, p. 33) has argued, 'on the ideological assertion that the disorder was orchestrated by a small number of subversive recalcitrants who, once identified, could be removed from the main body of the prison population before the contamination of deviance could be spread further'. Alternatively, the widespread problem of order in British prisons, especially in dispersals, might have instead been seen as 'a clear illustration of the still fragile nature of the modern prison's social order and the institution's lack of legitimacy in the hearts and minds of many of the confined' (ibid., p. 34).

In dispersal prisons, despite the privileges, the relative freedom and autonomy and various other material benefits, prisoners were still serving very long sentences, confined away from society, their families and the possibility of a normal life. The experience of confinement, therefore, inevitably overwhelmed anything productive the system was trying to achieve and prisoners rebelled. They engaged in significant power struggles with the staff and with each other that often resulted in violent confrontations, disturbances and riots. (The riots, however, were more often the result of prisoner resistance against staff or the conditions of confinement and were not often the result of power struggles between prisoner groups.) Operationally, the regimes lacked structure and that created high levels of uncertainty for both staff and prisoners, which, in turn, exacerbated the problems with order and control. Dispersal prisons, therefore, were largely unpleasant places to live or to work and were often fraught with confrontation.

> A lot of staff were made terribly miserable ... I remember a prisoner ... boiling up a pan of oil and pouring it over an officer's head and *he thought he could do that*. He didn't think he could get away with it, but he felt *able* to do that. And that is a horrendous indictment of the breakdown of trust ... There was a murder, in fact. There was a bloke on A-Wing, who was a notorious paedophile and he was murdered ... So these sort of cataclysmic events were happening ... This pervasive situation where staff were worrying, am I going to have something happen to me like oil poured on my head, which is horrendous. Prisoners were worried, am I going to be murdered in my cell? Am I going to be stabbed? And lower-level violence of prisoners throwing jars of excrement and urine and fires being set, televisions being thrown off the landings. It was a pretty unpleasant place all round. (former prison governor)

At the time the research on which this book draws took place there were several members of staff and senior managers still working in each of the five dispersal prisons who had witnessed, first hand, the disorder of the late 1980s and early 1990s (and even a few who had worked in dispersals in the 1970s). Characterisations like that presented above about the first era of dispersals were commonplace among them. Moreover, such accounts of the early years permeated and infused contemporary dispersal staff culture in myriad ways. As a result, institutional memory was to play a significant role in legitimating and justifying the changes that would eventually occur.

> To this day there is a bit of animosity amongst the staff who have been there a long time towards other staff who ran away when a wing went up [a serious disturbance broke out] and did not help their colleagues. People got really hurt; some have lost their nerve because of it. (long-serving prison officer)

Disorder and prisoner resistance continued to trouble the dispersal prison system until the mid-1990s. As Chapter 4 will discuss, however, the problems with disorder would not be recognised as a symptom of the contradictions and failures associated with the practice of imprisonment but would, instead, come to be constructed as the result of liberal policies.

Enter law-and-order politics

While problems of order persisted within dispersal prisons the policy and political context outside prisons began to shift. 'Tough on crime' discourses, coupled with those that firmly located causes of crime within individuals, had begun to emerge in the USA when Richard Nixon declared a 'war on drugs' in 1971, but such discourses rose most rapidly during the Reagan–Bush administrations (1981–92) (Simon, 2007). Law-and-order politics came to the fore in the UK in the 1979 general election (Hale, 1989; Sim, 2009). Although crime rates and crime policy had been part of political agendas in the UK to some extent since the 1960s, prior to 1979 the problem of crime was not overtly constructed as solvable by specific political policies. As a campaigning tactic leading up to the 1979 election, the Conservatives argued that the Labour government had undermined the rule of law and that its 'permissive' policies were the cause of rising crime rates. After Margaret Thatcher's election victory in 1979, the Conservatives implemented a variety of criminal justice policies and began to increase spending on law-and-order services (particularly police, courts and prisons) (Downes and Morgan, 2007; Sim, 2009). As has been recognised by a number of social commentators and criminologists, similar political rhetoric also began to emerge in many countries around the globe from the mid-1990s onwards (Garland, 2001; Pratt et al., 2005; Kury, 2008; Wacquant, 2009; Snacken, 2010).

In Britain, the Conservative government's politicisation of law-and-order issues gradually began to chip away at the conduct of government that had been preserved by liberal elites. Likewise, liberal values began to be constructed as blameworthy for problems of crime, moral and social deterioration and for limiting the economic potential of the nation. Sim (2009) has provided a detailed consideration of penal politics in Britain from 1974–97. Arguing from an abolitionist-informed view, he suggests that the ideological terrain of penal politics in Britain has supported 'the continuing presence of the prison as a bulwark against the criminality and disorderly behaviour of the powerless' (Sim, 2009, p. 8). He identifies the prison as a key state institution that contributes to the reproduction of a social order that reinforces structural inequalities based on class, gender, 'race' and sexualities. By tracing events and movements within the Conservative Party, Sim identifies the emergence of the 'Thatcherite bloc' and pays particular attention to the hegemonic role this bloc played in the setting of 'ideological parameters for establishing where responsibility lay and what should be done about it' (ibid., p. 16). His analyses reveal an intensification of law-and-order processes that combined with the rise of principles of the free market and a strong state which worked to simultaneously disadvantage the poor, discursively create 'enemies within' and prepare the scene for an expansionist prison complex. This coincided with the decline in liberal elitism or Platonic guardianship as outlined by Loader (2006). Loader argues that the Conservative Party engaged in a rhetoric that explicitly broke with the policy trajectory of the post-war period. He (ibid., p. 574) writes:

> [T]he Conservative government of the early 1980s launched a sustained, radical critique of the alleged weaknesses and indecisiveness of liberal rule, and its role in rendering Britain 'ungovernable' (King, 1975). The commitment of Platonic guardianship to patient, deliberative policy formation and its excessive zeal to protect individual rights and keep a lid upon public passions, failed, on this view, to recognise that good order and government require that 'enemies within' (whether they be burglars, muggers, rioters or striking miners) be identified and defeated. What followed in the early 1980s was, inter alia: a penal rhetoric dominated by deterrence and retribution … and a crime-fighting agenda.

Although this 'authoritarian populism' (Hall, 1980) included a change in the punitive tone of penal policy discourses and within penal politics, as already discussed, Sim (2009) has argued that punitivism has always been, and remains, a central feature of penal policy in Britain. Its evolution has been deeply influenced by this fundamental orienting principle. The persistence of punitivism notwithstanding, in the late 1980s and early 1990s a shift in penal discourse began as did the steady decline of what I described above as paternalistic liberalism in dispersal prisons. It also included a reintensification of Victorian ideas about the 'morally dangerous underclass' (ibid., p. 54), austerity and the principle of less eligibility. Further, as both Loader (2006) and Sim (2009) point out, the Thatcher government's law-and-order rhetoric included a vision that sought to identify enemies within. According to Sim (ibid., p. 55), this was 'an enemy who ranged from conventional criminals to illegal immigrants and from drug takers to single parents …'. Therefore prisoners were a key group to target as 'enemies' (a theme which will be picked up again in the next chapter) and dispersal prisoners were especially singled out to receive this label.

Whilst these shifts in penal politics were occurring outside prisons, the crisis within British prisons and the 'fragile nature' of their order (Sim, 1994, p. 34) persisted and spread. In 1990 the worst riots in English prison history erupted in Strangeways (now Manchester) Prison (Carrabine, 2005; Coyle, 2005, pp. 26–8). The riots took place over 25 days and spread across six other (non-dispersal) prisons. With the riots still in progress the Home Secretary appointed Lord Justice Woolf to lead an inquiry into the events that led to the riots. Lord Woolf expanded the terms of reference to include consideration of the general state of imprisonment and its use in England and Wales (Woolf, 1991).

The Woolf Report was widely acclaimed for its thorough consideration of the systemic issues that led to the riots and the endemic problems of the prison system generally. Penal reformers have described the report as the most enlightened blueprint for improving the prison system presented to any post-war government (Player and Jenkins, 1994). The report highlighted and reinforced the existing belief that humane, constructive regimes created controlled and secure prison environments. It also introduced the idea that a balance between security, control and justice (defined primarily as the fair treatment of prisoners) needed to be achieved. Roy King and Sandra Resodihardjo (2010, p. 69) have argued that '[t]he Woolf Report recognised that security and control would only be achieved if prisoners were also treated fairly and had access to justice.'

Somewhat in keeping with the beliefs of liberal elitism the Woolf Report set out detailed recommendations for the ways in which prison experiences could be made more constructive and the goal of rehabilitation more actively and humanely pursued. To some extent the Woolf Report recommendations were reflected in the White Paper *Custody, Care and Justice* (Home Office, 1991). However, as King and Resodihardjo (2010, p. 69) point out, 'a further high security escape from Brixton brought with it a retrenchment and many of Woolf's reforms were progressively undermined by [then Home Secretary Michael] Howard's claims that "prison works" and his insistence on "austere regimes"'. But it is important also to note that the Woolf Report did not challenge the acceptability of the prison as a means of managing the problem of crime (Sim, 1994), nor did it consider the political economic dimensions of the use of the prison. Although the Woolf Report may have provided a thorough consideration of the systemic causes of the riots, the systems it focused on were contained within the walls of the prison. The broader social system and structures that rely on prisons to manage the marginalised, socially excluded, disorderly and transgressive members of society remained unexamined by Woolf. The Woolf Report may stand as a significant blueprint for prison reform, but as such it can be seen as a proposed extension to an existing but fundamentally flawed apparatus. What was needed was a radical rethinking of criminal justice practice and social justice issues. The moment for undertaking such a task, however, quickly passed. The rationale for the prison was further reinforced, as King and Resodihardjo (2010) point out above, by Michael Howard's claims that 'prison works' thereby politically and discursively reinforcing the importance of the prison in the fight against crime. At the same time, two high-profile escapes from two dispersal prisons in late 1994 and early 1995 focused public and political attentions on prison practices. For my purposes here, it is important to note that it was at this point that the pursuit of security began to take on new meaning within the Prison Service and especially in dispersals. The extent and implications of this shift will be further developed in the next chapter.

Conclusion

By considering the intricacies of the development and early evolution of maximum-security prisons in England the sheer complexity associated with the use of imprisonment comes into fuller view. It becomes easier to recognise how it is that the failures of prisons and their inherent contradictions can be completely and repeatedly overlooked. The bulky apparatus of the 'prison engine' makes administrators, practitioners and policymakers (and often, academics) busy with and distracted by other concerns. The prison draws us in by presenting a number of administrative, managerial and operational challenges that prevent us from standing back and recognising that we are engaged in a futile exercise. Nevertheless, the examination of these intricacies also sheds some light on the way particular criminal justice policies, measures and approaches evolve.

In examining the precipitating events that led to the establishment of long-term, maximum-security prisons and the competing values on which they were based, the particular approach that maximum-security prisons in England took is better understood. Whilst social welfare concerns were present in their planning and founding policies, it is argued that these concerns were inevitably undermined by the contradictions associated with the practice of imprisonment and its fundamental orientation towards punishment. By the early 1990s, dispersals and lower-security prisons alike reached a point of breakdown and near collapse. The Strangeways riots and continued problems of disorder in dispersal prisons seemed to create the possibility of a defining moment in penal policymaking. These events may have been construed by prison administrators and political leaders as indicative of a failing system that needed to be carefully and thoughtfully reconsidered with a view to finding a way to be more parsimonious about prison use. However, at the moment that the breakdown was taking place, the political regime in power was one that heavily supported an ideology of imprisonment and was firmly opposed to social welfarist concerns. It had also begun to incorporate a law-and-order rhetoric within its discourses to be used as a tactic for garnering public support and gaining political legitimacy. And so the decision was made that 'prison works' and penal policy and practice were emphasised in order to address the breakdown, as the next chapter will elucidate.

4
A State of Security in Maximum-Security Prisons

Introduction

Picking up the story of English maximum-security prisons where the previous chapter left off, this chapter considers what might be seen as the second era of dispersal prisons, which, I argue, began in 1995 and continues up to the beginning of the second decade of the twenty-first century. It examines the policy and political contexts that contributed to the gradual decline of social welfarist principles in maximum-security prison policy and practice in favour of a more explicit emphasis on austere, harsh and repressive prison regimes. It argues that the decline in social welfarist concerns in penal policymaking was a deliberate political decision that was facilitated by key events and the responses to them. In particular, the introduction of security thinking into maximum-security prisons that coincided with the change in policy focus has proven to be a useful tool for introducing, retaining and legitimising austere and repressive policies.

This chapter argues that the transformation of the meaning of the concept of security and its new role as a primary purpose of English maximum-security prisons has somewhat diminished the contradictions inherent in the ideology of imprisonment (described in Chapter 2). By reorienting prison environments more heavily towards security, penal policymakers, prison managers and staff struggle less to devise and implement humane regimes that actively seek to neutralise the negative effects of imprisonment. In practice, the state of security in English maximum-security prisons amounts to a version of 'harsh justice' that is both overtly and covertly punishing (as will be discussed in more detail in Chapter 5). Moreover, it is argued that the infiltration of security thinking and its particular 'ideology' has meant that

English maximum-security prisons have become not only places of punishment – the end product of the criminal justice system – they are increasingly devices of exclusion where 'enemies within' are continuously controlled, judged, assessed and kept under surveillance.

A reorientation of penal thinking and practice

The political context

As Chapter 3 outlined, the political context in Britain in the early 1990s included an intensification of law-and-order processes. However, there was much controversy and political contention associated with criminal justice and penal matters. As Richard Sparks (2000, p. 128) has noted, political debate began to emerge around questions of public safety, sentencing practice, parole arrangements and the extent to which prisons delivered 'justice'. The then Home Secretary Michael Howard was the main proponent of a 'prison works' agenda, arguing in favour of austere and repressive prison regimes. Howard 'was critical of the breakdown in the family, lax discipline in schools, the role of television in promoting violence and the lack of individual responsibility for criminal behaviour' (Sim, 2009, p. 59). Implicit in his position was, as Mick Ryan and Joe Sim (1998, p. 176) point out, that prison works, but welfare does not. Such a position was somewhat incongruent with penal policy discourses and thinking at that time. As discussed in Chapter 3, social welfarist ideals had, in part, shaped some of the thinking about and the character of penal arrangements in Britain (albeit alongside paternalistic influences and punitive realities). Furthermore criminal justice policymaking at that time suggested a trend towards reductions in the use of custody. The 1991 Criminal Justice Act included a guiding principle of parsimony in the use of imprisonment for non-violent crimes (Millie et al., 2003, p. 378). Several key events, however, occurred in the early to mid-1990s that began to reorient directions of thinking on penal matters.

In early 1993, two ten-year-old boys murdered two-year-old James Bulger in Liverpool. This attracted immediate attention from the press and television news media that increased throughout the arrests, trial and sentencing. David Green (2008, p. 94) has argued that the Bulger case resulted in significant pressure on policymakers to act. The print media leveraged much of this pressure. Green (ibid., p. 247) astutely points out that 'press discourse can be a misleading indicator of popular sentiment, yet in England, as elsewhere, there is a tendency for policymakers to utilise newspapers as a primary index of public opinion'. In the early 1990s there was considerable opposition in the press with respect to what was seen as soft or liberal criminal justice and penal policy. As Millie et al. (2003, p. 378) have argued, 'elements of the press depicted the reforms introduced by the 1991 Act as liberal do-gooding at a time when crime was out of control'. Such discourses and their proliferation in the media were consistent with those of Howard and his supporters. The Bulger murder was significant enough to mobilise considerable public support for harsher criminal justice penalties. However, two escapes from dispersal prisons in 1994 (from Whitemoor) and 1995 (from Parkhurst) added momentum to the effort. Further, the way the escapes were discursively constructed and reported on in the official inquiry reports and in media coverage contributed to a climate in which law-and-order penal discourses could be reinforced whilst others, which foreground the need for humane prison experiences, were further subjugated and marginalised.

Sparks (2000, p. 131) has argued and illustrated that the Whitemoor and Parkhurst escapes provided a unique opportunity to examine the question: 'How do professional (calculative, pragmatic, results-led) and public (rhetorical, performative) "faces" of the penal question intersect, and with what consequences for each?' He suggests that although these extremely high profile events attracted much media attention, 'their longer-term significance lies in much less visible arenas, namely in the reconstruction of major aspects of prison management and regimes' (ibid., p. 129). Likewise, I will argue that the significance that these events were given and subsequently came to symbolise amongst prison staff and managers was an important element that established and legitimated the pursuit of security in maximum-security prisons as an all-encompassing aim.

Key events and policy influences

On Friday 9 September 1994, six out of the ten prisoners housed in Whitemoor's Special Security Unit[1] (SSU) escaped. All six prisoners were immediately recaptured. On Tuesday 3 January 1995, two category A prisoners and one category B prisoner escaped from Parkhurst prison on the Isle of Wight. They were all recaptured five days later, still on the Isle of Wight. The Woodcock (1994) and Learmont (1995) inquiries examined the events that led up to these two escapes and produced recommendations about how to improve prison security. Together the reports produced 191 recommendations, the majority of which were implemented. The implemented recommendations resulted in a range of new practices and procedures that significantly altered the working and lived experiences of, especially, maximum-security prisons, but also lower-security prisons too. The majority of the recommendations in the two reports were related to matters of either security or control. A few examples of the changes that were made include:

- more prescriptive procedures for searching staff, prisoners, visitors and cells
- volumetric control of prisoners' property
- tighter control over prisoners' movements
- dog patrols
- increased use of CCTV
- refortified perimeter security and increased procedures for monitoring it
- dedicated search teams.

In addition to changes in procedure and practice, the reports represented important shifts in the philosophy of dispersal prison administration. The Woodcock and Learmont reports included a scathing critique of dispersal prison practice. They conveyed the opinion that the liberalised aspects of the dispersal system had gone too far and new limits needed to be set. The Woodcock Report seemed particularly concerned with what were constructed as excesses in the treatment of prisoners. It presented the view that prisons should be austere environments and prisoners should not be afforded privileges. Stephen Shaw (1995, pp. 26–7) has argued:

> The Woodcock Report, in particular, is written in unusually and unhelpfully racy language ... No fewer than 12 pages are given over to listing the property of one prisoner, including such irrelevant details as the fact that one of his jumpers was made by Lacoste and his toilet water by Givenchy.

And in reference to conditions in the Special Security Unit (from where the Whitemoor escape occurred), the Woodcock Report (1994, para. 8.10, p. 63) stated:

> The underlying philosophy [of dispersal prisons] had been to provide a more 'humane environment' for all inmates and this approach had been extended still further for the SSU inmates. A by-product of providing greater privilege, however, had been to create an impression of pampering such prisoners.

In the above passage the use of inverted commas around 'humane environment' seems to indicate disagreement with what constitutes a humane environment. It is evident that humane and liberal approaches are being implicated here as the means through which privilege and pampering took place. They are deliberately not constructed as appropriate approaches to meet the needs of human beings who are being deprived of liberty for significant periods of time.

In practice, it was true that the SSU in Whitemoor did afford prisoners a variety of privileges. These had been put in place and were explicitly justified (by the Director General and the Home Secretary, see Appendix F in the Woodcock Report, 1994) on the grounds that due to the restricted activities available in the SSU, the regime needed to 'provide a modest counterbalance to some of the more draconian aspects of the environment and regime' (ibid., p. 142). These privileges included a virtually unlimited amount of personal property; the facility to order in foodstuffs (paid for with the prisoner's private cash) through designated prison staff; and the provision of one 15-minute phone call each week at public expense to anywhere in the world (the majority of the ten SSU prisoners in Whitemoor at the time were Irish political prisoners). However, the Woodcock Report condemned these practices on the grounds that there were significant abuses of each of these privileges and that established procedures were not being followed consistently. There was no recognition or acknowledgement of the draconian aspects of the regime or that long-term prison sentences were in themselves a severe punishment. In the view of the Woodcock Report, affording privileges to prisoners was simply not justifiable. In support of this view, the Appendices of the Report (Woodcock, 1994, p. 141) included a letter, dated 13 January 1994, to the Home Secretary from a Member of Parliament who had visited Whitemoor's SSU, that stated:

> I visited the SSU unit … It is far too comfortable. The wing has wall-to-wall carpeting, pictures on the wall, curtains, lampshades, soft furnishings, television and [a] sitting room where Satellite TV is available.

The inclusion of this letter in the Appendix of the Woodcock Report is used as further evidence that SSU prisoners were being pampered (see p. 63, para. 8.14), but it signifies a particular ideological position: that prison should be uncomfortable.

As already suggested, the then Home Secretary Michael Howard was of the view that prisons should be 'decent but austere' (see King, 1995,

p. 67). With this phrase the concept of austerity as part of the ideology of imprisonment begins to be reinforced once again in British prisons. This feature of imprisonment lost some of its weight during the first era of dispersals when it was argued that long-term prisons should provide opportunities for choice and variety. However, these more liberal ideas about choice and variety in the prison regimes were summarily dismissed in the wake of the Whitemoor and Parkhurst escapes. The Woodcock and Learmont reports and Howard's proclamations about prison life argued, instead, that prison experiences should not include anything that might be pleasurable or comfortable. Prisons should provide a bland, almost monastic environment in which, presumably, the prisoner is expected to 'reform'.[2] Further, as will be discussed in Chapter 5, ideas about rehabilitation became even more concerned with the 'individual pathology' of prisoners (who from the late-1990s were compelled to complete a number of cognitive behavioural programmes, which were and continue to be favoured over either vocational training or educational opportunities). It is evident that these shifts in emphasis marked a decisive return to and a reinforcement of central aspects of the ideology of imprisonment (austerity, less eligibility and reform), and are indicative of both a political decision to continue to use the prison and to ignore the opportunity to consider alternative responses to it.

That opportunity had arisen from continuous breakdowns in dispersal prison order and the two high-profile escapes. However, as briefly mentioned in Chapter 3, the decision was made not to enter into a radical rethinking of penal policy and prison use, but to continue to rely on prisons – indeed to rely on them more heavily – and to re-emphasise their harsher qualities. To this end, the long history of disorder and prisoner resistance in dispersals, the explosion of riots that began with Strangeways and the escape attempts from Whitemoor and Parkhurst were constructed as operational failings in the apparatus of imprisonment, not as symptoms of an inherently flawed social institution. Furthermore, both political and media discourses at the time were explicitly arguing in favour of the use of harsher measures.

With respect to political rhetoric it might be argued that the heavy use of the prison was in keeping with conservative government political economic policy. As Chapter 2 discussed, right-wing, conservative political rule can be a strong predictor of increased prison use. Media support of harsh justice, however, has perhaps always been a constant. As suggested in Chapter 3, public views as expressed in the media have generally always held punitive undertones. Debate over more civilised criminal justice approaches in the 1960s took place primarily amongst liberal elites, and not often in the media. The difference in the early 1990s and the reason the media held more influence was perhaps the beginning of what Anthony Bottoms (1995) has called populist puni-tiveness. This concept, according to Bottoms (ibid., p. 40) is 'intended to convey the notion of politicians tapping into, and using for their purposes, what they believe to be the public's generally punitive stance'. The moment at which the decision was made to move towards harsher criminal justice measures was made possible by a confluence of factors: the particular leanings of the government that was in power, the Bulger murder, a long history of prison disturbance, two high-profile prison escapes and the rise of populist punitiveness. Whilst these events may have created the conditions that enabled a seemingly justifiable shift towards a harsher approach to criminal justice, the way in which they came to influence penal practice should also be considered.

Dispersal prisons in practice from 1995 onwards

An examination of the changes in dispersal prison practice that occurred after the Whitemoor and Parkhurst escapes provides an opportunity to observe the way the transition towards harsh justice measures in pris-ons was accomplished and the particular means by which the punitive aspects of imprisonment have been intensified.

The research on which this book is based revealed that the escapes were a defining moment in prison staff and senior managers' retrospective accounts of Prison Service history. The Whitemoor and Parkhurst escapes (and the governmental and organisational responses to them) were universally identified by long-serving prison staff and senior managers within the Prison Service as marking the beginning of a new era in the Prison Service as an organisation and particularly in dispersals.

> Yes, I remember that they [the Woodcock and Learmont reports] gave zillions and zillions of recommendations ... there was this giant mushroom cloud exploding in the Prison Service. (senior manager, Prison Service)

The accumulated histories of maximum-security prisons, particularly their problems with disorder (discussed in Chapter 3), contributed to the acceptance of a new approach to prison administration and laid the groundwork for this to occur. The escapes took place at a moment when many of the dispersal prisons were still experiencing high levels of disorder.

When I went in in '93 it was very disordered. It was a very scary place and I'm not easily frightened ... Nobody was in control of the prison, not the staff and not the prisoners ... It was traumatic for staff on the wings ... I mean, it was really serious stuff ... There were lots of assaults, lots of staff intimidation. (former prison governor)

As outlined in Chapter 3, early dispersal prison policy had been based on three fundamental beliefs about how prisons work and how security was to be achieved:

1) The painfulness of long prison sentences needed to be ameliorated by attempts to neutralise the inherently negative effects of imprisonment in order to encourage compliance from prisoners (and prevent escape attempts).
2) A constructive regime and humane treatment facilitated prison security because such measures were thought to offer a disincentive to escape in that they provided the chance for prisoners to engage in self-improvement activities that were of personal benefit to them.
3) Repressive prison conditions would lead to disorder.

The first 25 years of dispersal prison administration, however, had illustrated that these beliefs about prison administration were not borne out in practice. Indeed, amongst prison staff and managers the approach of the dispersal prisons – to create a liberal regime by attempting to afford prisoners increased degrees of relative freedom within the confines of the prison compound – began to be seen as faulty. The above-listed assumptions, therefore, came to be viewed as mistaken and inappropriate for achieving prison order. However, prior to the escapes there was no clear consensus about how order should be achieved and there were still concerns about what the outcome would be if regimes became too repressive.

At the prison level, when the escapes occurred many prison staff were beleaguered and prison managers were uncertain about how to tackle the seemingly endemic problem of disorder in dispersal prisons. Moreover, as a result of the way the escapes were reported in the inquiry reports and in the media, prison staff felt that they were being publicly condemned. The escapes were constructed in disaster terms in public discourses. Prison staff who worked in these establishments at the time felt as though they had been complicit in a disaster.

The problem was that *everybody* jumped on the bandwagon, all the local papers jumped on it, led by the national press and the TV, and for days and weeks we had TV cameras outside the prison … so it was a bad time for the Prison Service in general. And then you had quite a delay until they published the report, the Woodcock Report that came out, and then there was a documentary on the failings of [the prison] again. So again you just get over it and then all the embarrassment comes back about it. (prison officer)

The public vilification of the Prison Service, of the establishments concerned and of individual members of staff, governors and senior managers (Lewis, 1997) was somewhat relentless:

It had a big impact on the local community, huge impact on the staff … Staff who worked [here at the time] were a laughing stock around the bars and in the schools. Kids got teased. And that hurt people. Everybody's chins were well and truly on the floor. (prison officer)

The recommendations of the Woodcock and Learmont reports, therefore, were implemented in dispersals – especially in Whitemoor – with something of a spirit of contrition. Prison staff and managers felt compelled to unquestioningly take forward whatever changes were deemed appropriate. This created a context that enabled a rapid shift in practice.

We went through a major process of changing. We changed the way we maintained order in dispersal prisons and that was wildly disruptive. To be taking something that worked that way for years and suddenly shaking it up and saying we're not going to do it any longer … and most of the time, surprisingly, just the sheer power of the approach, the prisoners didn't rebel against it. (senior manager, Prison Service)

The primary goal of security

The condemnatory tone of the inquiry reports and media accounts of the escapes, coupled with a pre-existing sense of discontent with the state of dispersals amongst prison staff, created a context in which staff were prepared to implement extreme and hitherto unthinkable solutions. The inquiry reports were effectively blueprints for the implementation of security regimes. Their recommendations were devoid of any consideration of the human element in prisons and were, instead, fundamentally concerned with establishing a state of security within them. Alison Liebling

(1999, p. 165), who was conducting research in one of the dispersals in the period when the Woodcock and Learmont recommendations were being implemented, has commented that:

> The prison world changed rather drastically between 1995 and 1996 … What our research project witnessed was a dehumanizing moment, whereby new managerialism met popular punitiveness. Prisoners (and staff) were on the receiving end of a rational choice model of human behaviour, a seemingly authoritarian era of prison management, and the concept of austerity. This latter vicious concept – all about excluding sympathy and humanitarian principles – dovetailed with a specific obsession with security – against a backcloth of authoritarian management by politics.

The process of implementing the recommendations translated into new ways of thinking. They established a new orienting principle for staff and managers: to pursue and maintain security. The Learmont Report explicitly argued that security should be seen as the primary goal of prisons. As Liebling (2002, p. 119) has observed:

> The concept of security was transformed. It was no longer about the perimeter, but was made up of thousands of daily practices inside the prison. The perimeter wall was only one small part of a secure prison. Procedures and practices mattered too.

Although, the centralisation of the goal of security was, at first, met with the discomfort of staff and managers (see Clark, 1997; Liebling, 2002), dispersal prisons did become more ordered and controlled after the implementation of the Woodcock and Learmont recommendations.

Part of the success of the security regime, it might be argued, can be attributed to the tendency in day-to-day prison practice to view almost all aspects of prison administration and management through the lens of security. Previously, King and Morgan (1980, p. 80) had argued that the difficulty in maintaining order and control in dispersals was related to a conflation of the concepts of security and control. They put forward the notion that there were two distinct categories of dangerous prisoners – those who posed a threat to security and those who presented control problems. Prisoners who have the wherewithal to escape and whose escape would pose a risk to the public, the police or national security were, they argued, dangerous to prison security. By contrast, those prisoners who presented challenges to prison order through the instigation of unrest amongst the prisoner population, the perpetration of staff or prisoner assaults, or other acts against the 'good order and discipline' of the prison posed control problems. Although, King and Morgan argued, there may be some overlap between the two, security and control were distinct operational concerns. However, with the implementation of the security regime each individual prisoner and all behaviours of prisoners began to be constructed as potential security threats. The loss of control, for example, could be seen as a potential security threat. When prisoners are viewed as enemies within (as discussed below), the loss of control is seen as a tactical failing on the part of the staff (who control the occupied territory of the prison, in a quasi-militaristic way) and a failure in security intelligence. Likewise, finding items of contraband is constructed as a security failure or a security breach because searching or other security systems have failed to detect the item at the moment it was smuggled into the prison. The circumstances surrounding the Whitemoor escape, in particular, helped to make this link between contraband and security because some of the items used to effect the escape were contraband items. Moreover, the compliance of prisoners is achieved, in part, through the management of their security classifications. Prisoners cannot be downgraded in their security categories unless they are compliant with the regime.[3] As a result of the benefits the security regime offered in terms of order and control, there began to be a gradual acceptance of security as an orienting purpose and the procedures that accompanied it.

> As far as the actual security/control ... if you asked most uniformed staff they'd probably say it [the escape] actually did us a favour. What it did was highlight a problem ... It was a disaster waiting to happen and it did but the ramifications for that were really to the benefit of [this prison], once we'd got over the embarrassment, the humiliation and everything else ... What it did was it gave staff the opportunity to regain control of the prison. (prison officer)

The escapes came to be seen as a fortuitous catalyst for change. The orientation towards security gave prison staff and managers a greater sense of purpose and a more concrete pursuit than attempting to create humane conditions within prison environments. In mundane ways reorienting prison practice towards the pursuit of security resulted in a deluge of new routines, systems and procedures. However, due to the nature of the pursuit of security and the tactics it employs, the importance of recognising the humanity of prisoners is replaced with new discourses that construct prisoners more as enemies rather than human beings in custody.

Prisoners as enemies within

Reorienting prison practice around the purpose of security introduced a new focus of prison work: the collection of intelligence information.

> I think the ... real bonus we got is in terms of security intelligence. It has improved dramatically, beyond recognition to what it was like before. The sorts of skills that we've enabled our staff to develop in those areas and the recognition [by] our staff of the value of security intelligence, the importance of submitting it, no matter how simple it appears, has paid huge dividends. And, I think, therefore we are able to predict and anticipate events much more accurately and therefore take pre-emptive action to prevent disturbances, prevent disorder and certainly prevent serious violence. (senior manager, Prison Service)

> A lot of what we do is listening, listening and anticipating. When you work in these places, any bit of information you might be able to pick up from a prisoner, you might be able to find a way to use it. Security is one of the main things you have going through your head when you're out on the landings. (prison officer)

Whilst the gathering of intelligence information may offer clear benefits to prison order and the avoidance of violent confrontations, the ways in which such practices are framed in security discourses implicitly construct prisoners as enemies. Staff–prisoner relationships have taken on a sense of military occupation in their character. In dispersal prisons there has been a worsening of the underlying general tendency towards an 'us versus them' mentality between staff and prisoners. However, in the now security-laden approach of staff this is transformed to a more tactical and subtle approach to staff–prisoner relationships where the aim is to extract information. In essence, there is a 'cold war' atmosphere, complete with espionage, covert surveillance and tactical planning.

The construction of prisoners as enemies of security was fairly explicit in the Learmont Report. Here prisoners were, for the first time in official dispersal penal policy, constructed as other. Citing Shaw (1995), Morgan (1997, p. 66, emphasis added) has argued that in previous inquiries into the state of prisons prisoners had been seen as real people: 'By contrast Woodcock and Learmont see prisoners as "dangerous phantoms who must be exiled or controlled. They are the *objects* of the Prison Service, not its subjects ..."'. One of the most explicit passages of the Learmont Report (1995, para. 4.45, p. 123), which objectifies prisoners in this way, states:

> A feature of prison life is that prisoners endeavour to manipulate staff. They may do this for malicious reasons or as a game played for psychological domination ... In manipulating staff, prisoners seek to take control from them and this threatens safe custody, leaving staff anxious and uncertain.

The discourse used here includes several emotive themes: domination, maliciousness, threat, anxiety and uncertainty. It might be argued that by using this language the Learmont Report sought to highlight the threat that prisoners could pose by playing on the emotionality associated with the general fear of crime and, more precisely, the fear of disorder shared by many dispersal prison staff. Prisoners became transformed from human beings in custody to manipulative, game players out for psychological domination. This reconstruction provided a strong justification for heightened security measures and left little room for debate about the extent to which such measures were necessary. It also made it less important and, indeed, potentially risky to view prisoners as ordinary human beings.

Amongst the features of security thinking are precaution and risk. Anticipating threat, according to security thinking, is best achieved when precautionary principles are employed (Ewald, 1999). Such principles require that action is taken (or prevented) based on what we *do not* know, rather than what we *do* know (Guldberg, 2003; Aradau and van Munster, 2007). When applied to human beings this means viewing other people as 'enemy combatants' who must be continually watched, anticipated and viewed with suspicion. The tendency of staff to take such a combative stance in relation to prisoners is strengthened, to some extent, by the way maximum-security prisoners are constructed in official prison discourses. Such constructions have proven particularly pernicious because they seem to reinforce ideas about the otherness of prisoners (see Drake, 2011 for a more focused examination of these same themes). They also align well with techniques of denial that prison staff may employ to actively avoid acknowledging the pains of imprisonment (Scott, 2008). As David Scott (ibid., p. 176) has found in his research with prison staff in lower-security prisons, prisoners can be 'effectively distanced as lesser human beings, constructed as essentially different and beyond the realms of prison officers' understandings of humanity'. The capacity for staff to essentialise prisoners is heightened within the security regime of dispersal prisons, making the tendency for staff to construct prisoners as essentially different not only more likely, but normalised.

As already mentioned in Chapter 1, maximum-security prisoners are described in official discourses as some of the most 'difficult and dangerous prisoners in the country' (see HMCIP, 1997, 2002). The extent to which this is truer in the current context than it was when dispersal prisons were first formed is a matter of subjective conjecture. The crimes current maximum-security prisoners have been convicted of do not suggest trends that are inconsistent with the longer history of dispersals. Dispersals have always housed the small proportion of prisoners convicted of very serious or prolific violent crimes, alongside those who could, theoretically, be allocated to lower-security conditions. This is the nature of the dispersal system. Indeed, it might be argued that this is one of the fundamental flaws of the dispersal system. It has always been its policy to disperse prisoners who require the highest levels of security amongst a population of those who do not require such conditions (Home Office, 1968; King and Morgan, 1980). As King and Morgan argued in 1980 (pp. 81–20):

> [I]t unwarrantably taints the long-term population with the high security or dangerous prisoner label. What all this suggests is that whoever is put into dispersal prisons, for whatever reasons originally, they soon come to be seen as needing or deserving maximum security.

The dispersal prison policy has a tendency to level-up assessments of risk, dangerousness, deviance and threat. However, in the first 25 years of the dispersal system these fundamental flaws of the policy were somewhat mitigated by the dominant discourses and political rhetoric of ruling liberal elites. These discourses included recognition of the humanity of prisoners and reinforced the belief that attempts needed to be made to preserve this within the punishing environment of prisons. Although such discourses may not have filtered down very evenly to become fully absorbed into prison practice in the first era of dispersals, they did create some tension for prison staff in relation to the extent to which their practice differed from the official prison policy. That is, if a member of staff or a staff group had a tendency to behave harshly or punitively towards prisoners, there was at least the possibility that managers might question this sort of treatment. One of the guiding principles of the early dispersal system had been to attempt to find ways of neutralising the negative effects of long-term prison sentences. Prisoners were therefore constructed as human beings in custody and not as dangerous or violent others. By contrast, current daily practices of maximum-security prison life constantly remind staff of the types of offences some dispersal prisoners have been convicted of. Further, there have been explicit messages from politicians that prison is for punishment and that prison experiences should not be easy. Therefore the tensions for staff and managers associated with finding ways to neutralise the negative effects of imprisonment have been, to a large extent, removed. Staff are now explicitly told that prisons are meant to be punishing, uncomfortable and, in effect, painful.

The implementation of a security regime has made a significant impact on the environment of maximum-security prisons. As Chapter 5 will illustrate, prisoner experiences have become relentlessly punishing. There seem to be no inherent or built-in limits to the delivery of their punishment, aside from legal protections (and even these are being challenged by parliament, for example, with respect to prisoners' voting rights). Likewise, there are seemingly no normative limits to punishment in maximum-security prisons. Indeed, political rhetoric has begun to explicitly argue that prisons should be *for* punishment. Therefore, there is less concern to ensure the humanity of prisoners is protected during their imprisonment. Prisoners as enemies of security are stigmatised and viewed more as objects to control and anticipate, rather than confined human subjects or fellow citizens whose treatment at the hands of the state should be carefully monitored and considered alongside the expectation that the vast majority of these prisoners will, one day, be released.

The ideology of security and its role in harsh justice

As has been mentioned in previous chapters of this book, the pursuit of security is an enterprise of increasing concern and expanding research both inside the prison and in wider society (Zedner, 2003, 2009). The inner workings of English maximum-security prisons can be looked upon to delineate the contours and parameters of what might be seen as an increasingly dominant ideology of security. Connections between the way security is constituted in the penal and the social realms will be more fully delineated in Chapter 6. However, it is useful to point out here how the rise of an ideology of security within prisons has been made possible and the way it both justifies harsh justice measures and gives them the appearance of legitimacy.

The pursuit of security has gradually become a powerful reorienting force within English maximum-security prisons. This concept and the range of beliefs, practices and discourses it is accompanied by have simultaneously achieved a greater sense of order in maximum-security prisons and resulted in more austere prison conditions. The discourses that accompany the ideology of security in prisons construct prisoners as enemies within or as dangerous others. Such constructions have proven useful for achieving a renewed and more heavily emphasised punitivity in penal philosophy and practice. This was an explicitly intended goal of members of the Conservative government who were in power at the time of the escapes and who sought to emphasise the need for harsher measures and wanted to dismantle social welfarist ideals, particularly in criminal justice policy.

Dario Melossi (2000, p. 296) has charted a cyclical pattern of differing representations of crime and criminals that, he argues, changes in accordance 'with the ways in which human agents perceive of and give accounts to themselves and others of phenomena of crime and punishment [that link with] regularly changing "structural" variables indicating specifics aspects of the economy, the polity and society' (ibid., pp. 314–5). Criminals are seen as public enemies, he argues, when it is perceived, at least from the perspectives of elites, that social 'fracturing and disorganization have reached "unthinkable excesses", and the want for reinstituting a unity of authority, purpose and hierarchy ... asserts itself as a matter of social life and death' (ibid., p. 314). The political rhetoric of Michael Howard and others in the Conservative Party in the early 1990s constructed society as fractured, disorganised and endangered in just the way that Melossi suggests. Further, the Conservatives seemed to be fundamentally concerned with finding ways to evidence the belief that liberal and welfare-based policies were, at least in some measure, to blame for societal breakdown. This was, in part, facilitated by the events taking place in the penal sphere, and the Woodcock and Learmont reports helped to provide some of the evidence the Conservatives wanted. The inquiry reports both include illustrations of the way liberal regimes and values had been at the root of the problem in dispersals. This sentiment was conspicuously similar to Michael Howard's apparent view that liberal or welfare-oriented policies were associated with social breakdown. It resonated with his implicit suggestion that prison works, but welfare does not. Furthermore, the emotional resonance that the use of the prison tends to hold for individual members of society (see Sarat, 1997) made the Whitemoor and Parkhurst escapes a good platform from which to advocate for both the increased use of prisons and tougher prison conditions. The security regime that the Woodcock and Learmont reports proposed for maximum-security prisons (which was implemented, in varying measures, in lower-security prisons too) included a move towards austerity. Prison security is more easily assured when prisoners are afforded less property, subjected to tighter controls and afforded few privileges. And by constructing prisoners as enemies to security or as dangerous others there was less need for prison staff and managers to struggle with the tensions of protecting the humanity of prisoners during a long prison sentence served in repressive conditions. Indeed, when prisoners are viewed as enemy combatants their humanity becomes less of a consideration. Moreover, the power of the security ideology and its capacity to alter thinking as well as practice enabled the disappearance, within penal thinking and policymaking, of the view that the loss of one's liberty is, in itself, a severe punishment. The introduction of the security ideology may thus be seen to provide a means by which harsh justice and law-and-order rhetoric can establish a strong foothold in public, political and penal contexts.

Maximum-security prison officer work now focuses on a persistent pursuit of absolute assurances of security. Other purposes and functions of imprisonment are subordinated to this agenda. In prison discourse (e.g., staff training and prison policy) prison work is often constructed as being primarily concerned with the safety of the general public. Prisoners, by contrast, are viewed as wholly undeserving, less eligible outcasts of society. Explanations of crime that focus on social causes are passed over in favour of explanations of criminality that locate the problem of crime within dangerous, pathological others who, as David Garland (1996, 2001) argues, need to be incapacitated and excluded. These ideas resonate with similar discourses within the security ideology. Dangerous others need to be neutralised, not negotiated with or treated in ways that aim to foreground their humanity or their rights. Prison officer work, therefore, has become more fundamentally focused on keeping prisoners in, on anticipating their actions and maintaining absolute control and constant vigilance. This security focus both enables and is enabled by the public view and the political directive that prisons should rightfully deliver punishment. The security ideology assists in the justification of the use of harsh measures. It also serves to legitimate them.

The security regime is a repressive regime (as Chapter 5 will illustrate). Therefore dispersal prisons are seemingly now more orderly places. There has not been a riot in a maximum-security prison since

1998. On outward appearances it looks as if the security regime works, that the elusive recipe for achieving order in prisons has been found. More importantly, however, it implicitly argues that harsh justice measures, austerity and punishment work too – at least in the sense that they produce compliant (or, more accurately, heavily coerced) prisoner populations. The failure of prisons is now even less publicly visible. The only evidence that can now be relied upon is the persistence of crime and recidivism. But, of course, these too can be explained away as individual pathology or the stubbornness of individuals who refuse to change or even as evidence of the existence of evil (discussed further in Chapter 7). In Britain now there is less of an incentive for any government – whatever their ideals or political leanings – to retain a social welfarist approach to crime or the treatment of prisoners. Therefore, one of the strongest predictors of the use of the prison (conservative political leadership) may be losing its significance and the retention of an unswerving commitment to the prison seems assured despite its fundamental flaws and insignificant relationship to crime rates. The example of English maximum-security prisons, therefore, provides a useful illustration of the way the transition towards harsh justice has taken place and the how the concept and pursuit of security have been instrumental in justifying the persistence of the use of the prison.

Conclusion

By examining the current state of security in English maximum-security prisons it becomes clear that there is little space for alternative ways of thinking and talking about prisoners to emerge amongst staff, governors or Prison Service senior managers. Further, the transformation that has taken place has ensured that the other functions of the prison in society are even less likely to become widely recognised.

The disillusionment with the liberal vision that dispersals had tried to achieve, coupled with sustained political pressure towards austerity and repressive measures, created a context where prison staff and managers were compelled to implement a new approach, despite its departure from previous ways of thinking about long-term, maximum-security imprisonment. Both inside the prison walls and in political and media discourses, maximum-security prisons have seemingly become symbolic holding tanks for those constructed as enemies within society, those excluded, dangerous others, who need to be kept safely away from decent, law-abiding citizens. For prisoners, they have become places of continuous control, judgement, assessment and surveillance. But, in essence, these prisons – like all prisons – continue to serve many of the same functions within the political economy that they have always served: to absorb the marginalised, the unemployed and the disadvantaged and to provide a repository for unwanted, excluded or deviant social members. The difficulty is, however, that the prison experiences that are now created within such heavily security-focused regimes are patently dehumanising and damaging, as well as futile. As the next chapter will illustrate, the consequences of heavily security-focused, individualising and punishing prison experiences seem to offer little in the way of reparation or opportunities for the improved social participation of prisoners or for improved social cohesion. They do, however, offer prisoners a relentless experience of vengeance, retribution, stigmatisation and punishment.

5
Long-Term, Maximum-Security Punishment

Introduction

> The general public knows practically nothing about the prison and appears to be little concerned about how it is managed and how prisoners are treated. Not until the average man finds himself behind steel bars does he realise how indifferent he has been to a problem in which he should have felt himself vitally concerned. (Debs, 1927, p. 128)

The above quotation is taken from the book *Walls and Bars*, by Eugene V. Debs, published in 1927. It is an unusual treatise within the literature on prisons. The book is not so much a study of the prison, but Debs's reflections on it as an instrument used in class warfare (ibid., p. 17). Debs himself was imprisoned twice and served a total of four years. He was also disenfranchised for life. His first experience of imprisonment was in 1895, when, as president of the American Railway Union, he was imprisoned in Woodstock (McHenry County) jail in Illinois for his actions during a railroad strike (ibid., pp. 27–9). The second time, Debs was imprisoned in Atlanta Federal Prison for violating the Espionage Act by speaking out against America's involvement in World War I. After his first prison sentence Debs became a prominent member of the Socialist Party and ran for the American presidency in 1900, 1904, 1908, 1912 and 1920 (on the last occasion he ran the campaign from his prison cell (ibid.)). His only book, *Walls and Bars*, is a critical account of prison life and the prison system. Many of the chapters were first published in the Bell Syndicate (though in a less critical form) and were Debs's attempt to educate the public about the degradations of prison life. He is often remembered for the statement he made at his sentencing hearing, a portion of which also appears at the beginning of his book under the title 'My Prison Creed'. Debs stated:

> Your Honor, years ago I recognized my kinship with all living beings, and I made up my mind that I was not one bit better than the meanest on earth. I said then, and I say now, that while there is a lower class, I am in it, and while there is a criminal element I am of it, and while there is a soul in prison, I am not free.

The sentiment captured in the above quotation is one that this chapter very much attempts to emulate. Although Eugene Debs's account of prison life is not 'academic', it provides an impassioned, first-hand critique of the prison that resonates more with my own examinations and analyses of experiences of imprisonment than much of the academic literature. Like Debs's work, this chapter seeks to cast light upon the prisoner experience. It attempts to illustrate – as starkly as possible – an unmediated exposition of what prison 'feels like' and the way it is designed to deliver punishment rather than reparation or to prepare prisoners for full participation in society. Unlike much prison sociology that has gone before, which has been concerned with analysing the influences and parameters of prisoner social life, this chapter focuses on capturing the essence of what it is like to be imprisoned. To do so it presents prisoners' views of their own confinement. It is argued that the suspension and minimisation of their rights creates a deepened sense of social exclusion whereby prisoners are left in a state of despair by the extreme disempowerment they experience as a result of what amounts to relentless punishment. The chapter considers some of the different forms that punishment takes during a long-term prison sentence and questions the extent to which such experiences can serve any of the assumed purposes of the prison.

The themes that are presented here were the strongest to emerge from the research on which this book draws. They are organised in a manner that seeks to best capture the overarching, broad experience of long-term, maximum-security imprisonment. In so doing the chapter sacrifices the individualised, interpretive meaning-making of prisoner experiences that can be found in many sociological studies of the prison. This is deliberate. There are, of course, myriad and often miraculous ways that prisoners learn to cope with, and manage, the pressures and strains of imprisonment. Although academic examinations of such individual experiences are valid and make valuable contributions to the prisons literature, they can obscure the fact that the act of imprisonment – the confinement of a human being, their removal and exclusion from the rest of society – is essentially a punitive one. Prison is, as Christie (2001) argues, the way pain is delivered to particular groups of people in a civilised society.

The chapter 'bears witness' (Quinney, 2000) to experiences of imprisonment in order to throw open the gates of the prison for closer public scrutiny. Drawing on over 200 in-depth interviews with maximum-security prisoners across the dispersal system, the chapter reveals the fundamentally punishing experience of long-term prison sentences. It is revealed that prisoners are offered few opportunities to make meaningful reparation for the harm(s) they have caused or to be safely and inclusively brought back into society as full and contributing social members. Therefore there is a disjuncture between the symbolic delivery of punishment by a long prison sentence, the experience of serving such a sentence and the question of its utility in making amends for harm or preparing an individual for their return to society. It is thus argued that neither victim nor prisoner needs are fully addressed or adequately met by the terms and conditions of long-term imprisonment. The social functions that the prison does serve, therefore, must be found elsewhere.

Before delving into the examination of prisoner experiences there are three caveats that need to be declared and explained. The first is to identify what this chapter provides in contrast to other, foregoing studies of imprisonment and, in so doing, identify what it does not provide. The second is to acknowledge the subjectivity associated with any assessment of prison conditions or experiences of punishment and how this chapter seeks to reconcile this. And, finally, the third is to set forth the proposition that in order to fully understand the experience of imprisonment one must, first, set aside the grave, immediate realities that bring people into maximum-security prisons. Each of these caveats will be considered in turn.

Foregoing studies of prison life

Academic study of prison life was first embarked upon by Donald Clemmer in 1940 in the United States. Since then a number of in-depth studies of the prison have been undertaken in a variety of penal settings (for example, Sykes, 1958; Morris and Morris, 1963; Irwin, 1970; Tittle, 1972; Jacobs, 1977; King and Elliot, 1977; Bondeson, 1989; Sparks et al., 1996; Liebling and Arnold, 2004; Kruttschnitt and Gartner, 2005). Three main theoretical models on prison social life have emerged from these and other works and have dominated the literature: those that identify a functionalist approach, those that argue in favour of an 'importation' model and those that integrate aspects of the two. In functionalist models, it is argued that prison life is shaped by the coercive nature of the prison environment. The purest branch of the functionalist model argues that any differences in the organisation of prison establishments are irrelevant because the experience of total institutions is so coercive that it homogenises prisoner responses to their environment (see Sykes, 1958; Goffman, 1961; Bondeson, 1989). By contrast, the situational-functionalist model argues that prisoners' responses to prison life are situationally contingent on institutional characteristics (Grusky, 1959; Wilson, 1968). Broadly speaking, both functionalist perspectives are known in the prisons literature as deprivation models because they seek to explain prison life and prisoners' adaptations to it as responses to the pains of imprisonment and the deprivations associated with the loss of liberty.

In response, and in contrast to, the functionalist perspectives, explanations that favour an importation model for understanding prison life emerged. Importation models argue that the social environment of prison life is shaped by the imported characteristics of the prisoner group and that these originate in the subcultures to which prisoners belong prior to their entry into prison (Irwin and Cressey, 1962; Irwin, 1970). Further studies of prison life have proposed slight deviations from these models (e.g., DiIulio, 1987; Useem and Kimball, 1989). However, much contemporary prisons literature tends to present integrated versions of prison social life which draw on aspects of both importation and deprivation models (Tittle, 1972; Goodstein and Wright, 1989; Toch and Adams, 1989; McCorkle et al., 1995; Liebling and Arnold, 2004; Harvey, 2007; Crewe, 2009).

One of the main difficulties faced by prison researchers concerned with examining the inner life of prisons has been untangling the complex relationships that influence it. Although many studies of the prison have ignored the diversity of prisoner experiences and the heterogeneity of prisoners' viewpoints on their own lives and their reflections on the experience of imprisonment, there have been some valuable contributions that have applied interpretive sociological theory to ethnographic or interview data. These works have illustrated the connections between human agency, intersubjective meanings and environmental or structural conditions of prison life (see Goffman, 1961; Irwin and Cressey, 1962; Garabedian, 1963; Cohen and Taylor, 1972; Jones and Schmid, 2000; Medlicott, 2001). Likewise, much insight has been gained in relation to our understanding of prison experiences from the work of 'convict criminologists'. This growing field of criminology was established in the United States by a small group of prisoners and ex-prisoners who became academic criminologists and who joined together to develop a new school of criminology (see Ross and Richards, 2003). The work of convict criminologists has provided an authenticity to ethnographic prison studies (in particular) that simply could not have been as succinctly or completely captured from an outsider perspective (see, for example, Irwin, 1970; Newbold, 1989; McCleary, 1992; Jones and Schmid, 2000; Austin and Irwin, 2001; Ross and Richards, 2003; Terry, 2003).

Prison ethnography, more generally, has offered a number of important recent contributions to the study of prisons. Despite Wacquant's (2002) lament over the dearth of prison ethnography in the US, there is vibrancy in ethnographic prison studies elsewhere (Piacentini, 2004; Jefferson, 2005; Harvey, 2007; Crewe, 2009; Waldram, 2009b). Although such in-depth studies of prison life have provided rich and nuanced insights about prison culture and institutional life, there is a tendency (particularly with single prison studies) to focus on the minutiae of institutional arrangements and the (pre-prison and in-prison) experiences of prisoners within particular institutions. Recent ethnographic studies of prison life, like much of the prison research that has gone before, can become caught up in questions about deprivation or importation, aspects of prisoner coping and adaptation or the peculiarities associated with prisoner social life that emerge as a result of living in a total institution (Goffman, 1961). By engaging in these sorts of questions much prison research sidesteps the problem of interrogating the broader social meaning of imprisonment as a form of punishment or the extent to which prisoner experiences serve the assumed purposes of imprisonment. That is not to say that in-depth studies of prison social life are not valuable. There is certainly much to be gained in continuing to carry out the types of detailed, contextually focused prison research that have gone before. It is important, not simply for its capacity to contribute to a wide range of fields of knowledge (including *inter alia* prison administration and practice, informing prison reform agendas and the furthering of academic knowledge in a wide range of disciplines, such as organisational studies, psychological and behavioural studies, interpretive sociology, legal studies), but also because it allows us – as social members – to remain vigilant and aware of the way prisons are run and managed and the way prisoners make sense of, and negotiate, their experiences of imprisonment. However, there is also value in considering the prison from a highly critical stance, which asks to what extent experiences of imprisonment fulfil the supposed or official purposes of prisons as a social institution. It is to these issues that this chapter now turns.

The subjectivity of assessing experiences of prisons and punishment

Rather than situating this chapter neatly within any of the above fore-going literature on prisons, it is perhaps better categorised as a critical examination of *punishment*. Therefore, it acknowledges that throughout many westernised nations, long-term imprisonment – the prolonged loss of one's liberty – is the most severe punishment available to the courts. Historically, this is perhaps a timely moment to consider the punishment associated with the use of imprisonment. The day-to-day practice of imprisonment in most Western democracies is not intentionally physically brutal.[1] Corporal punishment is not a feature of these penal systems (though capital punishment is still practiced in 34 American states). Surface or cursory evaluations of contemporary imprisonment in many countries may appear civilised and humane, depending on one's vantage point. Likewise, again depending on one's vantage point, uses of the prison, sentencing practice and prison conditions may appear too lenient to some who may argue for harsher (e.g., more austere prison environments) or more severe penalties (e.g., longer sentences).

The difficulty with assessing the punitiveness or lenience of prison life is that individual perceptions of relative social conditions differ with cultural understandings, social positioning and life experiences. Similarly, as argued by Mannheim (1939, p. 58, cited in Sieh, 1989, p. 169), evaluations of particular penal conditions vary according to personal reaction and opinion. The harshness, leniency or the extent to which penal conditions fulfil the official goals of punishment – deterrence, rehabilitation and retribution – are all subjective judgements that can vary according to one's perspective. Furthermore, as Sparks et al. (1996, p. 169) have argued, prisoners too 'speak from diverse vantage points, which vary in relation to their prior experience, their sentences and offences, their degree of optimism or otherwise regarding their current position and prospects'. Likewise, the vantage point of prison researchers should also be considered as a contributing factor to the way prison experiences are understood and constructed in the academic literature.

Bearing all of the above varying perspectives in mind, it should also be acknowledged that there is no objective measure of the degree of painfulness of imprisonment as punishment. In order to engage in meaningful analysis a baseline should be drawn. For the purposes of this book and this chapter it is assumed that the loss of liberty is, in itself, a severe and inherently painful form of punishment. This view is heavily informed by the research findings on which the book draws and on previous scholarly and policy considerations on this topic (Debs, 1927; Sykes, 1958; Home Office, 1968, 1984, 1990; Cohen and Taylor, 1972; Parliamentary All-Party Penal Affairs Group, 1986; Hudson, 1987; Singer, 1991). In addition to the empirical and scholarly grounds for taking such a starting point, it is also an informative baseline position from which to begin because it acknowledges the circumstance of being a prisoner. This in itself is a crucial point. The loss of liberty and the experience of being confined at the hands of the state by the will of the rest of society – which are the fundamental features of imprisonment – are frequently overlooked, dismissed or ignored in media coverage of sentencing or penal matters, common sense considerations of imprisonment and even some scholarly works that have examined prison life or prisoner experiences. With the increasing use of imprisonment and lengthening prison sentences in many nation states around the world, it is a timely moment to engage in a detailed exposition of what the long-term loss of liberty by imprisonment actually feels like, its meanings and the extent to which it, in essence, achieves its stated or assumed goals.

Understanding prisoner experiences

When examining the experiences of maximum-security prisoners in England some distinctions need to be made about the population we are discussing (for further details on the total population of maximum-security prisons see Figures A.1–A.4 in the Appendix and the surrounding text). As discussed briefly in Chapter 3, the vast majority of prisoners in English maximum-security prisons are not necessarily more violent or more prolific in their criminal activity than other prisoner populations serving time in less secure prisons around the country. As has always been the case with the English dispersal system, the vast majority of this population (nearly 75 per cent) are Category B prisoners and, therefore, need not strictly be housed in maximum-security conditions. Many of those who find themselves in dispersal prisons could have been allocated to a less secure, Category B prison. This does not mean that some of them have not committed acts of violence. A high proportion of them have (see Figure A.3 in the Appendix). However, that fact does not necessarily have any bearing on their allocation to maximum-security conditions. Many are there by chance, not by necessity.

In addition, even though English maximum-security prisons include a high proportion of prisoners convicted of violent crimes, the vast majority of this population – as with most prisoner populations – originate from lower socio-economic positions in society. It has been established in the research literature that there is a link between socio-economic conditions and interpersonal violent crime. Murder and assault, in particular, are closely associated with poverty and income inequality whilst robbery and rape show a less strong, but still significant association with these factors (Hsieh and Pugh, 1993). Crucially, it must be made clear that it is not simply poverty that relates to interpersonal violent crime – it is also *income inequality*. The larger the gap between the rich and the poor, the higher the levels of violent crime in a given society (see the extensive work of Michael Marmot, 2000, 2004; Marmot et al., 1997).[2] Moreover, the reliance on the prison and the persistence of individually focused explanations for causes of crime have continually obscured our ability to recognise the social, economic and structural factors and conditions that correlate with problems of violence (including interpersonal, corporate or state-inflicted violence).

Despite the confluence of complex and interactive factors that precipitate the occurrence of violence, the fact remains that it often occurs by the hands of individual human beings. And many of the men housed in maximum-security prisons in England – whose words will be presented below as we consider experiences of long-term imprisonment – have, indeed, committed acts of serious harm and violence against other people. Some of them have done so more than once. However, in order to fully understand the subjective experiences of imprisonment it is important to attempt to set aside the grave, immediate realities that bring people into maximum-security prisons. Although this can be a difficult task, given the severity of some of the harms committed by prisoners in these prisons, it is essential to do so in order to avoid clouding one's perceptions with the emotiveness of vengeance or revulsion. There is a wealth of psychological literature that identifies the importance of neutrality as a key element required for fully understanding the experiences of another human being (see, particularly, Rogers 1957, 1989, for the origins of this thinking). Further, recent path-breaking work on psychological therapy in prisons has argued that neutrality and a non-judgemental approach are especially important when seeking to fully understand and provide meaningful support to prisoners (Harvey and Smedley, 2010). Given these arguments, I would suggest that in order for us, as a society, to identify better ways to respond when one human being harms another, we should first strive towards a deeper understanding of the effects of our current means of responding to such events. The assumptions that imprisonment is a useful crime control tool, that it achieves its purposes and that it automatically protects the rights of 'deserving' citizens and generates a safer and more secure society simply cannot be made if there is not a genuine attempt to fully understand what the experience of imprisonment involves. In order to achieve understanding it is of central importance that a close and critical examination of the forms and uses of punishment takes place – even though it may be difficult to undertake and subsequently presents thorny and difficult questions. Although some readers might find it uncomfortable or even impossible to read with a sympathetic eye the perspectives of men convicted of serious, (often) violent harms, it is a useful exercise for us all – as social members – to examine the implications, efficacy and consequences of the means and methods we employ in an effort to achieve public protection, to improve inclusion and social cohesion, to pursue greater levels of human security and personal safety and to prevent further, future victimisations.

As the accounts presented in the following pages of this chapter will illustrate, and in contradiction of the portrayals in media accounts of maximum-security prisoners as 'depraved, conscienceless monsters', prisoners' perceptions of punishment and imprisonment reveal perspectives that are all too human. Despite the seriousness of the harms perpetrated by some of the prisoners in maximum-security prisons, the inconvenient and perhaps unpalatable truth is that the vast majority are not conscienceless. Although people sometimes perpetrate monstrous acts against one another, it is crude, unproductive and essentialising to define individuals solely in terms of the harm they have caused. Like all of us, people who have committed such acts have complex social lives, constrained and pressured by all sorts of structural and personal influences. The ensuing pages are, therefore, written with a view to gaining a fuller understanding of the experience of punishment and imprisonment, setting aside for a moment the immediate acts that brought these men into prison.

Long-term, maximum-security punishment

Constituting punishment

Drawing on prisoners' accounts of their experiences, it is evident that the forms punishment takes in maximum-security prison are varied, changeable, potentially cumulative, and multidimensional. Over a lengthy prison sentence, prisoners gain expertise on what constitutes punishment and its variety of hidden and overt forms. During the present research the adage that 'men are sent to prison *as* and not *for* punishment' was frequently offered by prisoners as an argument against aspects of the conditions of their confinement or treatment that seemed like 'too much punishment' (prisoner). The assertion of former Justice Minister Jack Straw in 2008, that 'prison is for punishment' (Travis, 2008), was a significant departure from the view of 'prison *as* punishment', which had been a precept of penal policy rhetoric and discourse (if not in practice) since the Gladstone Report of 1895. Indeed, with specific reference to dispersal prisons, the Radzinowicz Report (Home Office, 1968, para., p. 78) argued:

> We believe that even if a human being remained permanently in prison it would be right for the governor and the staff of the prison to endeavour to create a liberal and constructive regime. But if the most important fact about a prisoner is that he is a human being, the other vital fact is that, except in a very, very small number of cases, he is a human being who will be released and return to the community. The prison will have done part of its job for the community if the prisoner has been securely contained in humane conditions during his sentence, and has lost none of his mental or physical alertness in prison except the loss that comes to us all with the passing years.

The extent to which such guiding principles have ever been meaningfully translated into penal practice is highly questionable (see Chapter 3, and also King and Morgan, 1980; Scraton et al., 1991). As Chapter 2 illustrated, the goals of imprisonment set out in the Gladstone Report (1895) – namely that prisons are for both punishment and reform – are incompatible and contradictory (Thomas, 1972). In practice, prisons have tended to deliver punishment much more successfully than they have created opportunities for reform (Mathiesen, 2000). Nevertheless, in maximum-security prisons during the time that the research on which this book is based took place (2005–08), many prisoners (and a minority of staff) expressed the cultural value that imprisonment itself constituted one's punishment and that the conditions of confinement and the treatment of prisoners should not add further to this sanction.

Prior to entering prison, an individual may have particular expectations about what prison will or should be like. However, once the individual is imprisoned those opinions may be challenged. Prisoners' views on the goals of imprisonment are often that it should be punitive (Crewe, 2009, pp. 429–31). In the present research, most prisoners said they thought it was right that they should be punished for what they had done and that they deserved to be in prison. Prisoners often repeated such clichéd statements as 'if you do the crime, you have to do the time', which many heartily agreed with. Despite these firmly held beliefs, their experiences of imprisonment seemed to gradually contradict and undermine their beliefs about what constituted a harsh punishment.

Five overlapping forces seemed to account for prisoners' gradually evolving views about punishment which, over time, seemed to contradict their imported beliefs about what punishment does and should consist of. These five forces were that:

1) Over time, prisoners become experts on what constitutes punishment.
2) Prisons are slow to reflect progressive changes in outside society, which necessarily lowers the material standards in prisons (even if prison standards remain the same) and this is especially obvious to long-term prisoners.
3) Similarly, during the course of a long prison sentence penal policy may shift and change and, as has been the case more recently, may come to favour a more punitive stance. As a result of changing attitudes outside prison, and increasing prison populations inside, long-term prisoners may experience an actual worsening of material prison conditions during the course of their sentence.
4) Being continuously punished loses its meaning over a lengthy period of time.
5) Once an individual's threshold for 'enough' punishment has been reached, the experience of punishment feels gratuitous, cruel and against human dignity.

Each of these five forces seemed to influence prisoners' evaluations of their experiences of imprisonment and the views they held on punishment. The way these processes were activated, and how they connected to the domains through which punishment was enacted, will be examined as we delve further into examining experiences of punishment.

The principle of less eligibility

It should be acknowledged that in all reasonably civilised prison environments a proportion of the prisoner population will use neutral terms in their evaluation of the environment and some will even report favourably on aspects of their experience. A prison sentence may sometimes offer a period of respite from personal and social lives that were, on the outside, fraught with danger, unpredictability and chaos (Wacquant, 2002; Crewe, 2006; Rowe, 2011). For many individuals, imprisonment occasionally may provide an environment that is more containing, materially superior and less unsafe in comparison to the conditions in which they lived on the outside. Jeffrey Reiman and

Paul Leighton's (2010) work on who goes to prison in America reveals that it is people who are amongst the poorest. They argue (ibid., p. 157):

> [T]he criminal justice system does not simply weed the peace-loving from the dangerous, the law-abiding from the criminal. At every stage, starting with the very definitions of crime and progressing through the stages of investigation, arrest, charging, conviction, and sentencing, the system *weeds out the wealthy*.

The population of prisoners in British prisons is, likewise, drawn primarily from the poorest segments of society. The principle of less eligibility (discussed briefly in Chapter 2) in relation to prison conditions is, therefore, extremely difficult to fulfil. For British prisons to reflect conditions worse than the lowest significant social class on the outside, they would need to be extremely impoverished indeed. Given the fact that the vast majority of people in prison (both in England and elsewhere) tend to come from the most impoverished and socially marginalised segments of society (Coyle, 1998, 2005; Friestad and Hansen, 2010; Reiman and Leighton, 2010) many prisoners' own evaluations of the terms and conditions of their confinement may – to the 'un-imprisoned', outside listener – sound reasonable, acceptable, and perhaps to some, even too 'soft'. Although neutral evaluations of prison life should be respected as valid representations of prisoners' experiences, they need to be considered alongside various mitigating factors. For example, these may include the contexts from which prisoners often come prior to their imprisonment, our own subjective position on what constitutes harshness or lenience in relation to prison life, and the other factors that may influence prisoners' evaluations of their experience. For instance, there is the fact that many long-term prisoners use a variety of coping mechanisms in order to endure their sentence – including reassuring themselves that 'prison ain't so bad' (prisoner). Therefore it is extremely difficult to present any sort of consistent or generalisable evaluation of prison conditions.

Whilst some prisoner evaluations on the material conditions of maximum-security prisons revealed quite neutral or reasonably favourable assessments, others expressed deep concern with the circumstances in which they found themselves once they became imprisoned. Alternatively, conditions that may have appeared reasonable upon entry into a maximum-security prison could gradually come to be viewed as inadequate, as prisoners sink more deeply into their sentences. Further, even those who reported neutrally on some aspects of prison life inevitably identified other aspects of their confinement that they found intolerable. Assessing the adequacy of prison conditions was a key area where subjectivities (of different prisoners, staff, and my own perspective) played a role in how prison life was depicted and evaluated. Assessing the material conditions of confinement and the extent to which these appeared or were experienced as punishing (or not) varied from individual to individual, with some reporting feelings of severe material deprivation and others reporting reasonably favourably on material conditions.

The loss of liberty

I look at it like this: prison is the idea that we are losing our liberty. *That* is our punishment, not all of the inhumanity and cruelty in here. You know it should really be like we are living out there, in our houses, with everything else – access to the internet and stuff like that. But these people seem to think that … well, it's like double jeopardy because you're punished in your label – you've been labelled a criminal, but then when you come here and you are confronted with a second tier of punishment: 'you can't do this and you will not have that', and here they are forever coming up with new things and it's really cruel, so petty, so mindless. (prisoner)

As already stated, the most basic feature of long-term imprisonment is the loss of one's liberty. Few members of the public get the opportunity to fully comprehend the profundity and pain that is exacted through experiences of imprisonment due to the hidden forms of punishment that accompany a prison sentence. Christie (2004) has questioned when is enough enough and when is it more than enough? He asks: 'Where is the limit in modern societies? When has a prison population in a country reached a level when at least our intuitions say that this is wrong, completely wrong, unacceptable! And when are life conditions below dignity?' (ibid., p. 102).

Likewise, long-term, maximum-security prisoners, now serving (on average) the longest sentences in the history of British prisons, have come to question the extent to which the public, the media or even prison staff (see Scott, 2008) understand how severe a punishment the loss of one's liberty actually is.

I hate when people outside go: 'Look, they have got this and they have got that [in prison].' Well, come in then and live here. Alright, yeah, I deserve to be punished for what I done [*sic*], but what level of punishment do you want to give me? The people outside don't even know the ins and outs and yet they judge so quickly – being locked away is punishment enough. It is mind boggling to be locked in a room all the time. I always say to people outside: 'Go and get your bed and put it in the bathroom and lock the door. Keep that door shut for seven weeks and then tell me how you feel.' (prisoner)

Many of the ancillary consequences of the experience of imprisonment are directly associated with the loss of liberty. The examples provided below of the ordinary and profound losses that accompany an extremely lengthy prison sentence are compiled from interviews and field notes collected during the ethnographic research on which this book draws. They are all known (and perhaps obvious) accompaniments to the loss of one's liberty and may be understood without drawing attention to them, but they are included here in list form in order to attempt to begin to capture, and make meaningful for the 'un-imprisoned', the lived reality of long-term imprisonment. An extremely lengthy and/or indeterminate prison sentence consists of the loss and interruption of a significant portion of one's life, including, for example:

- The loss of ordinary experiences that most people take for granted:
  - intimate contact, intimate and sexual relationships;
  - opportunity for procreation;
  - participation in major life events (births, deaths, marriages) of family and friends;
  - collective sharing in significant social events (the experience of a recession, important national sporting events);
  - bathing or going swimming;
  - chance to go to the shops, the pub, a football game;
  - milestones of children;
  - payment of household bills.
- The loss of opportunities for self-actualisation, which may include:
  - the inability to attempt to participate in society, gain training, employment (these opportunities will also be severely limited if release is ever is granted);
  - little or no opportunity to make meaningful amends for the harm that has been caused (either to one's own family, victims, victims' families or to society).

The final point above, regarding the opportunity to make meaningful amends is a crucial one that calls into question the usefulness of imprisonment as the only option for the meting out of justice. This will be discussed in more detail shortly.

Thus, the length of a prison sentence necessarily compounds in myriad ways the punishment that is the loss of one's liberty. During a long period of imprisonment, society on the outside will inevitably progress, certainly with respect to technological advancements and often with respect to general improvements to standards of living (though not always and not for all segments of society). Even though long-term prisoners lose much of their awareness and connection to changes in outside society, the outside world penetrates the prison in various ways (Jewkes, 2002). As a result, long-serving prisoners may come to expect that prison conditions will progress too, alongside the standards of outside society (the principle of less eligibility notwithstanding). However, it has generally been the case that prison conditions in Britain, as in many countries, have either remained the same or worsened. Over the course of the present research in maximum-security prisons, there were a number of amenities and privileges that were withdrawn or curtailed. Certain material conditions were perceived by prisoners to be worsening (for example, facilities, sports equipment not replaced when broken, access to outside areas). In addition, there were inconsistencies between maximum-security establishments in relation to prisoner entitlements – inconsistencies prisoners were aware of. From their perspectives, this called into question why prisoners serving time in one maximum-security establishment should be subject to worse (or better) conditions than prisoners in another institution. A few examples of items or activities that might be subject to withdrawal or restriction or that differed between establishments included: cooking oil, glass jars, play stations, the writing of lengthy letters to loved ones or friends, restricted access to outside areas, or the number of children allowed on a visit. Prisoners identified such losses of amenities, inconsistencies in privileges or the differing or lowering of material standards as adding further to their experience of punishment. Such changes, they argued, felt punitive during the course of a long prison sentence because it felt as if there were 'never any rewards only further punishments' (prisoner).

It is inevitable that, in the time that passes during a lengthy prison sentence, aspects of penal practice and provisions for prisoners may change due to, for example, fiscal restraints, increasing/decreasing prisoner numbers and/or more punitive or more progressive penal policies. When, for example, prevailing prison conditions are improved due to decreasing prisoner numbers or systematic improvements, prisoners report more positively on the way they feel treated at the hands of the criminal justice system (Liebling and Arnold, 2004, pp. 45–8). However, when prevailing prison conditions are readjusted to become more austere, long-term prisoners experience a more punishing environment.

> There seems to just always be a constant tightening up, a constant closing down of little avenues and trimming of things. It feels like we're always being squeezed. I can't remember when somebody said: 'we want to extend this to you', you know? (prisoner)

Prisoners, naturally, become accustomed (in some cases over many years) to prison conditions that are of a particular standard and, as a result, they form reasonable expectations of their confinement. When these standards are reduced, prisoners experience this as adding significantly to their punishment. This, in turn, is perceived by prisoners as unfair and capricious because they are, of course, the same individuals, serving the same sentences they were serving before the standards were changed.

> It is confining and it just got more confining [access to the outside sports field had just been withdrawn] and, like everything else, you will get used to it, but one wonders in a transition to another life, later on the outside, is it going to make it that much more difficult? I really don't understand the reason why. It's repressive and it's progressively repressive and there just is no recourse and so there's a frustration there at the same time … But like everything else you grow used to what you're going into every day. [sighs] You get used to it. I wonder how it will feel in 20 years. What do you do to psych yourself into it in 20 years' time? (prisoner)

The maintenance of in/security

As described in Chapter 4, the concept of maximum security was an ideology that influenced mentalities, practices and beliefs in these prisons. The dominance of security as an organising feature of prison governance necessarily had implications for prison life and prisoner experiences. From the perspectives of prisoners, the concept of security was an instrument of penal power and authority. If security was the reason for or against a particular decision or course of action, it simply could not be disputed.

> Security. They give security as the reason for everything they do. Security, security, security, that's all you ever get out of 'em. There's no point in asking 'em 'cos they're not going to tell you. (prisoner)

The concept of security thus could become a form of ultimate power. It was unchallengeable, unquestionable and provided an infallible argument for taking any course of action that the prison authorities deemed necessary. Its invocation pre-empted any further discussion and withdrew opportunities to appeal decisions, consider alternative options or even question the details behind why a particular decision had been made.

> We can't get on the field anymore because of 'security'. Okay, I understand that. We can't have a situation whereby people are throwing certain items over the wall and compromising the jail. Drugs aren't such a major thing because, you know, they only last for a few weeks and they only have a very small impact, but I understand that there was knives being thrown over and these put people in jeopardy – both staff and inmates alike. I understand you can't allow that. But to close the field down completely and say you're not going out there again? I think it's draconian and I think they should have tried to find a solution. (prisoner)

Security, in that instance, as a mechanism of governance, formed a key basis for power. Further, its pursuit was diffuse and all pervasive, which meant that it felt as though 'everything [was] about security' (prisoner). As a result, it seemed to prisoners as though nothing else really mattered to prison authorities.

> It seems to me that all they care about here is security, which is understandable being a maximum-security prison, but that's like *all* they care about, you know what I mean? (prisoner)

Concerns over security and the commitment of prison authorities to maintain it – seemingly at any cost – suggested to prisoners that their status as human subjects was not fully recognised or considered.

> To me the whole thing about this prison right now that makes it unacceptable is losing [access to the outside sports field]. It's the only piece of true freedom that we get to experience in here, where we've got open space and air. I think that's very valuable. I can just about live with most other things, but that seems more valuable to me than anything and to know now that we're going to lose that … I guess we'll adapt and adjust and get over it and we'll live within what we're given, but it's a loss to our humanity. We're living in a pressure cooker environment and that was our safety valve – maybe [now]

a lot more things will become intolerable within this environment here. I really do worry about that. I worry about it for my own health and mental health as well as everybody else's. (prisoner)

In one sense, the disregard for prisoners' humanity in the implementation of security measures made them feel worthless and valueless. In another sense it made them feel as though the only value they held was a negative one. They felt that the prison authorities saw them as embodiments of threat and risk that needed to be managed, anticipated and controlled. They were the enemy, an object, an outsider – 'others' who could be afforded no rights, no legal status and offered no avenues through which to exercise agency. Prisoners argued that due to the way the concept of security was applied to them as individuals, they could not find a way to present themselves that could effectively challenge the way they were viewed.

> I just don't know how to get round it. It needs someone who's really, really clever to say 'this is what needs to be done' … to say, 'wait a minute, you have to give people a chance, you have to recognise that they are more than the crime they committed to get in here'. It feels like once you're here a lot of spin doctoring goes on, that's it. And then once it's done it's so hard to undo … you just can't undo it once it's done. Their security shield can come up at any time and then they won't tell you nothing and you're stuck. (prisoner)

The experience of being viewed – fundamentally – as a security risk was a source of uncertainty and created a sense of *insecurity* amongst prisoners. They felt as if there was no limit to what could be taken from them or to the sanctions that might be applied to them.

> The security thing in here is just absolute madness – it is. You're not seen as a man, as a human being, you're just seen as a 'risk', you know? A thing to be 'managed' and that can't be trusted. It's a scary thing because you think no one will care about this. No one on the outside will give a shit if no one in here sees me – a scummy prisoner – as a human being with rights … people will say 'good, he don't deserve no rights'. It makes you feel scared and insecure and like you just don't matter to anyone at all and they can do whatever they want to you in here … because you made a stupid, stupid mistake. (prisoner)

The combination of increasing austerity and increasing security measures caused prisoners considerable concern because they reported feeling that any amount of power could be exercised over them, at any time, for any reason and that they would have no recourse to challenge it. Security decisions were often explicitly associated with punishments or sanctions. Therefore they were, in essence, a means through which prisoners felt punishment was being delivered.

> Even though you get used to these things happening to you, enduring it day in and day out for weeks, months, years. It feels progressively more punishing ... and you feel, um, despairing. (prisoner)

Living in such an environment resulted in a sense of defeat in many prisoners who felt unable to resist or protest the increasing levels of control that they felt were being exerted over them.

> When I first come [*sic*] here, four years ago, it was just more relaxed. It seems now they put more pressure on you and they keep throwing things at you – 'don't do this, don't do that, you can't do this'. (prisoner)

> On the front of the gate it says their duty is to treat us with humanity and to help us to lead law-abiding lives and yet you see their behaviour and you think there is something really wrong with this. Any society where people can be treated like this, so repressively [pause] it's just [pause] not right. But people [prisoners] just seem to regard it all with a patient shrug, you know, 'I don't want it to happen to me', and they've begun this defeated way of thinking now where it's, 'I don't want to get involved because I don't want that to happen to me'. (prisoner)

Such impressions were, in part, formed as a result of physical expressions of control used by prison authorities and which were justified on the grounds of maintaining security.

> The regime has become really quite bland now ... There's not much imagination. There's been a gradual cutting back of everything ... At the other extreme, there seems to be an increase in security and searching, whereas before if they had to take you off the wing it would be quite informal. Now they always have to come with the MUFTI[3] stuff and they always rush in at you; they don't give you any opportunity to walk.[4] (prisoner)

The experience of imprisonment and what it felt like to be a prisoner were affected by tactics used to maintain security (and control) and continually reinforced the subjugated status of prisoners. Prisoners used the words 'unsafe' and 'insecure' to describe how they felt about their treatment in prison.

> This place is scary. The way this place is run is scary – I don't feel safe here because of that. For them to have the power that they do, the way they use 'security' against you, to obfuscate – makes you feel totally powerless. And who's going to care about a bunch of high-security prisoners? No one's going to care if they leave you here forever or if they are brutal or if they overuse the power they have. Who cares? And that's really scary. That's the scariest thing in this prison; other inmates aren't scary. It's the screws and security and the sheer power they hold over you. (prisoner)

Life-sentenced prisoners and those designated as Category A – those who have been deemed to require the highest conditions of security – felt the most uncertain and insecure, which resulted in these prisoners experiencing the very deepest sense of punishment.

> As a lifer, you will not get out being a Cat A, like after you've done your recommended time if you are still a Cat A you won't be getting released, so it is not good. It's the way the system works – you can be stuck. You can do your time and you can do it well and not cause any trouble but because you are still Cat A you will still be a risk so they are not going to recommend you for release. So its like, how does it work? What do you have to do? 'You have made the mistake already and you're just going to have to live with it for the rest of your life because we are not going to help you even if you're helping yourself.' So what are you supposed to do? It's serious. (prisoner)

Their uncertainty about their futures and whether they would ever be recategorised to a lower-security status or progress towards eventual release added significant weight to all other aspects of their experiences as a Category A prisoner.

> I am a lifer and I don't have a release date and one of the biggest issues, for me, is wondering if I'll ever get out. That is my greatest fear and sometimes I just wonder if it is somehow intricately woven into the fabric of the system to want you to feel like that. Certainly as a Category A prisoner, a Category A lifer, I feel that that status is, to some extent, used as a barrier to prevent you from progressing

because as long as I am a Category A prisoner I know that my chances of ever getting released are virtually nil. (prisoner)

Uses of power and authority

The comparatively civilised state of English maximum-security prisons may be postulated to result, in part, from fairly high staff–prisoner ratios and from a long-held tradition of engagement between staff and prisoners in British prisons (Crawley, 2004; Liebling et al., 2010). That is, despite the difficulties of order experienced in the early dispersal system and the new pressures on staff–prisoner relationships exerted by the security regime the fact remains that prisoners and staff in dispersal (and other, lower-security prisons in Britain) have always (and continue to) mix and communicate with one another. Staff regularly spend time speaking to prisoners on the landings, in prisoners' cells and in other private and communal spaces. This tradition is in itself remarkable and deserves sustained research attention given its distinctiveness in comparison with staff approaches in other similar prison systems, such as the United States, Canada and Australia.[5] Studies of the nature of British staff–prisoner relationships have argued for both the importance of interactivity (Liebling and Arnold, 2004; Liebling et al., 2010) and the careful use of authority by staff (Sparks et al., 1996; Drake, 2008; Crewe, 2009). Despite the potential benefits of these relationships in British prisons they necessarily present a number of complexities and perils (Scott, 2008).

There are, of course, numerous ways in which interactive staff–prisoner relationships can have real and significant benefits for prisoners, at times alleviating some of the pressure they experience as a result of being imprisoned. When used carefully, and with considered discretion, staff authority can be a source of support for prisoners, promoting safety and creating a more predictable and constructive prison environment (Harvey, 2007; Liebling and Arnold, 2004). In the prisons considered here, there were certainly many examples of such careful uses of authority by staff. These examples should not be dismissed or disregarded and they surely contributed a valuable dimension – in both explicit and implicit ways – to prisoners' overall experiences of confinement. However, it is essential to bear in mind that the everyday experience of being confined is a difficult condition to live within and consequently does not easily lend itself to positive influence. Even in comparatively progressive prison systems, which have endeavoured to provide conditions as close as possible to those on the outside, a sense of profound punishment can still be felt amongst the prisoner population. This, again, underlines the importance of recognising the pains associated with the loss of liberty when considering the various ways that punishment is delivered through a prison sentence (see Mathiesen, 2000, pp. 132–5).

Given the place that prisoners are beginning from – an inherently powerless and subjugated one – the ways in which power and authority are used by prison authorities are a crucial feature of prisoners' experiences of imprisonment and their perceived treatment at the hands of the state (see Sparks et al., 1996). The ideology of maximum security provided prison staff with a power base from which their authority was confidently exercised. Although the nature of prison environments is such that the staff must ultimately hold control, the overuse of power and authority by staff can add to prisoners' experiences of punishment. Further, security and risk 'thinking', combined with measures associated with maintaining security, seemed to pervade the way staff thought about prisoners, which, in turn, influenced the treatment of prisoners.

The use of power by staff and its manifestation in the implementation of a heavy security regime added weight and pressure to prisoners' experiences of punishment. There was inflexibility in the way the staff carried out security tasks. They fulfilled their security duties with vigour, determination and forcefulness that felt heavy handed to prisoners. The constant subjection to security measures was difficult to endure for prisoners because it reinforced their own powerlessness whilst at the same time it bolstered the power held by staff. Further, it added an extra dimension to their punishment that seemed to go unrecognised.

> The other day the DST[6] were there to spin[7] me and I had already had two spins in that week. So, you saw me, I said: 'fuck, you are not spinning me.' So, you know, they locked the gates there and all the staff walked over to me to restrain me and to put the cuffs on … Probably if the transfer[8] and everything else was not building up I would not have acted like that, but it comes to a point where you just feel like you're going to *break*. You can say 'be positive' and all that, but it is not possible. When you are in a place like this, you are away from your family, away from your kids, your girlfriend, your lifestyle – that's bad enough. I know that you've done the crime, you do the time, there is no moaning about that, I agree with that. But when you get treated like a scumbag in these places … it's just too much. (prisoner)

As a witness to this event, it seemed to me that this young man's protests about being searched again for the third time that week were understandable, controlled and valid. However, the immediate staff response to his outburst was significant and imposing. Further, the reasons behind these three searches were the result of unfortunate coincidences, rather than genuine security concerns. The first search was simply routine, the second one was as a result of an allegation made by another prisoner (which was subsequently proven to be false) and the third search was, in fact, a random selection by the dedicated search team (who operate separately from the wing staff who carry out the routine searches). This provided an illustrative example of the way in which security measures are routinely applied and the reluctance of staff to use discretion when such measures seemingly become excessive. That is, there was simply no question among the staff concerned that the third search would be taking place, even though the prisoner was obviously becoming distressed and two previous searches in the same week had already revealed no contraband (as discussed in Chapter 4, finding contraband in maximum-security prisons has come to be seen as evidence of a failure in security systems). This example begins to capture part of the essence of staff–prisoner relationships within a heavy security regime – where staff can hold an inordinate amount of power and exercise it regularly in order to doggedly pursue security targets.

The most significant way that staff–prisoner relationships were placed under strain by the heavy security agenda in dispersal prisons was through the collection and documentation of intelligence information. As discussed in Chapter 4, one of the means by which security was procedurally maintained was through security intelligence collecting and reporting. Staff were trained to be vigilant for evidence or even the suggestion that a prisoner or group of prisoners may be involved in activities that could threaten prison security or were in any way suspicious. The difficulty with this remit was that within the security-conscious environment of maximum-security prisons, where prisoners were perceived as enemies or dangerous others, there was a tendency among staff to view almost any aspect of prisoner behaviour or activity as potentially suspicious. The apparent security-thinking of officers seemed to permeate many staff–prisoner interactions with staff actively seeking out security information and recording anything and everything that they perceived as potentially suspicious. This was, again, another way in which the security consciousness of maximum-security prison administration felt unsafe and threatening to prisoners:

> No, as a prisoner, you feel very unsafe ... within the first week I very quickly became aware that there's a culture here where staff will go out of their way to be derogatory, negative, hostile against prisoners.

> They're writing reports on their day-to-day interactions with prisoners, and that creates a very unnerving environment for people, and that makes people feel unsafe. (prisoner)

In this information age, it is possible for prisoners to gain access, through the Data Protection Act, to the reports written about them. This, in turn, allows prisoners to become aware of the ulterior motives behind staff-instigated interactions. Prisoners reported feeling shocked by the way conversations they had with officers were being interpreted, recorded and potentially used against them.

> Under the Data Protection Act you can now have access to information they have about you. So like, say, you are an officer who I speak to every day, like we are now, and behind my back you are writing: 'There have been a couple of times when I have felt intimidated by him. I thought he was going to threaten me and he seemed mentally ill at one point.' And now I can get hold of this and I think 'what?!' And this is someone who you speak to on a regular basis and they go back and are writing this behind your back and because of the Freedom of Information Act you are entitled to this now and this is what people are being presented with. It's a real sort of two-facedness; there is no integrity in it. (prisoner)

From prisoners' perspectives there was a lack of sensitivity or carefulness about the way prison staff recorded or discussed information about them. Firstly, many of the comments recorded about prisoners lacked appropriate evidence and were substantially subjective. This was potentially of serious consequence to prisoners. Negative wing reports could affect prisoners' privilege statuses, their treatment by officers and other staff, their opportunities for employment or education within the prison and would even be considered (amongst other information) during deliberations regarding their suitability to progress through the prison system. From the point of view of prisoners the way information was recorded about them was a significant use of power and authority that was not always used carefully and could have long-term, life altering, detrimental consequences.

Secondly, there was a lack of sensitivity in the way some comments were recorded in prisoners' reports and, indeed, in the way officers spoke about prisoners.

> I've witnessed staff members openly verbally abuse disabled prisoners here, in front of senior staff and the senior staff member says nothing.

It was done in front of other prisoners, other officers, other prisoners, so it clearly implied that that kind of attitude was acceptable – it was condoned. But when people can see that going on here in an open environment, it makes for a very unsafe environment. (prisoner)

Derogatory comments about prisoners from those who held authority over them were experienced as 'extra, gratuitous punishment' (prisoner). It added to prisoners' feelings of insecurity because they felt as though they were not in safe hands and that staff could arbitrarily overuse their power against them – even in brutal ways – which prisoners could do nothing to protect themselves from.

They say things about us and write things about us that are really only half-truths or have been twisted in some way or taken out of context ... it is diabolical. What can we do about it? And if they're willing to do that, who's to say they wouldn't take it further? You sometimes don't feel safe around them, you know? (prisoner)

Although incidents of staff-instigated violence against prisoners were rarely reported during interviews with prisoners in the present research, each prison had a few reasonably well-evidenced anecdotes of significant overuses of power that served to feed prisoners' anxieties. Moreover there were more frequent occurrences of rigid or arbitrary uses of power that reinforced prisoners' feelings of insecurity.

Certain officers like to overuse their power. They go walking around like they're a big man, 'cause they know they can ... Like, for example, one time someone must have took too long to get out their bed to get their dinner, just didn't come out for his dinner at the right time, so they shut his door and didn't feed him. Now, that is not on. That is bullying tactics. (prisoner)

The derogatory language used by some staff and which sometimes appeared in prisoners' wing reports gave the impression to prisoners that the staff did not recognise their human dignity. Therefore prisoners found it difficult to respect staff as criminal justice professionals.

They're taught in the training school that all prisoners are scumbags, don't listen to a word prisoners say. Don't believe a word they say. Don't give 'em nothing. Don't ask 'em for nothing. Don't go near 'em. Anything they ask for has an ulterior motive to it – anything they *do* has a motive – there's always a reason and it's devious. They end up paranoid, that's why they end up so paranoid. It's drummed into them. So of course there's no respect in here. There is none whatsoever, that's where it all goes wrong. They've got this policy statement that says prisoners must be treated with humanity and dignity and respect, you see it everywhere. I always quote it and say: 'You know your policy statement that's up on the walls, don't you ever abide by it?' And that's what they're supposed to do, but they don't show nothing [inhales, long pause], they don't show nothing. (prisoner)

Overall, there was a lack of transparency and accountability in the way prisoners felt staff were using their power and authority and in consequence the punishment associated with overuses of power remained invisible. The way power and authority were being used in the contemporary English maximum-security prison was perhaps connected to the nature of the security regime and consequences of risk-thinking. Both of these aspects of contemporary imprisonment are brought into fuller view in the next section where condemnation and judgement are explored.

Condemnation and judgement: the context of rehabilitation

Condemnation and judgement are inherent features of any system of social control. In a criminal justice system, social condemnation is achieved when someone is proven or pleads guilty to causing harm and is convicted for their offence(s) by the courts. The moral and societal judgement of the severity of the act is expressed through the punishment prescribed to atone for the said harm. In theory, the social requirements for condemning and judging certain acts should be completed through court processes and should not continue to feature throughout the meting out of the prescribed punishment. The political and cultural values that have come to shape English long-term, maximum-security imprisonment, however, have led to a number of processes and means by which condemnation and judgement have become fundamental features of the ongoing experience of punishment. The way rehabilitation is pursued, for example, is one of the key ways in which prisoners' experience condemnation and judgement.

The form that rehabilitation has taken in English maximum-security prisons has always been influenced by knowledges drawn from various sources of expertise and has invariably included a narrowly defined normative element, imbued with particular moral values and often paternalistic undertones. Rehabilitation in contemporary British prisons is primarily organised around issues of risk and need and relies heavily on the expertise of forensic psychology and the use of offending behaviour programmes purported to target criminogenic needs. Ben Crewe (2009, p. 115) has argued that in this context 'prisoners' psychological "needs" [are] narrowly defined according to what is deemed desirable for the public rather than what prisoners might require to enhance their psychological well-being or address their social needs'. It is indicative of a more decisive shift towards public protection, individualism and rational choice theories of crime and has resulted in a reliance on particular knowledges, especially those associated with risk prediction and cognitive behavioural intervention (Kendall, 2002).

Risk assessment research and cognitive behavioural programming have both been criticised for being imbued with moral judgements, predominantly white, middle-class norms, and being unresponsive to personal narratives or developmental contingencies (Kendall, 2002; Aas, 2004; Hannah-Moffat, 2005). Crewe's (2009) research reveals that prisoners in his study of a Category C men's prison in England were deeply troubled by the normative standards that they were being held to and instructed to comply with, despite the fact that they bore no resemblance to their personal experiences of social life (see ibid., p. 130). In addition, Crewe found that the bases on which prisoners were being judged were not made entirely clear to them and could be both inconsistent and unreasonable, for example, using in-prison behaviour as a predictive measure of risk in the community (ibid., p. 124, and citing Hannah-Moffat, 2005).

The findings of the present study mirror those revealed by Crewe (2009), but were perhaps more starkly visible due to the extra weight that conditions of maximum security added. In these prisons, prisoners felt as though they were consistently under scrutiny, constantly subject to a punitive panopticon (Foucault, 1995):

> There's not just one judge anymore – there's the judge who sentences you – your sentence is ten years! And you say, well, I'll go and do my punishment, ten years in prison. No, no, no ... there's now all these other judges, everyday, all over the place. You have to go to this prison, you have to go to that prison, you're a Cat A, you're a Cat B. I don't like your attitude, you have to do this course, I'm fining you or I'm putting you on an IEP [incentives and earned privileges] level of standard or basic. Everyone wants to get in on the act, judges all over the place, all of the time, and they all want to condemn you. What's happened? Is this sophistication from the so-called cruel days, when they used to say go forth and do your sentence in a cell for X number

of years? I mean it's hard and its rough living on gruel and all this sort of stuff, but what is happening now? And even if they hang you, it was all over with, wasn't it? There's no messing around, you're not going to have people digging you up every few days and saying 'you're still a guilty bastard', and putting you back in the coffin. There was none of that; it was finished; it was finite. Not anymore. You're on trial and you're judged day in, day out. (prisoner)

As the above quotation eloquently illustrates, prisoners felt as though condemnation and judgement had become integral aspects of their sentence. Constantly being judged was another means by which prisoners felt they were being punished. Such judgement was often delivered through specialist staff, particularly psychologists, and their tools of risk and psychological assessment (see also Crewe, 2009). Further, the means of delivery of these judgements were often experienced by prisoners as damaging and painful.

I've seen some people come back [from a meeting with a psychologist], grown men on the verge of tears – saying 'I'm worthless, I'm this, that, and the other' – and it really is dangerous 'cos then they bang up in a cell and they just implode. They can't see any future for themselves or any self-worth and I think that is dangerous and horrible. These assessments are done in ways that are painful, and hurtful, and not at all sensitively communicated. (prisoner)

Moreover, it seemed to many prisoners that the way they were communicated with by specialist staff and officers alike was, in essence, contradictory to the lessons they were apparently supposed to be learning through pro-social modelling or other behavioural interventions.

I hate the way in which these people come into this place and conduct their business ... I have never known a place outside where you would ever have the type of interrogation that you get in here ... but all of a sudden because you have committed a criminal offence there is overt criticism about you as an individual, which can to a certain extent be justified – after all we have committed crimes – but the way in which they go about doing things is really detestable ... The way they confront you with these, these judgements they make of you, that really seem arbitrary and subjective. I mean psychology is not an exact science and yet people are coming in here and saying to you, definitively, that you have these so-called cognitive deficits or enduring characteristics that just seem to pigeonhole you ... it is actually really offensive, in effect a character assassination. Also it's not at all carefully communicated to you, which makes the courses they put you on seem totally hypocritical. Sometimes I feel like asking them if they've ever thought of doing ETS [enhanced thinking skills]. (prisoner)

The way in which prisoners were openly judged and verbally condemned in formal and official systems of reporting was, according to prisoners, degrading and emotionally difficult. There seemed to be no concern for the *person* or any recognition that negative assessments of an individual's personality or identity can be difficult to hear. Further, the goal of psychological assessment and intervention seemed entirely focused on security considerations and creating corresponding evidence that the Prison Service had done everything within its power to reduce the risk prisoners presented. They were not concerned with prisoners' individual needs *per se*:

The trouble is we're not psychology's client, the Prison Service is their client and we're secondary to the Prison Service ... It's a very worrying world, its worrying from our point of view ... And what the psychology and the prison system want is for you to become a robot and be what they expect you to be as a 'perfect person'. They want to take your personality away and replace it with a drone ... That's it in a nutshell. (prisoner)

What they want to do, they want to peel you like an onion until you're bare, and your soul is naked. And then they want to clothe you in their clothes. They want you to reveal your soul to them ... And then they want to clothe it with their clothes and send you out into the world a broken, defeated, soulless person, which is why psychologists, as far as I'm concerned, are the most dangerous people in prisons today ... they aren't interested in helping you be who you actually are, they want you to become someone they imagine you should be, in accordance with some standard they think is 'right' ... but it's according to their rules, their morals, their judgements ... which may not be the same as mine. (prisoner)

Meaninglessness

There are no meaningful rewards available to mark an individual prisoner's progress during the time they spend in maximum-security conditions. The high proportion of life-sentenced prisoners[9] in these prisons (around 60 per cent at the time of the research) must, by definition, serve the whole of their minimum tariff. Unlike some other penal systems there are no early release possibilities available for good behaviour. As already discussed, life-sentenced prisoners may be arbitrarily allocated to a maximum-security prison and most could, in theory, have been sent instead to a Category B lifer prison. Those, however, allocated to maximum-security conditions will generally spend around a third of their minimum tariff there (in theory this should mean between five and eight years, though significant numbers of prisoners will remain in maximum-security much longer than this).

Inevitably, people hold differing views about when 'enough punishment' has been reached. Victims of crime, different segments of the general public and opinions expressed in popular media may present wide ranging views about when enough is enough. Rowell Huesmann and Cheryl-Lynn Podolski (2003, p. 68) have argued that people – both those experiencing punishment and those observing it – become accustomed to it 'in such a way that the punishment no longer evokes an emotional reaction'. In some respects this statement held true for prisoners interviewed in the present study.

> I were thinking the other day with prison it don't matter if you do 6 months or 16 years, it is still the same because every day is monotonous. It is just there. So you have no memories. So if I think back over the last ten years, like what have I done? Hmmm, I have been sentenced, we had the riot at Full Sutton, after that I am lost. It is all the same, so it feels like you have only been away six months. Unless something out of the ordinary happens, it doesn't register. (prisoner)

Furthermore, some prisoners reported feeling that they had been hardened by their prison experiences, having learned how to shut off emotionally, and had adjusted to the confines, parameters and restrictions of prison life. More often, however, prisoners who are subject to punishment may come to a point within their sentence when it begins to feel like enough is enough. Although it might be suggested that this is not entirely their judgement to make, the threshold for when one feels relentlessly punished must differ according to personal limits. 'There's only so much more I can take' (prisoner). 'How much more punishment do you want to give me?' (prisoner). Once such a threshold is reached and prisoners feel that being continuously punished further would not make them any more repentant or contrite, then the benefits of further punishment must be called into question.

This place makes you think, what can I achieve in prison? It is making me worse. I am already being punished by my freedom being taken away from me but they are punishing me even more because I can't get anything done in this place. It is more punishment. That is what it seems like. (prisoner)

Once the prisoner reaches their own threshold for pain the further experience of more and more punishment (sometimes for a considerable number of years if they have a very lengthy sentence) can have detrimental, unintended and even contradictory consequences to those that punishment is meant to achieve.

You can see people basically sink into a rut and they more or less implode. Lifers seem to go through this. It happens a lot with lifers where if things are not happening for them, after a few years they seem to abandon all hope. Of course then it means nothing is going to happen because they are not asking for anything. They are not doing anything. They are just wallowing in their own misery. The prison system is saying we are not recognising that you have changed. You are not doing anything. So you carry on year-in year-out for basically 99 years of this. They really do sink into themselves and this is a real issue because how can you ever gauge anyone who is that emotionally unbalanced all of the time? How can they ever do anything or achieve anything or have any kind of self-esteem? They are never going to be able to pull themselves out of it. (prisoner)

As Christie (2004, p. 103) has argued: '[T]he delivery of pain is the core element of punishment, even in countries without torture or the death penalty. With imprisonment we do not take the whole life away. But we take parts of life away.' The meaninglessness of prison experiences made some prisoners more acutely aware of the ways in which they were being punished and it was difficult for these prisoners to contemplate the reality of their lives.

When I get out I'll be about 40. I'm 24 now, I'll be 40-odd by the time I get out. I just take it one day at a time. One day at a time. It's hard. I don't let nobody see me emotion and I've got nobody I can talk to in these places because people don't understand and there is nobody that cares. It is hard sometimes, but I have to just look to the future. I'm always just looking on my appeal, that's the only thing that keeps me going at the moment and me people out there. I've been on an emotional roller coaster since I've been here, ups and downs. Inmates that are doing normal fixed sentences, they don't realise. They don't get it because they know they've got light at the end of the tunnel, whereas I don't have that. (prisoner)

The experience of long-term, maximum-security imprisonment afforded no opportunities through which prisoners could engage in restorative or redemptive endeavours. Once a prisoner felt as though he had experienced enough punishment to be able to live with himself for what he had done, there was no means by which he could meaningfully start to rebuild, heal or restore his sense of self or begin to reinvent himself.

I think the trouble is if a person feels remorse, there is nothing they can do to feel better. They would feel better if they were able to get on with their life – at least then they could feel like they are doing something positive. Whatever that is, they may just end up being a road sweeper, but at least they feel like they are doing something. Put them in prison for 25 years and they can never achieve anything good – they can only ever achieve selfish things. (prisoner)

I want to do something constructive, but in here constructiveness is very hard – it's frustrating. You've got to pay your punishment, but I would rather go out and plough someone's field for them or put a roof on someone's house and work my guts off to pay back or raise money for the victim's family or pay them money, but I just want to give something back. I'm not giving nothing back by sitting here. They are getting bitter, they are angry, I am angry, we are tired. Yeah it's a bad system. Let me do something. (prisoner)

As is evident in the above quotations, the experience of being punished, in some respects, loses aspects of its meaning over a lengthy period of time. For prisoners the day-to-day experience of being punished can become fully disconnected from the act for which they had been imprisoned. From the perspective of the prisoner it was difficult to see how the practice of long-term imprisonment held any tangible benefit for the prisoner, for society or for victims of crime. From my own perspective, as a witness to it, it looked relentlessly painful. And prisoners' accounts of its meaninglessness were observable. It was, in the estimation of many prisoners, a poorly conceived solution to problems of crime and human conflict.

There was also a senselessness to the long-term prison sentence that made it difficult to understand how it is that we (as a society) are still holding so firmly to this practice as a solution to serious harms or other social problems. It seemed unjustifiable, even if differentiations were made between the different types of criminal offences for which maximum-security prisoners were serving sentences. That, is, if we divide the criminal offences of maximum-security prisoners into two crude groupings – those which were indicative of physical harm to persons (including threatening or conspiring to physically harm a person or persons) and those which did not explicitly include physical harm – there still seemed to be little justification or social benefit for the long-term exile of people convicted of either group of offences.

For those prisoners in maximum-security prisons who have been convicted of supplying drugs, burglary, purely acquisitive crimes or other crimes that did not result in physical harm to a person (e.g., arson, blackmail), long-term imprisonment seemed a disproportionate and ineffectual response. Those convicted for these types of offences accounted for around 10 per cent[10] of the total dispersal prisoner population and many were serving long-term sentences due to their repeated convictions. Imprisonment had thus far not solved the problems that brought these men into prison and it was difficult to see the logic behind exiling them for longer and longer periods as a means of encouraging them to live more law-abiding lives once they were allowed to return to society.

For those prisoners in maximum-security prisons who were convicted of serious harms which had led to the death of other people or who had seriously physically assaulted other men, women or children, or even those who had acted in extremely threatening ways (e.g., those convicted for armed robbery or related offences[11]), the long-term prison sentence also seemed like an ineffectual response. All but a very small number (around 30 men) of maximum-security prisoners have the expectation that they will, one day, be released. This, then, suggests that one of the implicit goals of imprisonment is to return people to society to safely live alongside other people. If the aim of imprisonment is the eventual social inclusion of those who have transgressed social norms or acted in unsafe ways, then long-term prison is particularly poorly designed to fulfil this purpose.

From prisoners' own accounts of the extreme form of punishment that is long-term imprisonment, it was evident that the use of this sanction was not well designed or equipped to restore or otherwise overcome the personal and social damage that can result either when one human being physically harms another or when other types of illegal offences are committed. It is, however, very well designed to punish relentlessly – to the point of meaninglessness. Those who were subjected to it had to struggle against every pressure inherent in the structure of the prison to retain a sense of identity, feelings of self-worth and of human dignity. Prisoners felt that their capacity to care for themselves and other human beings was being severely jeopardised through their experience, thereby suggesting that long-term, maximum-security punishment had effects that were in direct opposition to those that were intended.

Conclusion: a 'suitable amount of pain'?

Borrowing a phrase from Christie (2000), English long-term, maximum-security prisons are perhaps best placed within the penal landscape to shed light on the question: 'What is a "suitable amount of pain"?' They provide a helpful exemplar for examining the pain that is the loss of one's liberty and the extent to which this punishment is in keeping with prevailing cultural values. Christie (ibid., p. 201) has argued that '[a] suitable amount of pain is not a question of utility, of crime control, of what works. It is a question of standards based on values. It is a cultural question.' It may be seen, then, that our values allow us or drive us to decide how much pain is enough. But it is questionable if, as a society, we fully understand how much pain is being delivered through the use and experience of imprisonment.

A cursory examination of contemporary long-term, maximum-security imprisonment in England might suggest that prison conditions are relatively good and that experiences of imprisonment deliver a reasonable amount of pain. As mentioned in Chapter 3, these prisons have endeavoured to engage prisoners in a range of activities, including physical education, unskilled work, vocational training or educational opportunities. All prisoners live in single-cell accommodation and most have access to cooking and recreational facilities on their wings. On the surface it might appear that prisoners are treated neither too severely, nor too leniently. As can be expected, staff–prisoner relationships are complex due to the way power flows, is held and is used in a contained environment, but levels of engagement between staff and prisoners tend to be high and in their most positive guises range from perfunctory to superficially friendly. Official prison indicators suggest that these prisons are performing well according to the National Offender Management Service (NOMS) key performance targets (which include: public protection, safety and decency in custody, offender management and interventions, and pathways to reducing reoffending) (Ministry of Justice, 2011). These prison environments appear disciplined, orderly and ostensibly moderate. The English example is in many ways a civilised one. It provides an exemplar that is less confounded by the brutal prisoner-on-prisoner violence that is often a feature of many other similar penal systems, in, for example, the United States (Braswell et al., 1994; McCorkle et al., 1995; Silberman, 1995) or Canada (Forum on Corrections, 1992; Welch, 1995). Experiences of punishment in English maximum-security prisons provide a unique opportunity to carefully examine a seemingly moderate example of the delivery of pain. And yet, as this chapter has illustrated, despite (or perhaps as a result of) their apparent moderation, when one delves more deeply into how prisoners experience maximum-security confinement in England, the meanings, weight and hidden brutalities of long-term imprisonment become evident.

Long-term prisons deliver punishment. In this way they serve some purposes particularly well. That is, they are places that deliver retribution and vengeance. However, the degree to which these prisons deliver on some of their other purported purposes, for example, deterrence or rehabilitation, remains unproven (as Mathiesen, 2000, has illustrated). Furthermore, there is much evidence to suggest that retributive justice (and the use of punishment as a way of encouraging better human behaviour) is fundamentally flawed and ineffective. As James Gilligan (2000, p. 746) has argued:

> [P]*unishment is the deliberate infliction of pain on a person for the sake of attaining revenge.* And penitentiaries, or prisons, are institutions whose purpose is to inflict pain on people for the sake of revenge (a task at which they are all too successful). But ... the trouble with revenge is that it is endless; the moment one person gets revenge, the person on whom revenge was taken is motivated to return the favour, resulting in an endless vicious cycle.

The problems of revenge, vengeance and punishment will be considered more fully in Chapter 7. But what is important to highlight here are the negative experiences that prisons generate – from prisoners' own perspectives. In the current context of exponentially increasing sentence lengths, growing prisoner numbers and the apparent erosion of political will and resources for providing humane and constructive regimes for long-term prisoners it is imperative that closer attention is paid to what prisoner experiences actually involve. Prisoners who are serving the longest sentences and are doing so in the highest conditions of security are perhaps the most vulnerable to losing their sense of humanity, their faith in the system (if they had any to begin with) and their hope for the future. All but a very small number of these prisoners will, one day, be released.

Dispersal prisons, therefore, must be seen to have an obligation, both to the public whom they are meant to protect and to the prisoners who they house (who are after all suspended *citizens*), to provide prison experiences that do not blunt the sensibilities of prisoners (Downes, 1988) and – at the very least – aim to limit the damage that the experience of punishment inevitably causes.

The notion that prison should or could create law-abiding citizens is made unachievable by ignoring, firstly, the social or structural factors and barriers that contributed – in complex ways – to the circumstances that lead people to prison in the first place. Secondly, the orientation of prisons towards punishment ensures that few positive aims can be achieved through experiences of imprisonment. Moreover, preparation for participation in society after prison is made even more difficult by the removal from society of those who have been criminalised due to the compounding of their disadvantage by their long period of exile away from the rest of society and the indelible stigma that such a prison sentence brings with it – both inside the prison and after eventual release.

Prisoners occupy an unenviable position in society. At best their rights and interests are viewed as marginal and at worst they themselves are seen as undeserving of human rights or other legal protections that aim to safeguard citizens from state abuses or overuses of authority. The plight of prisoners and their marginal status in society is nothing new. As this and the previous two chapters have illustrated, prisoners are variously constructed as deserving of punishment, as dangerous others, enemies within or in need of some form of intervention that will facilitate a reformation in their character. In the contemporary context of English maximum-security prisons, there are few official discourses that speak in favour of prisoners' rights, their care or their humane treatment. The intensification and proliferation of security ideologies in prisons has further marginalised these discourses as well as welfarist approaches to imprisonment. The prison provides for us some vital clues about the way the concept of security can infiltrate different aspects of social life and the different meanings and powers it can hold. The linkages between how security is constituted in the penal and the social realms and the potential implications of its power and capacity for hegemonic influence are the issues of concern taken up in the next chapter.

6
Constituting Security in the Penal and the Social Realms

Introduction

The problem of security – defined as both an objective state and a subjective feeling – and the solutions that individuals, institutions, nation states and global powers pursue to solve it is of central concern to all humankind. It is a complex problem that can be considered at micro-, meso-, and macro-sociological levels. This chapter, somewhat ambitiously, attempts to consider all three, at least to some extent. It negotiates and unpacks aspects of this complex problem through various ideological lenses. The overarching concern of the chapter is the potentially hegemonic power of ideologies of security and the many covert and stealthy ways these ideologies have begun to infiltrate social and political life. In order to illustrate this, the chapter begins by considering the way security is constituted in the penal realm. The implications of the rise of security in maximum-security prisons in England that has been systematically developed over the previous three chapters are drawn into full view here. An examination of the prison clearly elucidates the potential power of the concept of security. It is shown that the strategies that flow from security ideologies are often covertly coercive and suggestive of a tendency towards totalitarian principles. It is argued, therefore, that the constitution of security in prisons offers some important insights for its constitution in wider social and political contexts and with respect to what the concept of security can make possible within so-called democratic and free societies.

The chapter goes on to examine the ways in which security has been considered within criminology in relation to social and political developments. The strength and parameters of security ideologies and the way they are used to justify and normalise exceptional measures are identified as key means by which security is used to obscure the nefariousness of some of its own methods and the way it surreptitiously reinforces other dominant ideologies. It is argued that the symbiotic, mutually reinforcing relationship between the prison and wider security agendas is uniquely positioned to contribute to this systematic obfuscation and to reinforce taken-for-granted assumptions about both the prison and the most effective and appropriate means for pursuing security.

The final section of the chapter presents data from extensive research by Finnish criminologist Tapio Lappi-Seppälä from which it is extrapolated that the very measures being employed in the pursuit of security may, indeed, be undermining it – at least at the level of the nation state and in relation to a subjective sense of security. It is argued that the pursuit of a subjective *sense of security* may be a more worthwhile endeavour, particularly at the level of the nation state.

Security in the penal realm

As illustrated in the previous two chapters, the emergence of a security regime in maximum-security prisons has resulted in security becoming the primary purpose and *raison d'être* of these prisons (and, indeed, many other lower-security prisons as well). Prison environments have become dominated by the constant operationalisation of security measures (for example, CCTV monitoring, routine searching of prisoners' cells, dog patrols, surveillance and intelligence information gathering). Such measures result in not only secure prisons (in the sense that they are apparently escape-proof), but also highly controlled and regimented prison environments. It is significant that there has not been an escape from a maximum-security prison since 1995 and no serious riot since 1998. The absence of prisoner disturbances in maximum-security prisons is particularly remarkable given their tumultuous history throughout the 1970s, 1980s and early 1990s. These facts are seen as successes by prison authorities who argue that the absence of breaches of security and control are evidence that prison practice is now founded on knowledge about 'how prisons really work', which has, in turn, created prison environments that are safer and more secure for both staff and prisoners (Wheatley, 2005; Drake, 2006, 2008). It would appear that security regimes maintain both physical and perimeter security and create a firmer basis for order inside the prison walls. However, if we consider more carefully the way the concept of security is applied in prisons there begins to emerge some fundamental questions both about the successes that have been attributed to its application and about its desirability as a pursuit and strategic priority.

A chimera of safety and security

The security regime results in prison environments that appear, on the surface, as orderly, efficient, highly routinized and controlled. The atmosphere of dispersal prisons stands in stark contrast to the chaos and disorder that characterised these prisons throughout their first 25 years of operation. It should be recognised that this change of atmosphere is significant and is, arguably, an important improvement. It is particularly salient for long-serving prison staff, many of whom recall having faced numerous incidents of serious confrontation with prisoners, which included threats of physical and verbal assault, often on a daily basis. However, if we look at some of the evidence for the so-called improvements to physical safety that have been achieved through the security regime, the success of the regime seems less impressive.

Tables 6.1 and 6.2 present average staff and prisoner assault rates across the five dispersal prisons between 1993 and 1999 and between 2000 and 2009.[1]

The data within each of the time spans presented in the tables reveal some important differences on a year-to-year basis. For example, Table 6.1 reveals that 1994 had an especially high number of prisoner assaults. This was just prior to the Whitemoor and Parkhurst escapes and when there were still quite high levels of disorder occurring in maximum-security and other British prisons. The early stages of what would become the security regime began to be implemented in 1995 and prisoner assaults started to decline, averaging out at around 16 assaults per year between 1996 and 1999. Staff assaults peaked in 1996 (arguably the height of the implementation of the security regime) and then averaged out at around 11 assaults per year between 1997 and 1999.

Table 6.1   Staff and prisoner assaults in maximum-security prisons 1993–99

	1993	1994	1995	1996	1997	1998	1999	Total Average
Staff Assaults	5.6	8.8	13	20	16.2	9.4	8.6	11.65
Prisoner Assaults	29.4	50.8	27	14	16.4	15	20.4	24.71

Source: FOI/62512/09.

Table 6.2 reveals a seemingly incremental increase in assaults on prisoners (and to a lesser extent on staff) between 2000 and 2009, with prisoner assaults peaking at 37 per year in 2008 and staff assaults peaking at 16.4 in 2007. These numbers suggest that levels of physical safety

Table 6.2   Staff and prisoner assaults in maximum-security prisons 2000–09

	2000	2001	2002	2003	2004	2005	2006	2007	2008	2009	Total Average
Staff Assaults	6.8	13	11.4	9.2	11.2	14.4	10.8	16.4	14.6	14.8	12.26
Prisoner Assaults	14.2	16.4	16	15.8	19.4	28.8	31	32.8	37	32.6	24.4

Source: FOI/62512/09.

in maximum-security prisons are not assured within the security regime of these prisons, particularly for prisoners. Furthermore, despite the data not being directly comparable in the two tables (due to changes in recording practices), the total average assault rates for staff (11.65 and 12.26) and prisoners (24.71 and 24.40) in each time span are nearly identical for both groups. Even if recording practices have significantly improved it might be expected that some difference in total average assault rates would be apparent, particularly since the official rhetoric concerning the safety levels of maximum-security prisons suggests that they are significantly safer for both groups. Moreover, data in each of the tables reflect that within each time period, irrespective of recording practices, the average of prisoner assaults is fairly consistently about twice that of staff assaults. So whatever the recording practices, prisoners have always been twice as likely as prison staff to be assaulted. This suggests that the security regime despite its apparent successes in creating more secure, and apparently orderly, environments does not actually create environments that are much safer. They create the *appearance* or a chimera of safety and security, particularly from the perspectives of the authorities (i.e., prison staff, managers and senior managers).

Part of the perceived success of the security regime relates directly to the power base it affords prison authorities, which both forestalls opportunities for collective prisoner protest and effectively silences individual prisoner voices. The security regime bears no resemblance to a consensual form of order, though the extent to which prison order is ever achieved with the consent of prisoners has long been questioned in the critical criminological literature (see particularly, Scraton et al., 1991; Sim, 1994). Nevertheless, there has been much research and policy attention directed towards identifying the prison conditions that led to higher levels of orderliness in prisons (Jacobs, 1977; Home Office, 1984; DiIulio, 1987; Young, 1987; Sparks et al., 1996). For example, Sparks and Bottoms (1995, p. 47) have argued 'that there are variable conditions which render it more or less likely that prisoners will accept, however conditionally, the authority of their custodians'. Consideration of the forms of order that prisons could achieve may have served useful administrative purposes when disturbances were a common feature of prison life. Such considerations do not seem as relevant when prisoner unrest is a relatively rare occurrence in the life of British prisons. By contrast, the reduction (or cessation, in the case of dispersal prisons) of prison disturbances is a phenomenon that should attract considerable attention (Carrabine, 2005), especially given the history of disorder in British prisons and the asymmetries of power that have always been an inherent feature of prison life. As will become evident below, part of the reason the chimera of safety and security in the security regime has become so well entrenched is due to the power of the security regime to forestall incidents of collective disturbance.

The invisibility of coercion in the security regime

Prisons are, by their very nature, coercive environments as Scraton et al. (1991, pp. 61–2) argue.

> All forms of incarceration imply the use of force. Regardless of the outward appearance of compliance few people taken into custody would accept their loss of liberty so willingly if the full potential of state coercion was not handcuffed to their wrists ... The authority imposed by the prison is not a consensual authority. It is not derived in consultation and agreement, nor is it legitimated by any process of representation and accountability ... The 'totality' of the institution, in terms of its political and professional autonomy, is underwritten by a degree of 'totality' or absolutism in power relations which virtually strip the prisoner of civil rights ... On paper the procedures exist and in theory all prisoners have equal recourse to the law. In practice the hurdles are often [as] insurmountable as the inaccessible world of the prison, the closed ranks of its professionals and the climate of fear and intimidation stand in the path of even the most persistent complainant ... Life in most British prisons is an unrelenting imposition of authority.

The above quotation includes a number of truisms about prison life. Authority in prison is not a consensual form of authority. It may be carefully and mercifully exercised, but the power of authority is not bestowed upon prison officers with the consent of prisoners or through any democratic process. There is an absolutism in power relations that can be invoked at any time (and is on a daily basis). Prisons are, in essence, total in their control over prisoners' freedom, dictating dominion over every realm of their lives (Goffman, 1961). Compliance in prison is achieved through both subtle and overt forms of power and coercion. It is never fully willing. Whilst there appear to be procedures in place for prisoners to protest the terms and conditions of their confinement, they must always do so from a position of extreme disempowerment. As a result it can be exceptionally difficult for complaints to be heard and fairly dealt with. Prisoners, therefore, are made vulnerable by their imprisonment. The depth and form of this vulnerability, however, varies depending on the structure of the regime that governs prison life.

In the first 25 years of the dispersal prison system the notion of a liberal regime within a secure perimeter created prison conditions that were characterised by an uneven exercise of power, which was sometimes brutal and heavy handed and at other times dilute and tentative. The vulnerability of prisoners resulted from the capricious use of discretion by prison officers. In prisons arbitrary and inconsistent uses of power can create intolerable staff–prisoner dynamics that can result in much confrontation and conflict between the two groups that is then manifested in prisoner unrest and riots (King, 1985; Scraton et al., 1991).

Within the security regime of contemporary maximum-security prisons, by contrast, the vulnerability of prisoners has taken on a different form. As already illustrated in Chapters 4 and 5, security has come to provide a firmer basis upon which staff exercise authority and control. The chronic problems of prison disorder have ceased to occur in long-term, maximum-security prisons. However, it cannot be argued that the reason for this apparent calm is due to having achieved a consensual, legitimate form of order (see Sparks et al., 1996). Whilst prison staff, as custodians of the confined, have always had a firm basis from which to wield their power, the security regime has created a much stronger and formidable power base, fortified by the logic and absolutism of the security ideology, which leaves prisoners more profoundly vulnerable and more effectively silenced in the wake of its awesome might. Within this ideology there is no space to question the extent to which staff are using their authority in so-called legitimate ways. As the pursuers of security, staff hold unquestionable authority.

The bolstering of the power of staff and the incontrovertibility of the regime are reinforced by three features associated with the maintenance of security, each of which results in invisible forms of coercion. Firstly, the concern within the security regime with information and intelligence gathering provides a seemingly limitless source of data and possible evidence that is used against prisoners to judge, exclude, stigmatise or categorise them. Secondly, security ideology is fundamentally concerned with the practice of 'othering' prisoners (as described in Chapter 4). Therefore, it provides grounds on which the dehumanisation of prisoners can take place relatively unabated, and in so doing can justify and normalise both human rights abuses and exceptional measures (particularly in the case of those convicted or detained for acts of political violence). Finally, the security regime combines well with the punitive functions of the prison to deliver greater levels of punishment and penal severity. Each of these facets of the invisibility of coercion in the security regime will be considered in turn.

The importance of information and intelligence gathering within the security ideology results in new sources of data and ways of collecting it. The *raison d'être* of the security regime is to pre-empt breaches of security. Therefore, whenever security intelligence information comes to light – even if it is based on unsubstantiated evidence – pre-emptive action is taken. For example, when intelligence information comes to light about a prisoner he may be subjected to a strategic move (i.e., where he will be relocated to a different wing or to a different dispersal prison altogether) or a heavy control response (i.e., when an individual prisoner is suspected of plotting some form of protest or an assault he may be removed from a wing by force and placed in the segregation unit while the matter is fully investigated). The preoccupation within security ideologies with precaution makes the use of information and data a key way in which power is exercised (Aradau and van Munster, 2007). The application of precautionary measures has resulted in a hybrid of practices concerned with highly bureaucratised, routine procedures and constant surveillance and vigilance. Whilst the more bureaucratic elements result in an assault on individual judgement and responsibility for agents of security (the watchers), the tendency towards hypervigilance provides greater volumes of information about individuals (the watched) by which they can be judged, held responsible, categorised and stigmatised. Any piece of information, however tenuously substantiated, can be used against a prisoner with varying serious consequences. Moreover, the security regime within maximum-security prisons has readily absorbed the concepts of risk and dangerousness and therefore places great emphasis on their importance in pre-emptive strategies. These concepts, which in and of themselves hold great power, can combine with the concept of security to stigmatise prisoners in effectively permanent ways (which will be discussed more fully below).

Similarly, the tendency of security discourses and practices to cast prisoners as others or as enemies has created a context in which prisoners are seen as enduring suspects (see also Chapter 4). They are always worthy of suspicion, always untrustworthy and essentially, fundamentally and incorrigibly criminal. 'They' are not like 'us'. These discourses and ways of thinking about prisoners provide grounds on which they are effectively dehumanised. Constructing prisoners as enemy others makes it possible for state authorities to justify exceptional measures and disregard human rights. This aspect of the ideology of security explicitly and deliberately silences the voices of those it deems enemy combatants, in this case prisoners. Thereby any avenues for prisoner protest are effectively blocked because, as enemies of security, disgruntled or protesting prisoners are implicitly constructed as insurgents against the regime, not as fellow citizens who may have legitimate complaints to make against their treatment at the hands of the state. Their opinions, experiences and circumstances simply do not matter because they are viewed as enemy combatants and thus they are outside the protections of the state they have supposedly waged war against. Applying such arguments against fellow citizens is, without doubt, a clear resort to totalitarian means where the ideology of the regime is used to justify illegal action (Goodwin, 2007). Due to the powerlessness and vulnerability of prisoners the potential use of such tactics is especially troubling.

Finally, the concept of security combines well with punitiveness – both in the sense that it can contribute to greater penal severity (more austere prison conditions) and deeper experiences of imprisonment (increased sentence lengths). With respect to prison conditions, increased emphasis on security has had a marked effect on the quality of prisoner experiences in dispersal prisons (as described in Chapter 5, but also see Liebling, 2002; Drake, 2006). It has been used to justify more austere and starker living conditions for prisoners, a reduced range of activities and fewer opportunities for and freedom within family visits (Learmont, 1995), and more repressive practices (i.e., more responsive and coordinated control and restraint teams, increased levels of searching of prisoners and less respect for privacy). Furthermore, security can be used to justify longer periods of imprisonment, particularly when a prisoner is categorised as high risk (Category A) and many prisoners are held well beyond their tariff expiry (Padfield, 2002) on security grounds. Prisoners, of course, are patently powerless to resist this deepening of their experiences of punishment and, indeed, are further disempowered by the combined efforts of the other invisible forms of coercion associated with the security regime. Moreover, as maximum-security prisoners – who are often labelled 'the worst of the worst' in official prison discourse – their protests are discounted because they are viewed as deserving of the measures and the punishment they are experiencing. The security regime, therefore, adds the full weight of security measures to the punitive character of prison experiences. By doing so, it establishes a form of order that is total in its absolute power and delivers a form of punishment that is both overt and stealthy, but also silencing.

The invisible means by which coercion is exercised within the security regime means that it is capable of exerting high levels of control over prisoners in seemingly benign and rational ways. Beneath the surface, however, forms of coercion are operating, applying covert elements of totalitarian methods. This is especially troubling given the apparent capacity of the security regime to operate by stealth and conceal the pernicious nature of its methods, its own failings (with respect to improving levels of safety, for example) and the continuing perennial failings of the prison.

The security regime and the art of concealment

The infiltration of security into the penal realm and the apparent result of more secure prison environments have become instrumental in the external legitimacy of the use of imprisonment as a crime control tool. In addition, the hegemonic power of the ideology of security has made penal severity a key tactic in the pursuit of security in the social and political realm. This latter point requires some significant unpacking and will be more thoroughly examined in the next section of this chapter. However, the former point regarding the role of the security ideology in bolstering the external legitimacy of imprisonment relates to the art of concealment, which serves the concept of security particularly well and needs some further consideration before moving on to wider concerns.

The apparent success of the security regime and its ability to effectively silence the voices of prisoners has made its hegemonic power absolute, drawing attention away from the persistent failures of prisons. Security-thinking in the prison – due to its capacity to foreclose debate and its power once evoked (Zedner, 2009) – makes it even less likely that the failures of the prison will be noticed. The ideology of security subjugates other ideologies (e.g., welfarist ideologies or rehabilitative concerns) and marginalises other discourses. One of the central problems with which this book is concerned relates to the purported purposes and hidden functions of the prison. Chapter 5 demonstrated, from the perspectives of prisoners, what prison experiences entail. It established the purposes that are, to some extent, fulfilled, depending on how those purposes are defined (i.e., temporary incapacitation or justice defined as vengeance) and those that are patently unfulfilled (i.e., rehabilitation, justice defined as fairness, individual deterrence or general prevention). In essence, experiences of prisoners in English maximum-security prisons confirm Mathiesen's (2000, p. 141) assertion that 'the prison is a fiasco in terms of its own purposes'. This is not anything new. The prison persists, as Mathiesen points out and outlined in Chapter 1 of this book, because it fulfils a number of hidden and symbolic functions. What is new is the extent to which the concept of security and its application within the penal realm have been able to effectively conceal and distract attentions away from the chronic problems and fundamental contradictions of prison administration.

As discussed above, the sense of safety and security in prisons is a chimera. The environment created by the implementation of a wide range of security procedures, measures and practices is one of regimentation, discipline, control and apparent functionality. But upon closer inspection it is revealed that it is not an environment that is necessarily physically safe, it does not provide a sense of security (in subjective terms) for prisoners and it does not reconcile the contradictory purposes of the prison – that is, to punish and to reform. These contradictions persist, but they are transformed somewhat as they too have become infused with elements of security. The concepts of risk and dangerousness, which are handmaidens within the security ideology (Zedner, 2009), transform both the character of punishment and the parameters and requirements of reform. Within this ideology prisoners come to be seen primarily as representations of the crimes they have committed. They are, in effect, embodiments of risk and dangerousness. As Nikolas Rose (2000, p. 200) has argued:

> On the one hand, confinement becomes a way of securing the most risky until their riskiness can be fully assessed and controlled. On the other, a group of individuals emerge who appear intractably risky – 'monstrous individuals', who either cannot or do not wish to exercise the self-control upon conduct necessary in a culture of freedom. Sexual predators, paedophiles, the incorrigibly anti-social are representatives of a new 'human kind' – individuals whose very make up as human beings appears somehow faulty or incomplete, and whose very nature thus seems to place them permanently beyond the limits of civility.

Nowhere are Rose's theorisations more applicable than in maximum-security prisons which are, by definition, institutions which house some of the most risky individuals. The management of risk in relation to prisoners has become a central aspect of prison administration. As Malcolm Feeley and Jonathan Simon (1992, p. 452) have suggested, the penal realm is '... concerned with techniques to identify, classify, and manage groupings sorted by dangerousness'. This has created an environment in which the individuality of prisoners is not acknowledged or seen as relevant. As already discussed, prisons have become not only places of punishment – the end product of the criminal justice system – they are increasingly places of continuous control, judgement and assessment. They are persistent in their pursuit to find objective evidence that prisoners – as risks that need to be managed – can either be safely returned to the community or detained indefinitely. As David Garland (2001, p. 12) suggests:

> Today there is a new and urgent emphasis upon the need for security, the containment of danger, the identification and management of any kind of risk. Protecting the public has become the dominant theme of penal policy.

The preoccupation with risk and dangerousness within the prison context obscures one of the fundamental flaws of a punitive criminal justice system: that rehabilitation, healing or restoration cannot take place in the social isolation of the penal realm or in an environment that is relentlessly punishing. By orienting the so-called rehabilitative aspects of prison life around the concepts of risk and dangerousness the role of prisons is, in part, redefined. As Rose (2000, p. 200) has argued, prisons have become repositories for the secure containment of risk and, thus, offer progressively fewer meaningful opportunities for prisoners to improve their circumstances. In practice, prisons have become concerned, above all else, with maintaining prison security and containing risk and dangerousness. The other traditional purposes of the prison (i.e., individual deterrence, general prevention, rehabilitation and incapacitation) are secondary to these goals or are subsumed and transformed within them. Therefore, the security regime very effectively conceals and obscures the chronic failings of the prison and, indeed, proffers new goals for it, which are, at least in appearance, seemingly more achievable. At the same time the symbolic functions of the prison and the ideology of imprisonment have begun to be more deeply embedded in social and political structures. As these processes have begun to take place, much focus has been lost on other social problems, social welfare concerns and other aspects of social life that contribute to public feelings of insecurity, fear or, conversely, social trust. Likewise, due to the concealment inherent in the mechanisms and practices associated of with implementing security, its failings and the more malignant aspects of the methods associated with the pursuit of security remain hidden from view.

Security in the social realm

Concerns with security within the penal realm have been raised as a result of events and developments inside the prison walls, and also due to a heightened concern with security in society at large. Many social theorists have examined the growing preoccupation with subjective feelings of *insecurity* in contemporary societies (Giddens, 1990, 1991; Bauman, 1991, 1997, 2000a; Beck, 1992, 1995). Amongst the most influential, Ulrich Beck (1992, 1995, 1998, 2009) has argued that since the late 1970s there has been a growing sense of insecurity in Western societies accompanied by widespread public disillusionment with scientific expertise and with the capacity of existing social institutions to effectively manage the risks and hazards of contemporary social life. The rate of human progress and technological advancement that accompanied modernity seemed to suggest that continuing economic development would create a self-perpetuating, opportunity-rich society (Hudson, 2003, p. 43) and would eventually result in more even distributions of wealth and economic security. However as greater levels of widespread economic security have remained elusive and the problems caused by modernity itself have begun to exact new sources of manufactured risk, the positive possibilities of modernity have become transformed into negative ones and concerns over increasing hazards and risks have started to permeate all levels and areas of social life. As Beck (2009, p. 11) argues:

> It does not matter whether we live in a world that is 'objectively' more secure than any that has gone before – *the staged anticipation of disasters and catastrophes obliges us to take preventive action*. This holds especially for the state, which is forced to take anticipatory precautionary measures because guaranteeing the security of its citizens is one of its pre-eminent tasks. This is true even if the relevant authorities (science, the military, the judiciary) do not have the corresponding instruments at their disposal (e.g., because their ability to respond to global risks is confined to the horizon of the nation-state).

There is inherent difficulty in *securing* a state of security, especially in an increasingly globalised world. The pursuit of security is necessarily a continuous one. Chaos, it seems, is a perpetual feature of the human condition (Bauman, 2000b). Therefore certainty and predictability in social life remain out of reach and a sense of insecurity continues to permeate the public consciousness. Whether *objective* – defined as the condition of being without threat – or *subjective* – defined as a sense of personal safety – absolute security can never be assuredly achieved (Zedner, 2009). Nonetheless, in the early twenty-first century, nation states around the globe struggle with heightened public concerns over human and global security (Goold and Lazarus, 2007). Zedner (2009, p. 12) suggests that these concerns may be most obviously attributed to 'the extraneous threats that have recently provided the very justification for security laws, policies, measures, services, and products. The events of 9/11, subsequent terrorist atrocities, the threat of guns, drugs, international serious and organised crime ... licence extraordinary and exceptional measures ...'. The occurrence of such events in an already risk-wary social and political context has increased generalised levels of pubic insecurity and raised the prominence of security measures in a variety of institutional, national and international arenas. Further, it has also raised the prominence of, and the collective social concern with, the problem of crime.

Crime and security as political projects

Much criminological theorising has considered the way the issue of security and problems of crime are often closely intertwined in both policy and rhetoric (see *inter alia* Bauman, 2000b; Hope and Sparks, 2000; Garland, 2001; Furedi, 2002; Hudson, 2003; Zedner, 2003, 2009). Likewise, the role of crime and punishment in politics and state governance have been extensively theorised and examined both within and outside the criminological field (Garland, 2001; Simon, 2007; Aradau and van Munster, 2007, 2009; Wacquant, 2009). Concerned with the problem of social insecurity and mass imprisonment in the United States, Wacquant (2009, p. 11), as discussed in Chapter 2, has offered an impressive contribution which argues that with the atrophy of the welfare state there has been a corresponding 'hypertrophy of the penal state'. Wacquant integrates his analysis of penality with social and political structures and culture and implicates the prison as an aspect of state-building (Lacey, 2010, p. 780). He (2009, p. 11) argues:

> The resolutely punitive turn taken by penal policies in advanced societies ... does not pertain to the simple diptych of 'crime and

punishment.' It heralds the establishment of a *new government of social insecurity* ... [exemplified by] the turbulence of economic deregulation and the conversion of welfare into a springboard toward precarious employment, an organizational design within which the prison assumes a major role and which translates, for the categories residing in the nether regions of social space, in the imposition of severe and supercilious supervision.

Whilst Wacquant's emphasis on the importance of the prison, its role in the government of social insecurity and the way these developments are inflected by contemporary political economic arrangements is justifiable, the suggestion of the emergence of a penal state is perhaps a misnomer. By contrast, Simon Hallsworth and John Lea (2011) have theorised the emergence of what they have called a security state, which seems to better orient and broaden our gaze towards social and political developments, allowing both greater sensitivity to the specific dynamics of particular states and the capacity to take account of the manifestation of wider global pressures within them. They argue that the security state 'heralds a new type of authoritarianism which, beginning at the periphery and pre-occupied with the management of the marginalised and socially excluded, is gradually infecting the core social institutions, the criminal justice system in particular' (ibid., p. 141). They argue that this new state project has emerged gradually. Furthermore, its meanings and manifestations did not arrive ready formed nor does its emergence suggest the disappearance of other state projects (such as welfare or welfarism). Its characteristics and features have, instead, incrementally appeared in a variety of social policy areas, social institutions and state practices.

Hallsworth and Lea (ibid.) make the point that the ascendancy of crime control on political agendas has, in part, increased the prominence of security and vice versa. Criminalisation has begun to be relied upon more frequently by social policy makers as a means of social control and as an alternative to welfare-based approaches. As a result, coercive interventions now underpin policy areas that were previously constructed in terms of rights and entitlements. They (ibid., p. 144) argue that 'the emerging security state reconstructs marginality and its symptoms as risks and dangers that need to be coercively managed' by drawing on new technologies of power and risk management. But the most important characteristic of the security state, according to Hallsworth and Lea (ibid., p. 150), is the interplay between warfare and criminal justice.

The problem of terrorism and the events of 9/11 provided the context for a blurring of boundaries between criminalisation and warfare. Terrorism is simultaneously external and internal. Constructing this problem as a hybrid between an act of war and a criminal act extends the measures that can, firstly, be applied to specific acts of terrorism or individuals suspected or accused of it. Secondly, it allows the application of exceptional measures in criminal justice and other social policy areas that may play a role in the pursuit of security. That is, the overarching concern of security, the link between the pursuit of security and crime control, and the interplay between crime control and warfare all have the potential to justify exceptional measures in the areas that security has infiltrated. Hallsworth and Lea (ibid., p. 151) argue, for example, that: '... punitive welfare reforms, rather than appearing as a frontal assault on welfare citizenship, and the virtual criminalisation of weak poor individuals, appear as sensible innovations dealing with a marginalised, risky population against whom "citizens" need security and protection.' The social divisions that security-thinking has the capacity to delineate can be drawn on any scale or border (nation states, neighbourhoods, certain groups, such as prisoners, activists, asylum seekers, immigrants from particular countries). Furthermore, the slow infiltration of the issue of security into so many areas of social and political life and its taken-for-granted importance are manifest in a set of attitudes that 'welcomes and accepts the actions of the State as a necessary exchange between liberty and security' (ibid., p. 152), despite the fact that it is unknown whether any real increase in security will result. Moreover, Hallsworth and Lea (ibid., pp. 152–3) argue that '[i]n this process, policies that would have been wholly unthinkable within the welfare state have become acceptable and celebrated'. The infiltration of the concept of security into private, social and political life has made its justification nearly a foregone conclusion.

Taken-for-granted assumptions about the importance of the pursuit of security and the most effective strategies for engaging in this pursuit seem to be gathering hegemonic status at the level of the nation state and in international relations contexts. The proliferation of ideologies of security has been facilitated by the war on terror and its amorphous and apparently global reach. Young-Bruehl (2006, p. 62) has argued that this 'war' and the fact that NATO for the first time invoked its 'one, all' doctrine created an arena wherein coordinated action would need to be agreed amongst different and potentially adversarial states. This action provided a platform where collective, global concerns about security could influence the shape and scope of security strategies both within individual nation states and in collectively agreed and coordinated global security measures. Whilst the developments related to a global strategy for security are still unfolding and will, inevitably, continuously change and evolve, the seeming propensity for particular security ideologies to gain hegemonic status may have troubling implications for individual nation states, as well as social and personal lives the world over.

Zedner (2003, 2005, 2009) has written extensively on the concept of security and its pursuit both within areas of crime control and as part of wider governing strategies of nation states. She points out the ambiguity of the meaning of security and its resistance to simple definition. Zedner argues that this 'imprecision not only means that many divergent measures can be justified in the name of security, it also gives license to exceptional measures that might otherwise appear indefensible' (Zedner 2003, p. 158). She further states that even in relatively stable social conditions, the risks of negative consequences can swing decisions towards precautionary measures, despite uncertainty about precisely what negative consequences might transpire (2005, p. 528). Zedner persuasively argues the dangers associated with pursuing security, stating: 'The deployment of security as a pursuit is potentially hazardous ... because it presumes an endless quest, which must continually anticipate and forestall the next challenge by pre-emptive measures. Security becomes a moving target' (ibid., p. 528). Further, in a national context the quest for security can be used to invoke repressive measures that may actually be serving other state purposes. Zedner (ibid., p. 531) states that 'one of the ironies of pursuing security is that whilst claiming to protect liberty from one source – terrorism – it diminishes the protections from another – the state'. Whilst these issues are troubling enough within the confines of the nation state, the spread of security concerns across international and global contexts may result in the widespread adoption of highly prescriptive ideologies of security that are imbued with other symbolic functions and hidden purposes. In this context the prison stands to play a crucial role within the reinforcement and propagation of security ideologies, serving to obscure and justify the potential dangers of a global conceptualisation of the problem of security and its solutions.

The place of the prison within security agendas and global economic relations

The hegemonic power of the ideology of security has made the prison (as well as an 'assemblage' of other punitive measures (De Giorgi, 2007)) a commonly used tool in the pursuit of security. Indeed, the power of the ideology of security is reinforced and strengthened by the ideological and symbolic functions of the prison. The symbiotic relationship between prison and security ideologies is fostered both by global and nation state security agendas and globalised capitalist markets and networks. A re-examination of the ideological purposes of the prison set out by Mathiesen (2000) and outlined in Chapter 1 in light of the increased prominence of security in national and global affairs makes clear the particular role the prison can play in the building of a security state.

Firstly, the expurgatory role of the prison, where the prison serves to house a proportion of the unproductive, surplus population that is produced in (particularly, but not only) capitalist market economies, becomes even more important within the context of insecure labour market conditions which have the capacity to produce vast swathes of dispossessed populations. The prison becomes a repository for the 'immigrant, invisible, insecure and disposable labour-forces whose hyper-exploitation takes place *across* the thin border separating "subordinate inclusion" from downright poverty' (De Giorgi, 2007, p. 18, citing Gorz, 1999).

Secondly, and related to its expurgatory role, the power-draining function of the prison – where prisoners remain non-contributing members to the system that contains them – ensures that surplus populations have no power base from which to register their protest against the social and economic conditions that led to their dispossession. Further, the way security is enacted and deployed within the prison guarantees that, as prisoners, the dispossessed can marshal little power with which to protest the terms and conditions of their confinement. As enemy combatants prisoners can be seen as undeserving of citizenship rights and protections. These rights can be legally curtailed or even illegally withdrawn, but in ideologically justifiable ways. Public support for such tactics against prisoners can be gathered by concurrently constructing prisoners as dangerous others. In particular, prisoners who have been convicted of crimes that attract significant public condemnation (sexual offences) or evoke high levels of fear or anger (murder, terrorism) and calls for vengeance may be constructed in the media or in the public consciousness as particularly undeserving of rights and protections. Importantly, when such thinking becomes acceptable with respect to certain prisoners it becomes easier to apply the same sorts of ideas to a more general prisoner population.

Thirdly, the diverting function of the prison continues to focus attention towards state-defined crimes, obscuring the danger and harm posed and caused by powerful groups. However, within a highly security-focused social and political climate, the capacity for obfuscation of the harms of the powerful becomes heightened. State-defined crimes and prisoners convicted of all types of crime (be those crimes seriously physically harmful or not) can begin to be defined as security risks, either with respect to individual safety and security or in reference to national security. The ambiguities associated with the definition of security make this blurring between potential 'security' threats possible, at least in part. Furthermore, attention can become acutely and disproportionately focused on prisoners convicted of terrorist activities, which also helps to facilitate the spread of security within prisons as prison administrators become concerned with the threat of radicalisation within prisons (Liebling et al., 2011). Harms of the powerful remain unconsidered within this context. Moreover, the harms associated with the pursuit of security itself remain unconsidered and can be justified through the diverting function of the prison. Constructing prisoners as security risks serves to justify the use of increasingly repressive measures within the penal realm. Engaging in such practices within the realm of the prison then creates precedence for their use, potentially making them possible and thinkable outside of the prison. Trade-offs between liberty, human or civil rights and security are justified and deemed as necessary. The harms associated with such trade-offs, as well as the question of whether such trade-offs actually result in more secure conditions, remain unconsidered.

Finally, the symbolic function of the prison to stigmatise those it holds, setting them apart from us, is reinforced by and, in turn, reinforces these same principles of othering in ideologies of security. Security ideologies rely on segregation and exclusion in fortification processes. Marginalised, risky populations are identified and earmarked as potentially threatening in contrast to citizens who need to be protected from such groups. Prisons have long been instrumental in the project of identifying the deserving and undeserving, the less eligible from the eligible. Here security agendas can be instrumental in serving the interests of global market capitalism by assisting in 'configuring a paradigm of *global less eligibility*', which extends the relationship between punishment and social structure 'well beyond national borders' (De Giorgi, 2007, p. 18).

Totalitarian elements and means can be observed within the above ideological purposes of the prison and their synergy with ideologies of security (Arendt, 1968). Whilst it is unthinkable in our contemporary globalised world to suggest that the deployment of totalitarian elements could crystallise into the formation of a fully totalitarian state, it should be recognised that previous totalitarian regimes had a 'built-in limit' – the regimes were not global (Young-Bruehl, 2006, p. 58). Human social history reminds us that it is always necessary to remain vigilant and resistant to the emergence of ideologies that are capable of justifying repressive regimes and policies, that can alter the way reality is constructed, that employ methods of dehumanisation and othering that are justified on ideological grounds and that can make the unthinkable thinkable. This vigilance is especially urgent when such ideologies seem to be gaining hegemonic status beyond the confines of the nation state. It might be suggested that the symbiotic relationship between the ideology of the prison and ideologies of security may be well placed to build the hegemonic capacity of the security state. This relationship may be poised to play a key role, as described above, in serving the interests of global market capitalism or simply legitimating and perpetuating prevailing distributions of wealth and power.

Pursuing a subjective sense of security as a more viable security agenda

The taken-for-granted nature of the prison and its symbolic purchase in social and political life uniquely situates it to play a key role within nation state security agendas. Furthermore, the symbiotic relationship between the ideology of the prison and ideologies of security has the capacity to promote the hegemony of the practices of imprisonment and punishment as essential features of both national and global security. These are troubling prospects, given the persistent failure of the prison to fulfil its purported purposes. Furthermore, the proliferation of penal severity in many countries suggests that this persistent failure is of little relevance. The growing importance of the symbolic functions of the prison in security agendas, its role in justifying particular security measures and in obscuring the potential social harms associated with, for example, the possibilities of global market capitalism make the prison an invaluable political tool. This means, however, that the paradoxes of the prison (that is, that it does not solve the problem of state-defined crime, that it prevents us from engaging more carefully with how to respond when one human being harms another and that it does not actually improve either objective conditions of security or subjective feelings of security and safety) remain unchallenged and underexplored.

As already discussed, a permanent state of security can never be fully secured. Although there is much to consider in terms of determining how objective security may be sensibly and carefully pursued, nation states must be diligent in ensuring that social conditions are not worsened and compromised in the process. Furthermore, given the elusive and unpredictable nature of securing a permanent state of security, it may be that government attentions would be more productively focused on a security agenda concerned with a subjective sense of security (i.e., promoting feelings of security amongst the populace) and less concerned with pursing an endless and inevitably fruitless quest for objective security. Identifying the social and political conditions which promote a subjective sense of security may be a much more achievable goal that may result, more often, in higher levels of perceived political legitimacy as well as lower levels of fear amongst the general public. It is to these ideas that this chapter now turns.

Penal severity and the globalising myth of security

Recent empirical research on how penal severity relates to differences in a number of social, economic and political factors suggests some important implications for the way a sense of security might be better conceived, achieved and constituted. This research, undertaken by Tapio Lappi-Seppälä, Director General of the National Research of Legal Policy in Finland, provides strong empirical support for the linkages between particular political economic regimes, political and social cultures, repressive penal measures, levels of social trust, and political legitimacy. Lappi-Seppälä's research is detailed and extensive. It draws on data from across Europe, the US, Canada, Australia and New Zealand. Due to the importance of his findings and their centrality to issues of concern in this book, a thorough summary of his findings is required. As will be revealed, this research is instrumental in demythologising some of the taken-for-granted assumptions encompassed within particular political economic ideologies and within the logic of punitive criminal justice policies.

Using cross-sectional and trend analysis of a variety of international surveys,[2] Lappi-Seppälä (2007, 2008) has examined a number of factors related to crime – social, economic and political factors – and survey data on sentiments, fears and public beliefs. His findings hold crucial relevance both for understanding the social policies, practices and cultural characteristics that influence penal severity or parsimony and for identifying relationships between particular social, political and economic variables. Hence this research is particularly useful in identifying the factors that, in different combinations, can detract from or promote a subjective sense of security.

Lappi-Seppälä (ibid.) undertakes a number of analyses that examine international trends in imprisonment rates and the problems with imprisonment rates as policy indicators. These analyses include examining: the relative numbers of foreign prisoners and prisoners who are awaiting trial and detained on remand; prison admissions and durations of sentences; imprisonment rates relative to recorded crime and victimisation; criminal convictions and unsuspended prison sentences relative to prison population and crime; and the relationship between imprisonment rates and capital punishment. His findings that relate to the relationship between imprisonment and the use of capital punishment provide an excellent alternative measure of punitiveness, revealing (2008, p. 332) that:

> In the global sample of 99 countries, countries that abolished the death penalty have lower rates (150 per 100,000) [of imprisonment] and countries retaining the death penalty have higher rates (252 per 100,000). Between these two groups are countries that abolished the death penalty for ordinary crimes (180 per 100,000) and that retained the death penalty in the criminal codes but have not enforced it during the last 10 years ... Factors associated with the use of imprisonment are associated with the use of the death penalty (with weaker correlations) ... It should be no surprise that the same structural, political, and social factors that explain the use of imprisonment also explain the use of the death penalty.

This finding suggests that ideologies of punitiveness might work on a continuum of severity. The use of the most severe criminal sanction (i.e., death) does not serve as an alternative to imprisonment; indeed, its availability – on the whole – correlates with even higher imprisonment rates. Further, other research has consistently shown that the threat of this sanction does not result in a reliable deterrent effect. Figures from the United States, which compare states that retain the death penalty with those that do not, reveal consistently higher murder rates in those states that retain the death penalty (Amnesty International, 2008). Taken together these findings provide some useful data that firmly challenge taken-for-granted and common sense assumptions that often proliferate in public discourse whenever debates about the social benefits of the harshest of all punishments (the death penalty) arise.

Lappi-Seppälä's research also examined associations between crime and imprisonment rates cross-sectionally and over time. This work provides some quite definitive evidence that uses of imprisonment bear little relationship to levels and trends in criminality. His analyses (2008, p. 340) revealed that:

> It is possible to reduce the number of prisoners during times when crime rates are increasing (Finland 1980–90 and Austria 1985–90). It is also possible to increase the imprisonment rates during times when crime rates are stable (Netherlands 1985–2000) and to maintain both of them as stable (Denmark 1985–95, France 1985–2005). And it has been possible to increase imprisonment rates when crime rates were falling (England during most of the 1990s, New Zealand 1995–2005, and the United States 1990–2005).

The above findings establish that trends in penal severity relate more to political decision-making and ideologies of imprisonment than to any of the assumed, common sense or taken-for-granted assumptions about the role of the prison as a crime control tool. However, according to Lappi-Seppälä's analyses, a number of social, political and economic variables are also associated with penal trends.

As discussed briefly in Chapter 2, trends in penal severity, it seems, are closely associated with public sentiments, welfare provision, income inequality, political structures and legal cultures. Furthermore, a number of ancillary factors also play a role in shaping the way social and penal policies unfold in different countries and at different times, suggesting that effects are context related and cultural contingence must be considered in policy implementation. The ancillary factors identified in his research include: differences in media culture and in the responsiveness of the political system to the media; judicial structures and legal cultures; and demographic homogeneity and its capacity to facilitate liberal policies (though this does not suggest that multiculturalism necessarily leads to harsher regimes, indeed there is evidence to suggest the opposite when there are high levels of diversity).

For the purposes of thinking about the factors that might assist in promoting a greater sense of subjective security, it is useful to consider the interrelationships between the social, political and economic factors identified in Lappi-Seppälä's research. Firstly, an examination of the data on unemployment, levels of gross domestic product, income inequality, social expenditure and population demographics revealed that there is a connection between a country's welfare orientation and its penal culture – with different welfare regimes operating different penal policies. Levels of social spending correlated with imprisonment rates in countries that had decreased social spending. The steepest increases in imprisonment rates were found in countries with the lowest levels of social spending (ibid., p. 356). Secondly, Lappi-Seppälä conducted further analyses that added data measuring public sensibilities, including levels of fear, trust and perceptions of political legitimacy. The outcome of these further empirical examinations showed a strong inverse relationship between levels of repression, legitimacy and social trust. Furthermore, higher levels of trust were associated with higher levels of welfare provision and trust was intercorrelated with particular public sentiments. For example, public fears were associated with punitive demands (the higher the fear, the greater the levels of punitivity) and these varied inversely with trust (punitiveness increased when trust decreased and low public fears and high levels of social trust resulted in lower levels of penal severity). Interestingly, the findings revealed that trust, public fear and welfare provision were also intercorrelated with strong welfare states (e.g., those with high levels of social spending), revealing higher levels of trust and lower levels of public fear in countries with higher levels of welfare provision. Furthermore, Lappi-Seppälä (ibid., p. 375) suggests that 'behind less repressive social policies are feelings of solidarity and a broad, less individualistic understanding of the origins of social risks'. It seems social tolerance can be 'afforded' when socio-economic conditions are more secure, because solidarity is higher. Less eligibility loses relevance when material standards are relatively high across social groups. He (ibid., p. 378) argues:

> In general, needs-based social policy concerns 'other people,' those who are marginalised and culpable for their own position. Those in need are different. This feeds suspicion and distrust. Universalistic social policy that assigns benefits to everyone, grants social equality, and makes no distinctions between people, has a different moral logic.

In essence, growing social divisions and policies that promote exclusion and individualisation seem to raise public suspicions, fears and feelings of otherness. Therefore pursing a sense of security may be best achieved by implementing more inclusive, universalistic and less individualised social policies. Such policies, in turn, may have a variety of other social and political benefits, including reductions in poverty, a smaller gap between the rich and the poor and greater political legitimacy.

Conclusion: rethinking security?

The concept of security is difficult to constitute, pursue and to question. It holds a great deal of meaning in a variety of different areas of social and political life. In its most frequently used current form it is employed to both establish and reinforce a status quo that takes for granted the need for security measures, security protections, and security-thinking. Increasingly, this application of the concept is becoming more widely used in both national and global contexts. This is a worrying trend. As discussed and evidenced here, the way security is constituted, legitimised and pursued serves to reinforce its own ideologies, making them seemingly unquestionable. Indeed, part of the power of security is to make the questionable unquestionable and the unquestionable possible. It operates with stealth and invisibility using seemingly undetectable coercive means. It has great capacity to silently silence (Mathiesen, 2004). It is a firm basis for power, authority and right-ness. But its power, once evoked, can be applied to other purposes, as examinations of the relationship between prisons and security so clearly demonstrate. Exposing the many dangers that can result from the vigorous pursuit of security, calls into question the legitimacy of this pursuit. Further, Lappi-Seppälä's (2007, 2008) research provides strong empirical support for thinking about security differently. Although his work cannot shed light on better ways of fortifying borders, anticipating enemy combatants or more precise means by which to predict where the next global threat might come from, it does provide a great deal of insight about how to pursue another form of security – a form of security that garners trust, reduces public fears and suspicions, improves social well-being and increases political legitimacy. These are not empty goals for any nation state. Taken together his vast array of findings takes us some considerable way in identifying the social, cultural and political conditions that seem to promote a subjective sense of security rather than undermining it. These findings are invaluable in helping to demythologise some of the taken-for-granted assumptions encompassed within particular political economic ideologies and within the logic of punitive criminal justice or social policies.

7
The Duplicity of Criminal Justice, Violent Crime and the Problem with Punishment

Introduction

Much of this book has thus far been concerned with demythologising the assumed purposes of the prison by highlighting its symbolic functions both as a place of punishment and as a mechanism through which dominant ideologies and existing political and economic structures are reinforced. It has also focused on revealing the role the prison is poised to play in socially and economically precarious, yet simultaneously more security-focused global conditions. This chapter moves on to consider, in more detail, the reasons why the failure of prisons and criminal justice systems remain obscured from public view and why it is that they are not the most effective means for responding to problems of harm and violence. To do so, it reflects on and grapples with a number of moral, philosophical and practical problems.

The chapter begins by examining some of the contradictions on which the criminal law and criminal justice are based. It is argued that their opposing logics and foundations in unequal power relations obfuscate their continued failings to effectively respond to complex social problems. The chapter goes on to reflect on the other issues that both obscure and are obscured by the imbalances and contradictions of criminal justice. Of particular relevance is the persistence of common-sense thinking about problems of crime that perpetuate ideas of good and evil and feed public desires for vengeance. The chapter argues that democracies that adopt law-and-order rhetorics on crime as well as a populist approach to criminal justice policymaking actively play on these common-sense assumptions about crime, offering simple solutions to complex problems. In this context, criminals are easy targets for political posturing and victims' rights can similarly be used to justify more repressive state strategies. It is argued that such tactics can serve to erode human rights protections that have been put in place to limit the use of state authority.

The contradictions and convolutions of criminal justice processes, and the political purposes they serve, distract public attention away from the evidence of their failings and prevent wider considerations of alternative ways to respond to social and personal harms. The problem with punishment is presented towards the later part of this chapter. Drawing on the work of James Gilligan (2000) it is argued here that, in contrast to popular belief about the appropriateness of the use of punishment and its capacity to solve the problem of crime, our vast experience with its continued use reveals that it tends to produce the opposite effect than that which it is expected to achieve. That is, the continued use of punishment increases the likelihood of further continued violence. The chapter concludes by suggesting that the moral underpinnings of criminal justice processes obscure the ways in which the criminal justice system fails. It argues that the symbolic justice that criminal justice processes provide through the use of harsh penalties serve to undermine our actual levels of safety and security and only add to the levels of harm human beings perpetrate against one another.

Duplicity and contradiction in law and criminal justice

As with the prison, the law and criminal justice systems serve other purposes that have little to do with administering justice and much to do with reinforcing dominant ideologies and protecting the interests of powerful groups (Box, 1983; Pashukanis, 1989). In 1898, Peter Kropotkin published *Law and Authority*. In this work he launched a scathing critique of the criminal law and those who held the power to create it. He argued that processes of criminalisation were heavily biased in favour of lawmakers and property owners. For him, the law served three purposes – 'protection of property, protection of persons, protection of government' (p. 18) – and he famously concluded that such underpinning rationales highlighted the 'uselessness and hurtfulness of law' (ibid.). Although the protection of persons may be seen, by many, as the taken-for-granted central purpose of the law, in practice it serves to protect only some people and only from certain kinds of harm. Hudson (2006) has taken this recognition of the inherent biases in law and criminal justice further through her considerations of 'white man's justice'. She argues that both the law and criminal justice in modern Western societies are founded on and continually invoke the subjectivities of white, affluent men and that, therefore, their reasoning and logics are grounded in the perspective of the dominant male (ibid., p. 31).

Criminal justice practices in many countries focus disproportionately on certain types of harms, on particular categories of criminals and only recognise certain kinds of victims. The law and systems of criminal justice focus almost exclusively on individualised targets. They rarely focus on crimes of the powerful, such as environmental damage, occupational health and safety violations, corporate manslaughter or other forms of corporate crime, state crimes or war crimes – all of which cause harm on a much greater scale than, for example, street crime (Tombs and Whyte, 2003a, 2003b). At the same time other social injustices and harmful activities also remain unrecognised by the criminal law, as Hudson (2006, p. 30) suggests: 'Critics of law in general and criminal justice in particular point out that law treats women in the same way that dominant society treats them: law cannot be expected to remedy injustices legally before they are recognised as injustices socially.' Further, as Kropotkin noted, the law serves to protect the interests of the powerful and of government. Therefore, it is inextricably bound up with a number of political, economic and moral pursuits. However, this role of the law in reinforcing dominant ideologies and protecting the interests of more powerful and dominant groups in society is obscured by its formidable image as an institution of justice that is constructed in rhetoric as representing the interests of everyone in society equally (Reiman and Leighton, 2010). Moreover, this image likewise obscures and is contradicted by the moralistic underpinnings of the modern legal system.

The institution of law, and in particular the criminal law, is underpinned by two seemingly contradictory and duplicitous logics. On one hand it includes a rhetoric that firmly embraces rationality. In this view it presents an image of justice that is dispassionate and concerned with balance, equality and fairness. On the other hand it pronounces a particular kind of moral truth about what is right and what must be done to atone for harms that have been caused. The former logic presents the criminal law as a non-partisan institution. However, the latter logic sees the administration of criminal justice as an expression of societal censure. Far from being non-partisan, the criminal law serves dominant moral purposes as well as ideological ones. The condemnatory function of criminal justice is imbued with emotional undertones that are based on firmly held beliefs about what societies 'must do' to maintain social order or what sorts of actions will symbolically atone for (certain types of) social or personal harm. These two faces of the criminal law and justice process work together to obscure the inherent problems, biases and resultant failings of the particular means by which justice is sought and administered. Each of them will be considered, briefly, in turn.

The rhetoric of rationality in law and criminal justice

Through a formidable and persistent rhetoric, the law is elevated as a venerated institution, built on principles of rationality, equality and fairness. This rhetoric promotes beliefs that all are equal in the eyes of the law or that the law affords society an impartial means by which to deliver a fair and proportionate system of justice. This rhetoric centralises the neutrality of the law as a non-partisan institution, founded on cool rationality that is not swayed by emotion, moral indignation or political will. Indeed, the legal philosophical heritage of modern criminal justice rests in the capacity of the law to intervene with dispassionate clarity in the emotional aftermath that follows when one human being has harmed another. Its apparatus is designed to take the conflict out of the hands of both victim and perpetrator in order to get to the bottom of what has transpired and judge what is to be done about it for the good of all parties concerned and for society as a whole. In legal philosophy it has been argued that the role the state takes on in these matters was developed to suppress a natural, irrational desire for vengeance, which was seen as capricious and without internal limits (Vlastos, 1991). Austin Sarat (1997) has argued that criminal justice processes are founded on reason and due process and thus were designed to keep public passions at bay in the interests of administering a proportionate system of justice. However, there is an inherent contradiction in this. Sarat quotes Terry Aladjem (1990, p. 9) who writes:

> This inclination to make revenge over into a rational principle of justice has roots in democratic theory and in certain suppositions of natural law. It arose in claims about the founding of the state, where it was said that a process of consent converts the laws of nature into those of civil society and that the state acquires its right to punish from consenting individuals who thereby relinquish a natural right to avenge themselves. From the beginning, however, that reasoning presents a paradox: the state is supposed to arise from the inclinations of individuals as they might be found in nature, but it must rescue them from the very same inclinations.

That is, the state is brought into action by emotional outcry and indignation, but is relied upon not to act upon this emotion but to keep it in check and to proceed with rationality, arbitrating a proportionate and civilised system of justice (Hegel, 1942; Kant, 1965; Pelczynski, 1971; Vlastos, 1991; Zaibert, 2006). The state is also relied upon to act on behalf of social and personal interests and, in this way, may be seen as a means by which societies can collectively condemn certain actions, atone for injuries caused and express collective moral outrage in the face of actions perceived as abhorrent or unacceptable. Criminal justice, therefore, is, in part, concerned with fulfilling a moral task that is based on dominant beliefs. It is not solely concerned with impartiality and rational thinking.

The morality of criminal justice and punishment

Émile Durkheim (1997) emphasised the role of the law in serving two moral functions concerned with the building and maintenance of collective social solidarity: restitution (ensuring there is compensation for the damage that has been done) and punishment (the infliction of pain). That is, in order for social equilibrium to be maintained there needed to be some form of atonement for harms that were caused. The means by which this atonement was to be achieved was through the role of the law and criminal justice processes. As prosecutor on behalf of the public, the law and its administration of punishment (in particular) are imbued with religious and moralistic values. As Durkheim (ibid., p. 52) suggested, punishment is 'an impassioned reaction, varying in intensity, that society enforces through the intermediary of an organised body upon whoever violates certain rules of conduct'. The inherently moral element that is implicated in this practice of retributive punishment is often overlooked, as is the emotionality associated with its practice. Indeed, as Nietzsche (1969) identified, and recent philosophical debates attest to (Zaibert, 2006), there has been something of a spurious division drawn between revenge and punishment and an erroneous tendency to strip the emotional dimension from retributive punishment and criminal justice administration. There remains a tendency to overemphasise the dispassionate rationality of the law, which prevents us from thinking about its moralistic undertones. But, in practice, the decision to punish and to administer such punishment is imbued with emotionality and, it can be argued, is a state-sanctioned manifestation of revenge.

Leo Zaibert (2006) provides a compelling philosophical argument for the similarity between punishment and revenge. He systematically examines Robert Nozick's (1981) famous contrasts between retributive punishment and revenge and convincingly illustrates their similarity.

His argument is too lengthy and detailed to reproduce in its entirety here, but what is important for my purposes is to highlight some of the points he makes with respect to Nozick's discussions on the emotional element of revenge versus that of punishment. Nozick (1981, pp. 366–8) argues:

> Revenge involves a particular emotional tone, pleasure at the suffering of another, while retribution either need involve no emotional tone or involves another one, namely pleasure at justice being done.

Zaibert points out that there is a rarity of situations where a punisher would feel no emotion at all in response to the wrongdoing for which s/he is delivering the punishment. He (2006, p. 110; see also 2005) states: 'punishment is part of a continuum which also includes blame, and since blame, by definition, contains an emotional component, then ... this contrast would never hold ... it is never the case that the punisher feels *nothing* at all.' Those who work to administer criminal justice processes are, after all, human beings with emotional lives and the occurrence of serious interpersonal harms inevitably stirs emotional responses. Moreover, the symbolic function of punishment is, in part, atonement. It is enacted, in part, to avenge the harm that has been caused. These emotional and moral dimensions that underpin the foundations of criminal justice practice are heavily obscured by the rhetoric of rationality.

Despite the persistent notion that the criminal law is firmly grounded in rational thought, it remains responsible for establishing and protecting particular moral beliefs that inevitably include emotive inflections. Criminal justice fundamentally seeks to judge and to condemn certain types of behaviour and due to its unequal foundations in wider power relations it tends to focus more heavily on the activities of certain segments of the population. Further, it bases these judgements on dominant beliefs that also dictate what should or ought to be done in response to certain harmful events. Durkheim (1997) argued that religion, punishment and morality played key roles in forming the embedded structures of society. Despite growing secularisation, and increasing plurality in many societies around the world, the moralistic foundations of criminal justice remain intact. Furthermore, many traditional or common-sense beliefs about good and evil and about the importance of retribution and punishment in affirming social solidarity and retaining social order remain firmly held to and are evident in popular, political and media discourses and in contemporary criminal justice policy and administration. The persistence and proliferation of these common-sense beliefs also work to obscure the problems associated with the way criminal justice is administered and serve to prevent alternative considerations of the problems of social and personal harm.

The next section of this chapter discusses some of the emotional dimensions that accompany the occurrence of serious interpersonal harms. These emotional dimensions, it might be argued, form the basis of some of the common-sense beliefs that fuel calls for harsh approaches to justice and ensure prisons and criminal justice processes remain firmly entrenched features of social and political life.

Violent crime, the question of evil and the call for vengeance

Acts of violence and interpersonal harm, such as murder, rape or serious assault capture public attention and stir collective emotions. Moreover, those who are the direct or vicarious victims of acts of violence at the hands of another human being attract widespread sympathy and heartfelt public support whilst those who perpetrate such acts draw out public indignation. When such events happen they are, of course, painful. They provoke anger and frustration. They also result in a collective sense of loss and outrage. Such emotions are provoked both because of being forced to hear of the circumstances under which a human being has been harmed or taken from the world and because of having to face the knowledge of the depths to which human depravity can reach. We are forced, in these moments, to face the capacity for harm that is within the nature of human beings and it is hard to comprehend.

Across many societies and throughout human history there has been a tendency to hold firmly to binary notions of good and evil, especially when serious harms are perpetrated by one social member against another. When such events occur they tend to ignite a range of emotions, public passions and moral sentiments because they threaten our sense of security and belief in humanity. They provoke such questions as: 'How can a human being do such a thing?' Indeed, some acts that people perpetrate against one another seem unthinkable. As a result, a common-sense assumption that is often made is that some people are inherently evil. It is a convenient thought and it makes the terrible act that has been perpetrated easier to understand. Greer and Jewkes (2005) have argued that establishing the otherness of those who commit serious or unusual offences allows us all to maintain distance from them. It allows us to expel them from 'the social, moral, and cultural universe of ordinary, decent people' (ibid., p. 21). Greer and Jewkes suggest that this process is facilitated in contemporary society by a collusive relationship between the public and the media, where public punitiveness is fed by unrestrained media constructions of demonised, criminal others whose crimes are described as unthinkable and unknowable. We simply stop asking the question about how a human being can do such a thing and decide, instead, that it is unknowable because some people are inherently evil. Further, Greer and Jewkes (ibid., p. 29) argue that there may also be a collective unwillingness to think and to know (see also Jewkes, 2004). We want to avoid thinking about the fact that it is within the capacity of human nature to commit acts of serious violence and, because we do not want to face this, we attempt to distance ourselves from those who have done such things. As they (2005, p. 29) note:

> Through a process of alienation and demonization, we establish the 'otherness' of those who deviate and (re)assert our own innocence and normality ... Yet the repulsion we express (not least through the medium of mass communications) frequently denies the fact that those who commit crimes are not 'others.' They are 'us,' and are of our making.

The concept of evil allows us to avoid facing up to the fact that there is no difference between 'us' and 'them'. Given the right circumstances anyone is quite capable of committing a terrible act of violence and those who have are not inherently abhorrent or innately wicked. These are unpalatable truths, however, which many of us avoid or refuse to accept and, as a result, remain convinced that some people are essentially evil. The decision to see those who commit serious acts of harm as evil also prevents us from thinking about the way we treat them in our criminal justice processes.

The question of evil

It should be remembered that the population on which this book has based its discussions in earlier chapters include men who have committed serious acts of violence against other people. This is the grave reality about many, though not all, long-term prisoners. It might be argued that the other functions that prisons may serve are made somewhat irrelevant when confronted with the problem of violent crime. Some of the men housed in maximum-security prisons, for example, have committed serious acts of violence against men, women or children and a small number of them have done so repeatedly. So even if one is convinced by arguments that point out that the criminal justice system focuses its gaze disproportionately on those who commit interpersonal and property crimes and ignores white-collar crimes, or that prisons are largely repositories for the poor or surplus populations, or that imprisonment rates are more the result of a range of political, economic and cultural factors than crime rates, the fact remains that sometimes they serve a key role in society: they keep in custody those who have caused serious harm to other people.

As alluded to briefly in Chapter 1, the question of evil or 'monstrosity' arose whilst undertaking the research on which this book draws. Official prison discourses have long constructed men in these prisons as the 'most difficult and dangerous in the country' (HMCIP, 2002, p. 9). The security training that I had to complete prior to beginning field work in each of these prisons made it very clear that during my research in these prisons I would need to 'maintain constant vigilance'. The training warned that:

> These sorts of prisoners are masters of manipulation who cannot be trusted. They are not only dangerous, but cunning. They will take whatever information you give them and use it to their advantage, so you must be on your guard when speaking to them. Remember these are depraved individuals who have committed terrible acts of violence against other people and they have no compunction about doing so again. (excerpt from field notes)

Despite having spent a considerable amount of time during the research with men who are described as some of the most difficult and dangerous in the country, who have, indeed, committed some extremely serious acts of violence against other human beings and who may even still, despite their imprisonment, remain unsafe for cohabitation in free society, I have yet to meet a monster. Instead, I met people who, due to a confluence of factors, had developed ways of interacting with other people that increased the likelihood of violent confrontations. I met some people who had a variety of complex mental health needs. I met other people who had difficulty understanding where their own needs ended and another person's needs began. There were also a number of individuals who had just made unthinking, yet deadly, mistakes. But I did not meet anyone who was not essentially human. Indeed, in most every respect these men were essentially *ordinary*.

As I noted earlier, Arendt (1971, p. 180) has argued that: 'The sad truth of the matter is that most evil is done by people who never make up their minds to be or do either evil or good.' This is the banality of evil of which she wrote. Evil acts can be as much accidental, unintended and the result of thoughtlessness (as Arendt argued) as they can be deliberate, intended and planned. But the concept of essential evil remains unproven. Furthermore, it is an unhelpful concept that closes down opportunities for thinking about what to do about living with fellow human beings who sometimes commit serious acts of violence either at an interpersonal level or on a larger scale. By spending an extended period of time with people who had acted violently, it became abundantly clear to me that, firstly, their paths towards violence had not developed in a vacuum and, secondly, human beings are complicated and never one-dimensional. These are not revelations; but, due to the persistence of a belief in the concept of evil, we (despite being social beings) often overlook the mul-tidimensional facets of being human and of the importance of the social condition in accounting for the actions of human beings. Ideas that some people are incorrigibly or essentially bad are extremely unhelpful con-structs that stand in the way of developing a deeper understanding of the complexities of human beings and what conditions lead to problems of harm and violence. Further, such constructs seem to feed more vengeful desires, thereby preventing us from thinking more carefully about what to do in the aftermath of serious interpersonal harm.

Vengeance and criminal justice

There is a seemingly primeval drive to call for vengeance in the face of the suffering and pain that results when people cause serious harm to one another. Such events seem to instigate a deep, emotional desire to right that which has been wronged, to make the perpetra-tor understand – first hand – the nature of the suffering he or she has caused (de Beauvoir, 1946). Simone de Beauvoir argued that the desire for vengeance is the natural desire of others for a perpetrator of harm to experience the pain he or she has caused the victim, to *understand* this pain. We want revenge and the feelings of satisfaction that we are sure it will produce. 'The taking of revenge usually produces an emotional or psychological state in the avenger, a feeling of pleasure, a sense of accomplishment, a high' (French, 2001, p. 69, cited in Zaibert, 2006, p. 108). The private, emotional desire for revenge and the public call for vengeance can be powerful forces that are difficult to suppress (Nietzsche, 1969).

Across societies there are a variety of both legal and moral responses that can be evoked when violent actions take place between social members. Durkheim (1997) discussed the relationship between crime and collective sentiments. He (ibid., p. 40) emphasised 'we should not say that an act offends the common conscience because it is criminal, but that it is criminal because it offends that consciousness'. Indeed, with respect to some of the acts we define as crimes, they are designated as such because they offend the collective conscience (for example, murder, rape, violent or sexual crimes against children). As already discussed, when such events occur we rely on criminal justice systems to respond and to deliver justice. As Zaibert (2006, p. 111) suggests, what we really want is for something to happen 'in the world in order to somehow bring it back to the state in which it was before the person acted'. De Beauvoir (1946) has argued that when human beings are degraded there is a collective sense of injustice that cannot be ignored. This is especially heightened in the face of individual, interpersonal harms. People call for a reaction and for punishment. These strong emotions invoke intervention from the state on behalf of society. But, as discussed above, there are inherent contradictions in what is asked of the state, the founding principles of the law and criminal justice, and how justice is administered in practice. This has continually raises questions about the role of the state and the efficacy of criminal justice.

Populism, politics and punishment: barriers to thinking differently about justice

Whilst some Western European countries approach problems of crime, the practice of imprisonment and the treatment of prisoners by engaging in consultative processes that include public and academic debate, other nation states (both within the Council of Europe and outside it) have taken on what Sonia Snacken (2010) has called a more populist form of democracy (similar to what Bottoms (1995) has called populist punitiveness, discussed in Chapter 4). This approach to political action places much emphasis on the perceived will of the majority at the expense of the interests of unpopular and less powerful minority groups or those who have been labelled as other. It is also often associated with law-and-order approaches to crime and justice and the use of harsh criminal justice measures. In these populist climates, the print media, politicians and the general public produce and reproduce constructions of crime and criminals that are simplistic and one-dimensional. They focus attentions disproportionately on criminals as individuals and explain crime as a function of individual pathology. Such common-sense constructions are instrumental in reinforcing existing fears and dominant beliefs about the problem of crime and about how those who break certain laws *ought* to be treated. They may also reinforce personal beliefs that some people are just evil. It might be argued that such beliefs, amongst many others, float around the social consciousness intermittently, particularly when certain heinous acts of violence occur and are brought to public attention by the media (Maruna et al., 2004). They may be an inevitable feature of human social life that will perennially arise at particular moments of social uncertainty, increasing feelings of insecurity amongst the general public. Therefore it is important to question how governments respond to these fears and to think more carefully about the potential consequences of their responses. In particular, do their responses worsen or allay public anxieties? And are there further harms that may result in particular actions being taken?

Once again, the work of Arendt is relevant here. She (1958, p. 5) signalled the importance of considering the 'human condition from the vantage point of our newest experiences and our most recent fears'. In drawing attention to such a project she was highlighting the importance of both thinking and thoughtlessness. Arendt saw the problem of *thoughtlessness* (defined as not taking the time to reflect on and think about our actions as a society) as a particularly dangerous problem for public and political life. She (1971b, p. 445) writes: 'When everybody is swept away unthinkingly by what everybody else does and believes in, those who think are drawn out of hiding because their refusal to join is conspicuous and thereby becomes a kind of action.' Those who think, according to Arendt, are those who question the taken for granted. The absence of thought was of particular concern to Arendt who associated it with the banality of evil – when people go along with ideas, unquestioningly, without noticing what they are doing. She defined thoughtlessness as 'the heedless, recklessness or hopeless confusion or complacent repetition of "truths" which have become trivial or empty' (ibid., p. 445). She proposed, simply, but significantly, to 'think what we are doing'. Arendt's words are important to bear in mind when contemplating calls from the public for increasing punitiveness in criminal justice matters. Barriers to thinking more carefully about the actions we are demanding states take against our fellow citizens are created when we begin to construct human beings – even those who have committed serious acts of harm – as other. Not thinking more carefully about these actions also prevents us from anticipating or noticing their potential consequences.

When the state constructs citizens as other

Dominant political ideologies that include assumptions and discourses that seek to divide or single out particular types of individuals or segments of the population should be viewed as suspect and considered with caution (Arendt, 1968). Identifying some social members as deserving and others as undeserving or suggesting that there are enemies within or dangerous others can begin to fragment societies and diminish social cohesion. They may also be seen as key tactics employed by states both in times of crisis and when there is a need to build state legitimacy or reassert authority.

The link between moments of state or economic crisis and the tendency to construct as 'other' segments of the population who may be deemed – either erroneously or legitimately – as threatening has been examined by social psychologist Hèléne Joffe (1999) in her work on risk and the other. As an extreme and exceptional example of where these linkages can lead she draws attention to Nazi texts to illustrate the way crisis and the concept of the other can work together. She argues that the economic crisis in Germany, which had contributed to feelings of uncertainty and vulnerability amongst the German people, created the backdrop against which the Nazis demonised Jewish people, blaming them, in part, for the crisis. Nazi texts described Jewish people as 'vermin', 'bacteria', 'pests' and 'international maggots', and also as 'satanic', 'devils' and 'demons' (Bar-Tal, 1990, cited in Joffe, 1999, p. 22). Joffe argues that through such processes of othering, which drew on categories of non-human creatures, dehumanisation of the Jews was accomplished. She (1999, p. 23) states:

> The 'other' is not only represented as a threat in that it embodies that which must be kept at bay symbolically if the society is to feel safe. As a consequence of being a symbolic repository for that which societies, cultures and groups want to expel, 'the other' comes to be seen as a material threat.

The othering to which Joffe refers to here is of a type that was perpetrated on a massive scale and on an entirely innocent population of people. The Jewish people were vilified on the basis of ethnicity alone and had done nothing to warrant being singled out in this way. The process of othering they were subjected to, and the suffering that was subsequently inflicted upon them, was gratuitous. Their position in German society was, therefore, incomparable to the situation of prisoners or people who have committed illegal acts. Those who break the law and are imprisoned may, by social and legal standards, very much warrant being segregated for a period of time – either as punishment or for public safety. *This is an entirely different situation to that of Nazi Germany*. However, the processes by which human beings come to be constructed by state authorities as other – even when they have behaved in ways that are legally prohibited, collectively condemned, viewed as repugnant or are extremely harmful – should not be left unexamined or remain unquestioned, particularly when they become excessive. Indeed, if processes of othering can assist in creating conditions that tolerate the persecution of human beings who are entirely innocent, then they hold even greater power when applied to the guilty.

As mentioned briefly in Chapter 4, Dario Melossi (2000, pp. 149–50) has argued that in societal periods when there is rapid change and fragmentation and consequently the need to re-establish unity, authority and hierarchy, the image of the criminal becomes that of a public enemy. The criminal is constructed and represented (in media, in fiction and even by criminologists) as morally repugnant and fatally threatening to society's moral order. Thus an exclusionary penal mode is activated where society is described as being in a state of crisis. Like Joffe (1999), Melossi (2000, p. 153) identifies a link between the tendency 'to other' and moments of crisis.

> In the exclusionary penal mode … order needs to be re-established and the social fabric mended and brought back to unity after having been lacerated and torn apart. Here it is often the metaphor of the state to appear: leviathan as a purveyor of order and unity or better, of unification … and hierarchy … Because one of the main powers of the state is the power to punish … penality is particularly apt to be used to define powers and boundaries of sovereignty.

The public vilification of criminals and prisoners often does not differentiate between the severity of harms committed by those who contravene the law. There is, instead, often a blurring between criminals and dangerous others with the label of dangerous other being wantonly applied to anyone who commits the narrow range of individualised harms most often prosecuted by the criminal justice system. The word criminal often conjures up images of threatening, dangerous individuals and the worst kinds of interpersonal harms. When the problem of crime arises in public discourses violent and non-violent crime are rarely differentiated. It is of little importance that most prisoners are, in fact, the surplus population that Wacquant (2009), Mathiesen (2000) and others identify. When the words criminals, prisoners, dangerous others and evil monsters begin to coalesce, deviance and dangerousness are defined up, as Garland (2001) has argued. Within this context, anyone designated as a criminal or a prisoner is a potential enemy and a potential source of danger, fear and insecurity. With the increased reliance on the prison, as discussed in Chapter 2, this means that increasing numbers of human beings potentially begin to be viewed as other. As Wacquant suggests (2009), such measures may serve a crucial function in state-building. These tactics are of particular importance within a context of heightened security thinking, which seems to begin from a Hobbesian premise that defines the human condition as a war of all against all (Hallsworth and Lea, 2011).

Thomas Hobbes argued that men are all equal in their capacity for violence. '[T]he weakest has strength enough to kill the strongest, either by secret machination, or by confederacy with others, that are in the same danger with himself' (Hobbes, 2008, p. 84). His view of social life was that people live in 'continual fear and danger of violent death' (ibid., p. 86) and 'have no pleasure, but on the contrary a great deal of grief, in keeping company' (ibid., p. 85). This dystopian view of society and misanthropic view of human beings form the foundation of security ideologies discussed in Chapter 6. It justifies the use of any measure of state violence against those who are constructed as threatening. As Young-Bruehl (2006, p. 94) has argued:

> [A] bleak, misanthropic vision like Hobbes's stands behind every justification (including the ideological totalitarian ones) for perpetual state violence or what Hobbes called state power ... And the idea is that Leviathan will shock and awe not only external enemies in the perpetual war that Hobbes accepted as natural; it will keep its own citizens in a state of awe at its power and violence.

State constructions of prisoners as enemy combatants, evil others or as undeserving of rights or other protections could be viewed as the state taking public demands more seriously. Indeed some authors have argued that greater public influence on penal policies might be seen as more democratic (Brown, 2005; Ryan, 2005, cited in Snacken, 2010, p. 280). Alternatively, however, such political manoeuvres may be viewed as a way of justifying overuses of state power against particular social members designated as other. Such manoeuvres may then paradoxically result in undermining democratic principles or lead to a 'tyranny of the majority', as de Tocqueville (1965, p. 240) argued and as Snacken (2010) has recently considered in light of contemporary penal arrangements in Europe. Likewise, as discussed in relation to the work of Lappi-Seppälä (2008) in Chapter 6, they may also paradoxically result in diminished feelings of trust and fear amongst the general public.

As already discussed, there is not a straightforward relationship between crime rates and imprisonment rates, and prisons serve a whole range of other functions within global and nation state economies that have little to do with one person harming another and much to do with maintaining class hierarchies and masking failing political economic policies. The construction of prisoners, who are only temporarily expelled citizens, as others opens the door to repressive measures being applied in the penal realm, and in so doing, may justify their application against other populations who become constructed as threatening. Furthermore, part of the othering process can include the withdrawal or withholding of fundamental human rights (prisoners' voting rights, for example) or the use of other exceptional measures (for example, circumventing due process rights or rights to privacy). These are areas that have received increasing attention in the UK and Europe, where the European Convention on Human Rights has set out protections for citizens (including prisoners) that some nation states (Britain, for example) have found it difficult to abide by.

A battle of rights: protection from the state and protection from each other

To some extent the populist rhetoric, and the policies that go along with it, play on the public fears and the emotions that erupt when one member of society inflicts serious harm against another. The connections between populism and emotions will be discussed more fully below. But briefly, the public, media-fuelled, indignation within a populist climate that surrounds the problem of violent crime – and the people who commit it – creates a context in which the rights, protections and obligations that citizens have under the criminal law become somehow confused with the rights and protections that citizens have under human rights provision. It should be remembered that these are two separate areas of legal protections working for very different purposes. And we should be careful when contemplating the withdrawal of legal protections from any social members.

Populist criminal justice rhetoric seems to inevitably descend into a zero-sum game where victims' rights can only be won at the expense of the rights of accused persons or prisoners (Williams, 2005; Hall, 2009). The binary positioning of perpetrators or prisoners versus victims is a powerful ideological one. It casts victims and those accused or convicted of criminal conduct as distinct, polarised opposites (Zedner, 2004; Dignan, 2005). Further, by politicising the issue of victims' versus prisoners' rights, and by making it a zero-sum game, a clear delineation is drawn between those who are deserving of legal protections and those who are not. Such delineations encourage the proliferation of discourses which view the criminal or the prisoner as having actively forfeited their rights and are in keeping with discourses that define prisoners as other or delineate an us versus them dichotomy. It might be argued that constructions of deserving versus undeserving or victims versus prisoners run parallel to, and intersect with, the presumed binary trade-off between liberty and security. This trade-off includes an implicit reference to the provision and protection (or withdrawal and suspension of) rights.

Much has been written in the critical criminological literature about the trade-offs between liberty and security associated with, for example, the use of increased levels of surveillance and CCTV in social and public spaces and the implications of such tactics for social control (e.g., Coleman, 2004, 2009). Further, within the specific context of the criminal justice system, security and liberty are often explicitly cast in binary opposition (Zedner, 2005, p. 508). The rights of the few must be withdrawn or curtailed for the security of the many. The powerful state is cast as the protector of the rights and security of good citizens. Within this context it is not only that some people are constructed as undeserving of rights, the argument suggests that by recognising the rights of those who have contravened the law or proven themselves as threatening we will somehow undermine our collective safety and security and the very foundations for social order. Such reasoning is underpinned by a utilitarian logic that suggests prisoners' rights, or those of accused persons, can be overridden in the interests of political stability and national security. Zedner (ibid.) has pointed out, for example, the abandonment of due process rights for those who are cast as enemies of national security. But she warns (ibid., p. 514) that such actions, seemingly motivated by our collective desire for greater levels of security, come with a price:

> If security-gains for most people are being balanced against liberty-losses for a few, then we need to pay attention to the few/most dimension of the balance, not just the liberty/security dimension … We need not have recourse to a Rawlsian veil of ignorance in order to see that in designing security policies we should assume a priori that they might be used against us, as well as against putative terrorists.

Similarly, with prisoners' rights it is helpful to project ourselves into the position of subject rather than aligning ourselves with the majority on this issue.

[I]f rights make sense at all then the invasion of a strong right must be a very serious matter. It means treating a man as less than a man or as less worthy of concern than other men. (ibid., p. 519)

In all the debates surrounding the rights of victims and the rights of prisoners, the most frequently touted, common-sense argument that is raised (particularly in the print media) to counter arguments in favour of rights for prisoners is encapsulated in the questions: Where was the respect for the victim's human rights when this crime was taking place? Do their human rights count for nothing? Such questions misuse the terminology of rights. That is, by being a victim of a violent crime at the hands of another member of society, it is not a human right that is violated. The violation that occurs when one member of society chooses to act violently against another may be a violation of one's humanity, it may be a violation of criminal law, it may be an affront to collective public sensibilities, but it is not a human rights violation. It is not in our capacity as fellow citizens to grant human rights to one another or to withhold them. Human rights legislation and protections are in place *to protect us from the state not from each other*. The decision to disregard prisoners' human rights (e.g., by refusing them the vote) is not made in the interests of creating a fairer criminal justice system that better protects the interests of victims. Such a decision is taken in order to protect state interests and to appeal to popular opinion. Human rights legislation, it should be remembered, was, in part, put in place to protect us all from dictatorial and authoritarian rule. Further, as Sonia Snacken (2010, p. 281) has argued:

The protection of *human rights* is at the very core of the political construct of a democratic constitutional state ... [Human rights] work as a shield or a bulwark to protect individuals against excessive steering of their lives and entitle individuals to determine freely and autonomously their lives and choices and to participate in the political system.

The confusion over rights seems to prevent serious consideration of what can be seen as the most crucial questions that arise when one human being harms another, namely: How are the individuals who directly experience such events either as victims, families of victims or as perpetrators of the act meant to make sense of what has happened? And how are societies to grapple with how to repair the serious damage that has been caused in the social fabric? As stated above, what people really want is for something to happen that will somehow bring things back to the state they were before a terrible event took place. Of course this can never be achieved. But by holding firmly to a Hobbesian view of society as a war of all against all, cycles of perpetual violence continue. Moreover, the pain and suffering of victims of crime remains unacknowledged and unrecognised in any meaningful way, whilst perpetrators (and the prisoners they become) remain beleaguered losers in this war. In current criminal justice arrangements nothing is, in effect, resolved in the aftermath of serious violence. Further, the continued construction of prisoners or other people who have contravened the law (such as illegal immigrants, accused persons or terrorist suspects) as outsiders or undeserving or as 'threatening others' invokes public fears and emotions. These emotions now play – politically – a more explicit role in criminal justice policy and administration, particularly in populist democracies.

Populism and emotion

The importance of emotion within populist democracies and in relation to crime, criminal justice policymaking and administration has not received enough attention in theoretical criminology (though see the special issue of *Theoretical Criminology*, 6:3 (2002); and Valier, 2004; Walklate, 2009). And yet emotions have continually influenced and become progressively more prominent in the practice of criminal justice (Sarat, 1997; Valier, 2004). A key way through which this has taken place has been via the voices of victims of crime, pressure from victims' rights movements and the politicisation of the victim (Miers, 1978; Walklate, 2005). The injury to victims and the role of emotion in criminal proceedings and in lawmaking have recently become more prevalent in many adversarial (and democratically populist) criminal justice systems (Walklate, 2009, 2011). One of the first ways these changes in criminal justice began to manifest themselves was the introduction of victim-impact statements in sentencing proceedings, or in death penalty cases, in the United States.

Whilst the criminal justice system has historically failed victims of crime (Dignan, 2005), and greater victim involvement in its administration has been seen by many victims' rights groups as a positive (if still tokenistic) development, such tinkering with the procedures of modern criminal justice has been argued, by some (for example, Sarat, 1997), to be undermining the foundations on which the system was built. Incremental, though significant, changes to the administration of justice have been seen as signalling a cracking of the foundations of criminal justice processes. This, in turn, has begun to erode inbuilt protections in criminal law procedures (Sarat, 1997). As suggested above, emotionality has always been an underlying factor in the invocation of criminal justice, but its recent encroachments into existing criminal justice procedures marks an important shift. Furthermore, highlighting the emotional aspects of violent crime or other harmful criminal acts has become a key means used by pressure groups and the media to prompt and promote political action. The work of single-issue pressure groups and victims' rights campaigners has successfully leveraged emotions and the support of median voters in favour of harsher criminal justice policies. Conversely, the emotional reservoir that surrounds the problem of crime can be dipped into to garner public support for law-and-order politics and harsher criminal justice policies. Lacey (2008, pp. 69–70; see also Sim, 2009) argues that:

> both the popularity of harsh criminal justice policy among median voters and the relative simplicity of enacting such policy – the lack of need, for example, to develop complex new bureaucracies to administer or implement increased criminalisation – has proved a potent temptation to US politicians and other elected officials.

Public support for these sorts of movements is driven by the deep emotion that results when interpersonal harm occurs and from the desire to *do* something to ensure that there is some sort of reckoning of what has happened and to try to prevent such an event from ever happening again. Whilst there may be satisfaction on the part of victims' rights campaigners and segments of the general population when attempts to alter foregoing criminal justice processes are successful, incremental changes do not address the failings and inherent biases of adversarial criminal justice as a whole, as described above in this chapter. The biases inherent in the foundations of criminal justice and the criminal law cannot easily be overcome. Although it is imperative that demands for justice made, for example, by women, on behalf of children, or by ethnic minorities, be taken more seriously, appealing to a fundamentally biased and unjust (and arguably violent) criminal justice system will surely only make matters worse. Likewise, demands that perpetrators of white-collar or corporate crime become better recognised in existing criminal justice arrangements also seems a futile pursuit. Current criminal justice processes are flawed at their very foundations and the means by which justice is pursued (via prisons and punishment) do not solve even the problems they were supposedly designed to address (property crime, other acquisitive crimes). Any amount of augmentation or restructuring is not likely to address these fundamental failures.

Returning to the plight of individual victims, incremental changes to existing criminal justice practice do not result in a more serious and meaningful recognition of the loss experienced by victims of violent crime. The suffering that results from interpersonal harm is not a pain that criminal justice systems are well designed to attend to. Further, according to Sarat (1997, p. 169), by attempting to personalise existing criminal justice arrangements, sentencers and punishers are being asked to declare their alliance with either victims or offenders. He argues (ibid.) in reference to victim-impact statements in particular that: 'Criminal sentencing thus becomes a test of loyalty ... [ensuring that] the criminal knows that his or her punishment is an expression of personal loyalty and connection between state and victim.' The trouble with such incremental changes to existing criminal justice practices is that they largely serve to further destabilise an already precarious, ill-conceived and unequal system of justice. They do not make the criminal justice system – overall – more fair or equitable.

The role of victims within criminal justice policy formation often seems more symbolic and rhetorical rather than meaningful (Bottoms, 1983; Karmen, 1992; Walklate, 2007). Further, it also seems to be the case that the voices of victims are not listened to in equal measure. Sim (2009, p. 158) has pointed out that victim surveys have revealed that victims can be sceptical of the capacity of the prison to solve problems of crime. These voices are generally ignored and policymaking is more heavily influenced by those calling for a retributive response. Moreover, Aradau (2004) has suggested there is a 'politics of pity' in relation to policy responses. She discusses the problem of human trafficking and notes that there are different government strategies for legitimating or delegitimating the suffering of victims and for delineating which victims are deserving of policy interventions and which are not. Such strategies can become closely tied with strategies of security, as Aradau points out in the case of human trafficking. It seems that victims' rights movements can provide an opportunity for state posturing (Walklate, 2009) instead of a more serious grappling with the difficult issues associated with problems of crime. Through such posturing the strong arm of the state exercises its will and might over criminals for the purpose of gaining political legitimacy. In this way, victims are symbolic recipients of state benevolence in the form of increased policy focus and greater representation and voice in criminal justice proceedings. Harsher policies, or increased victim involvement in criminal justice proceedings, can be popular and relatively easy to implement. They represent a win-win strategy in building political legitimacy. Prisoners, by contrast, are a relatively vulnerable population over which to exercise excessive authority because they are, firstly, unpopular and often the subjects of public hatred and, secondly, they are a safely silent (or silenced, see Mathiesen, 2004) population over which to exercise symbolic power. However, the politicisation of victims (as opposed to thinking more carefully about how to support them) and the introduction of incremental changes to criminal justice process make it more difficult to observe the other purposes that the criminal justice system may be serving or to contemplate its failures, biases and contradictions. All of this, therefore, continues to prevent us from thinking differently about criminal justice. Further, the methods that are currently employed to try to move forward after violent events occur rarely result in restoration or reconciliation. Indeed, the main action taken by most societies when human beings harm one another is to punish. However, as the next section will discuss, this action serves to make the problem of harm a great deal worse.

The trouble with punishment

I want to return now to focusing more closely on the problem of violent and serious crimes. Traditionally, such events have most often led to the enactment of some form of punishment. As outlined above, punishment, according to Durkheim, is one of the primary functions of the law. It is the symbolic and real manifestation of society's censure. It is also an inherently moralistic practice, concerned with, as Christie has identified, the delivery of state-sanctioned pain. With respect to the pain associated with imprisonment, in particular, Christie (2000, p. 25) argues that there is 'nothing … so total in constraints, in degradation, and in its display of power as … the prison'. It might be said that one of the key ways public safety and social order are pursued in many societies is by inflicting high levels of pain on particular social members through the use of imprisonment. As Paddy Hillyard and Steve Tombs (2007, p. 14) have argued:

> The state – via the criminal justice system – proceeds to seek to inflict suffering, once a crime, and a criminal, has been defined. It inflicts punishment on offenders, of which the prison sentence is the ultimate option and symbol … Indeed, the inflicting of pain by the

state through the criminal justice system is a process that involves a number of discreet, but mutually reinforcing, stages: defining, classifying, broadcasting, disposing and punishing the individual concerned.

Using the concept of social harm, Hillyard and Tombs (ibid.) make a compelling case by which punitive penal measures can be seen as fundamentally socially harmful practices. In particular, they consider the wider social harms produced by prisons and the criminal justice systems that rely on them. Such harms, they argue, follow a different trajectory and are disconnected from the original harm and pain caused. They point out that ex-prisoners are subjected to symbolic, tangible and enduring ostracism by society; prisoners and their families may lose their home or the opportunity to have children or a family life. Further, they are removed from the labour market (if they were in it in the first place) and their future employment prospects may be severely limited upon their return to society, thus ensuring that they remain on the margins as non-participating members of society. Hillyard and Tombs (ibid., p. 14) point out that such harms tend to fall disproportionately on relatively vulnerable members of society and that the reliance on criminal justice processes to respond to those events that we define as crimes necessarily prevents us from considering other ways of responding to these events.

As Hillyard and Tombs imply, the use of prisons and punishment contribute to wider social harms that are, perhaps, unintended and which do not result in net effects that make our social world – as a whole – any better than it was before, and indeed, it may even worsen it. But what about the delivery of punishment; what effects does it have on those it is intended to correct? Above, when discussing the desire for vengeance, it was suggested that what is wanted when a terrible harm occurs is for the person who perpetrated it to understand the suffering s/he has caused and to be made to suffer him or herself. It was argued that the idea of revenge and the idea of punishment are not actually all that different and that the emotional desire for revenge is, to some extent, meted out in the delivery of punishment. Further, the delivery of punishment is seen as a necessary reckoning of the harm that has been caused, serving a functional role to restore the social balance and build and maintain social solidarity. But are these instinctive desires and common-sense or reasoned beliefs about punishment really the best ways of responding to violence? Is punishment the most effective means for helping someone to understand the extent and depth of the harm they have caused?

Punishment causes violence

James Gilligan is a psychiatrist who has written extensively on the subject of violence. His writings are based on over 25 years of experience working with violent people in American prisons and other secure settings. In 2000 he published an important article entitled Punishment and Violence: Is the Criminal Law Based on One Huge Mistake? The article (Gilligan, 2000, p. 745) begins with the following:

> For the past three millennia ... [w]e have been conducting a great social experiment to test the hypothesis that we could prevent violence by defining it as a crime (or war crime), and then punishing those who commit it with more violence of our own (which we define as justice). Three thousand years is long enough to test any hypothesis, and the results of this experiment have been in for a long time now. This approach to violence, which I will call the *moral and legal* approach, far from solving the problem of violence, or even diminishing the threat that it poses to our continued survival, has, instead, been followed by a continuing and ever-accelerating escalation of the scale of human violence – to the point that the century we have just survived has been the bloodiest in all of human history.

He (ibid., p. 746) goes on to say that 'history is the ultimate refutation of the theory that punishment will prevent or deter violence. On the contrary, punishment is the most powerful stimulus of violence that we have yet discovered'. This is a sobering revelation. It is contrary to intuition. It is contrary to what common-sense ideologies argue will be achieved by pursuing vengeance. That is: *if only the person who has perpetrated this terrible act of violence could himself experience the suffering he has caused then we could ensure he would never do such a terrible thing again.* Despite how obvious such an assumption may seem, its practical application has shown that punishment does not have the desired effect. As Gilligan (ibid., p. 749) notes:

> In short, what I learned from decades of clinical experience with the most violent people our society produces is that many of those who murder others are survivors of their own attempted murder, or of the murders of their closest relatives; their fathers, mothers, sisters or brothers, whose murders they often witnessed. *If punishment did inhibit or prevent violence, then these men would not have become violent in the first place, for they had already experienced the most severe punishments that it is possible to inflict on people without actually killing them.*

Gilligan (ibid.) presents a similar analysis from his prison work where he has regularly observed that 'the more severely prisoners were punished by the prison authorities, the more violent they became, and the more violent they became, the more severely they were punished'. His observations and conclusions deriving from his clinical work (Gilligan, 2000) suggest that the emotion that is necessary (though not sufficient) for the development of violence is shame and/or humiliation. He argues (ibid., p. 763) that 'being treated as if one were insignificant, unimportant or worthless' or 'when [one] suffer[s] an indignity' leads to rage and potential violence. This presents a problem for the role of punishment within criminal justice practice, which is, in part, designed to stimulate shame and, in practice, draws out feelings of worthlessness and social ostracism (as Chapter 5 illustrated). It also presents a problem for the instinctive, common-sense reactions about what to do about violent crime. That is, the strong, seemingly natural human desires that prompt people to call for punishment, and the main means by which most societies currently respond to the problem of violent, interpersonal harm both turn out to be the worst possible ways to respond if the aim is to interrupt cycles of harm and find better ways of preventing reoccurrences of interpersonal violence.

Our long experience with punishment illustrates – as Gilligan points out – that harsh, excessively long, punishing and painful prison sentences do not tend to result in reformed, non-violent ex-prisoners. At the same time, however, it is probably the case that short or community-based sentences will not satisfy the public thirst for vengeance when violent crimes occur (though there is evidence to suggest the public is less punitive than the media and much political rhetoric indicate, see Roberts et al., 2003). So we may be at an impasse. If punishment does not work to 'teach people a lesson' and it instead makes them more violent, then it surely must be worth considering abandoning. But there are firmly held moral beliefs about the need for punishment. If punishment causes violence, then is it possible for human beings to imagine abandoning beliefs about the need to make perpetrators of harm pay for the pain they have caused by, in turn, extracting pain from them? The use of punishment, it would seem, directly undermines the safety and security of the wider society because it results in an increased likelihood of the recurrence of violence. If, as human beings, we can come to accept this, then the first question we might ask ourselves about the use of punishment might be whether or not the moral belief in atonement is worth the sacrifice of safety and security. The second question might be whether we are also willing to maintain and potentially increase the levels of harm that we cause one another in society. Does the collective or natural desire to punish preclude us from better examining the consequences of harsh criminal justice measures, the use of prisons and punishment and the continued extraction of pain? Such questions are perhaps perennial and unlikely to be seriously considered within societies currently embracing harsh justice measures. Nevertheless, they form part of the basis for the discussion that follows in the final chapter of this book. Before coming to this, however, it is useful to acknowledge that there are no simple solutions to the problems of serious interpersonal harm. Despite the many ways in which public attention is directed and deflected by dominant political ideologies and existing criminal justice practices, the fact remains that human social life and human beings are complex entities that pose complex problems. Therefore the problems of violent crime, criminal justice and punishment are all areas that constantly require further and careful thinking and do not easily lend themselves to simplistic or one-dimensional explanations or solutions.

Conclusion

It is evident that the trajectory towards intolerance and vengeance fuelled by populist democratic rule and law-and-order penal thinking is difficult to reverse. The ideologies that underpin such thinking and the powerful interests that they serve make them especially difficult to refute or disrupt. The difficulties associated with eliciting political commitment to think about crime and punishment differently are seemingly insurmountable in societies where punitive approaches to crime and justice have established a strong foothold. In addition, the ways in which justice and rights are enacted in punitive criminal justice systems (such as that of England and Wales or the US) are shaped by firmly held moral beliefs and deeply embedded power structures, social divisions and inherent biases. Moreover, the apparent hostility within some public and political spheres to showing tolerance to certain groups, such as prisoners, adds further complexity when attempting to debate the rationale for current approaches to crime control, criminal justice and increased levels of human security. Questions such as whether public protection and human security are incompatible with the goals of tolerance and reconciliation serve to illustrate the density of issues at hand when considering problems of human security, justice, rights and social harm.

So where does this leave us? It might be argued that one of the ways to begin to shed more clarifying light on the depths and associated injustices of existing criminal justice practice is by continuing to debate, and draw attention to, the inherent harmfulness of the persistent social divisions, mechanisms of exclusion and overuses of state power that we currently observe in much criminal justice policy and practice. This chapter has attempted to grapple with questions surrounding the apparently competing agendas associated with criminal law and justice, the interests of the state, the interests of victims of crime, the interests of those who perpetrate violent crime and society as a whole. By drawing out the symbolic meanings associated with the trade-offs being made between liberty, rights, state power and the public will it has attempted to illustrate the dangers and harms associated both with punitive criminal justice practice and overuses of state authority.

It may seem (and feel) justifiable for the state to construct as other those among us who have committed violent, high-profile or particularly serious crimes. Moreover, it may even be seen as uncontentious, given that they have acted in ways that offend public sentiments or have shown they have difficulty living harmoniously alongside other people. However, state constructions of prisoners as other, and not as temporarily suspended citizens, create a space in society where it is acceptable to disregard the humanity of a certain group of people. Whilst this may be acceptable amongst individual members of the public who find it difficult to see the humanity in a person who has committed a serious act of violence against another human being, it is wholly unacceptable for the state to take such a position. When human life is disregarded at a structural or state level it is quite a different order of disregard, with the potential for far more harmful consequences. It perpetuates an ideology that makes it acceptable to denigrate other human beings. It also means that it is acceptable to dehumanise them. In doing so it increases the vulnerability of all. As Desmond Tutu (1999, p. 35) has argued, the greater whole of humanity is diminished when we agree that others within it can be treated as less than human. This idea will be discussed more fully in the final chapter, but for now it is sufficient to point out that the seemingly justifiable decision to view as evil others those who have committed terrible acts of violence against other people must be considered with caution, especially when it is taken on the part of the state and when there begins to be a tendency to construct the general prisoner population in such dehumanising terms. This is not to say that the harms private citizens can sometimes pose to one another should not be taken seriously and carefully responded to by the state, but the way societies and individual social members respond *matters* both for our mutual rights of liberty and freedom and for the preservation of the value we all place on human life.

8
Making the Unthinkable Thinkable

Introduction

> The delivery of pain, to whom, and for what contains an endless line of deep moral questions. If there are any experts here, they are the philosophers. They are also often experts at saying the problems are so complex we cannot act. We must think. That may not be the worst alternative when the other option is delivery of pain. (Christie, 2000, p. 202)

> [C]ritical thought needs continuous rethinking in order to remain up to its task ... the hope and chance of striking an acceptable balance between freedom and security ... need to be placed at the centre of the rethinking effort. (Bauman, 2006, p. 176)

This book has used a critical criminological standpoint to draw attention to and think through what may be seen as three interrelated concerns: the persistence of the prison, the potential dangers of security ideologies in both the penal and the public realms and the counterproductive nature of punishment. It has argued that prisons, punishment and the pursuit of security form a triad of overlapping ideologies, each apparently focused, in part, on responding to social threat in the interests of creating safer social conditions for all. However it has been shown that these ideologies also serve a number of other functions associated with maintaining political economic structures and prevailing distributions of wealth and power. As a result it is more difficult to recognise the failings and contradictions in the way security and safety are often pursued and to consider alternative solutions. This chapter reflects on the key issues that this book has highlighted. It seeks to make clear the value of the critical standpoint in making the invisible visible.

It concludes the book by examining some of the moral stumbling blocks that prevent us from thinking the unthinkable and considers the kinds of thinking that may be required for us to overcome them.

The denigration of humanity in the pursuit of security

One of the central tasks of this book has been to problematise the use of the prison and trends towards penal convergence. Through the close examination of maximum-security prisons in England, the book has endeavoured to illustrate the way that the bulky machinery of prisons distracts attention away from their contradictions and failures. It has been postulated that due to the taken-for-granted role of the prison in crime control agendas and its association with commonly held beliefs about safety and security, it is well placed to play a significant symbolic role in the pursuit of security. At the same time, the ideological functions that the prison has always served in political economic relations remain intact. Furthermore the increased use of the prison across different nation states may be suggestive of a troubling trend towards increased levels of social exclusion, othering and individualising social policies.

Alongside these considerations the prison has also been examined in this book as a device through which to consider the consequences of repressive security strategies and the way they can begin to infringe on legal protections and human rights. The detailed examination of English maximum-security prisons revealed the power of security-thinking, as well as the effects it has had on prisoner experiences. It brought into fuller view some of the key features of security ideologies and also illustrated the way security in the penal realm coalesces and mirrors the way it is pursued and constructed in the social realm. The potency and power of ideologies of security have long wielded a significant, if often invisible, force in national and international politics, warfare, and national defence strategies and security services. Such ideologies that were once only found under the auspices of clandestine intelligence agencies and obscure government departments have gradually begun to suffuse other areas of society where they influence or transform existing practices or aspects of social life. Indeed, the prominence of security measures and of security-thinking has become increasingly discernable in many arenas, including government agencies, airports, universities, policing practices and in the emergence of gated communities and the manifestation of widespread CCTV usage and other systems of surveillance. Further, examinations of the concept of security within the prison have illustrated its power and capacity for domination.

Whilst security strategies within individual nation states may combine with other political economic agendas, their seemingly global trajectory raises particular concerns. Moreover, the influence of global market capitalism on social, political and economic conditions complicates the analysis of the problem of security. The valorisation of conformity, individualism and objectification within some free-market economies (Sim, 2009, p. xi) and the political regimes that remain heavily committed to them (such as those who some classify as neo-liberal[1]), have served to reinforce ways of thinking that justify xenophobic security measures and perpetuate and widen existing social divisions and tensions. The extent to which such ways of thinking and approaches to security have the capacity to garner collective global support remains questionable. However, as discussed in Chapter 6, the unprecedented cooperation invoked by NATO, between allies and adversaries in the aftermath of 9/11, suggests that coordination and collectively agreed strategies of security are not outside the realm of possibility. It is important to recognise the possibility of widely agreed security strategies and tactics because such agreements may signal a move towards a global ideology of security that holds a hegemonic status more powerful than any we have previously seen.

As the book argues, security ideologies also rely on constructions of individuals and groups as other. They promote precautionary logics that foreclose possibilities for human agency and they inevitably seem to require that liberty and rights are traded off in favour of security gains. Further, they often dictate that if a person, segment of a population or other categorisable group of people are deemed to be a potential security threat, then from the perspective of the state there is full justification for whatever measures are necessary to neutralise the threat. Moreover, there is a collective expectation – seemingly on a global level – that such measures will be taken and are necessary. Whilst the use of particular measures may be justified when a threat is proven and imminent, it is often not possible to guarantee with certainty when threat *is* imminent. And yet security procedures and tactics may be (and often are) invoked without definitive evidence of impending danger.

The work of Arendt (1968) on totalitarianism recognised a built-in limit to foregoing dangerous and authoritarian political strategies, namely that they were not global. It is premature to suggest that there is a fully discernable security regime operating in any nation state. However Hallsworth and Lea (2011) have argued that we may be witnessing the emergence of security states. If elements of security-thinking are also beginning to radiate outside the confines of the nation state and towards a more widely agreed conceptualisation of how security is best pursued and if that conceptualisation is founded on ideologies of security that 'other' and denigrate human beings and human rights, then this should be cause for collective concern. As Young-Bruehl (2006, p. 76) has argued:

> Globalisation certainly distributes some beneficial features of advanced technology, such as education ... it puts people in touch with one another, promoting a sense of humankind. But it also implicates the entire world with a mentality that ... identifies people as superfluous and leads to imperialist techniques of ghettoization and massacre that [Hannah] Arendt, portrayed.

The disregard for human rights that has taken place in Guantanamo Bay is a recent example of the justification of the any means necessary type of logic often used in security strategies. Guantanamo is a clear state of exception, but where exception is becoming normalised. Importantly, according to Agamben (2005) the state of exception may be viewed as a political act, justified on the grounds of preserving the rule of law and the pursuit of security (see also Davies, 2008, p. 78). Although the treatment of the detainees held there has been condemned by European Union members, Amnesty International and Human Rights Watch and calls for recognition of detainees' human rights and legal status have been made, there has been transnational complicity with the decision to pursue security in this way. The fact that such tactics can be used against human beings at all and justified under the guises of security logics or intelligence gathering is troubling. The problems that terrorist attacks or other unpredictable threats perpetrated by human beings (including the occurrence of violent crime) pose are not easily solved. Nor can such events be conclusively anticipated. As Chapter 6 suggested, an objective state of security is a fruitless pursuit. It may, therefore, be more viable and desirable for states to direct a greater amount of attention towards improving the sense of security amongst its citizenry, focusing more heavily on building social trust, well-being and social cohesion.

In relation to the problems of danger and insecurity it is important to recognise that the fear and pain that result when unpredictable events occur are not easily overcome. As argued in Chapter 7, when such events occur there is a collective desire for every effort to be taken to prevent such events from recurring. However, the harm that can be associated with the *means* by which prevention is sought can also be significant and have devastating consequences. The processes by which societies attempt to ensure higher levels of safety and security should include within their aims the principle to do no further harm. This idea holds relevance both for security strategies and for those associated with criminal justice processes. Strategies that rely on the exclusion, othering or denigration of individuals or groups should be cause for collective concern. As has been argued, it is important to *notice* when human beings are treated as less than human – either at the hands of other social members (as in the case of perpetration of violent crime) or at the hands of states. It is also important to think carefully – and critically – about the strategies being used to pursue security and to consider whether the measures being employed are actually making us any more secure or safer or if our objective state of insecurity remains the same, despite the measures taken.

Recognising the coefficient of harm

> The purpose of a critical understanding of crime … is to expose the meaning of law and order … The false reality by which we live, the one that supports the established system must be understood and demystified … We must build a body of ideas that will allow us to critically understand crime and the legal order … In this way we will not only understand our contemporary experiences but we will be able to change our social world. (Quinney, 2000, pp. 90, 94)

If one begins from a critical standpoint when considering the problems of human security, crime, justice and punishment the seemingly black and white nature of the law, the question of right and wrong and the legitimacy of the state to punish, all become problematic. As this book has illustrated, the actual purposes served by the law, prisons, criminal justice and punishment have little to do with their stated functions. They are more heavily concerned with maintaining existing dominant and political economic structures. They are altogether less concerned with fairness, equality and justice. This, however, means that there are no simple answers either to the problem of injustice inherent in criminal justice systems or to problems of crime, social harm, human insecurity or punishment. Considering these problems from a critical perspective, therefore, allows us to see what is not at first evident. It enables our ability to notice and it opens up the possibilities for thinking differently about the problems that trouble us. This chapter now turns to the task of examining some different ways of beginning to think about some of the problems considered throughout this book.

One of the tensions that troubles critical criminology is the disjuncture between theory and action (de Haan, 1987, p. 322). That is, there has been difficulty in translating the critiques of critical criminology into practical, moral or political directives. Willem de Haan (ibid., p. 321) has argued that 'moral issues are intrinsic to the criminological enterprise'. But, he suggests, much of critical scholarship has neglected the moral dimensions of crime and criminal justice, suspending engagement with the conventional morality that crime should be condemned and criminals punished to focus solely on critiquing mainstream criminology and jurisprudence. Moreover, de Haan (1987), Cohen (1985), Christie (2007) and Quinney (2000) have all argued that criminologists cannot ignore the moral dimensions of their subject matter, because doing so undermines the credibility to argue for 'other "arrangements" besides the penal system of the state' (de Haan, 1987, p. 330). Whilst moral issues have intermittently appeared on the agendas of many critical scholars, they are an area that still lacks significant critical attention and debate.

As Chapter 7 suggested, moral questions are unequivocally amongst the most difficult ones when considering the myriad problems associated with crime and punishment. Human societies the world over are a long way from agreeing any answers to them. I do not intend to provide any unequivocal answers here. However, it might be suggested that in our contemplation of the problems of crime, justice and punishment we consider aiming for one simple goal: the overall reduction in the coefficient of harm. This position very much coincides with one taken by Christie in *Limits to Pain* (1981, pp. 10, 11), where he argues:

> One of my basic premises will be that it is right to strive for a reduction of man-inflicted pain on earth ... I see no other defensible position than to strive for pain-reduction ... One of the rules would then be: If in doubt, do not pain. Another rule would be: Inflict as little pain as possible ... Look for alternatives to punishments, not only alternative punishments. It is often not necessary to react; the offender as well as the surroundings know it was wrong. Much deviance is expressive, a clumsy attempt to say something. Let the crime then become a starting point for a real dialogue, and not for an equally clumsy answer in the form of a spoonful of pain.

It is important, as Christie makes clear, to think very carefully about the net result of our actions as human beings living together in an increasingly globalised world. Specifically, we may want to begin to pay closer attention to what might be seen as the coefficient of harm that we accumulate when we inflict pain on one another. In our pursuit of greater levels of security and personal safety, in our responses to problems of crime and social harm and in how we react to our own seemingly instinctive desires for vengeance and the call for justice, we need to consider whether our actions will be adding to an overall accumulation of harm and human suffering. We also need to consider whether if, by doing so, we are making ourselves any safer and more secure or whether we are, in fact, continuing to contribute to human distress and instead working to guarantee that we remain both subjectively and objectively insecure. But how do we begin to think about such a proposition?

Thinking the unthinkable

How is the unthinkable made thinkable, both in terms of how societies can come to justify cruel and inhumane treatment of individuals or certain segments of the population and in terms of how we might begin to retreat from such ideas and forge new terrains? A great deal of human suffering has come about as a result of ideological or moral beliefs or a combination of the two. If we think about the problems of prisons and punishment it is evident that a great deal of our decision-making around what to do about the problem of crime has been heavily influenced by moral ideas. We have founded our legal processes and procedures more on sets of beliefs than on evidence or on goals aimed at a reduction in human suffering. How might we think about doing things differently? Perhaps the most radical idea we might consider (and also the most difficult to imagine in practical terms, but which is still worth examining) is to do nothing. As Gilligan (2000, p. 767) has stated:

> What then can we do about crime and punishment? ... The first and most important principle might be to start doing nothing; in other words, to stop doing the things we already do that stimulate violence, such as responding to the kind of violence we call crime with the kind that we call punishment.

Writing about punishment in Canada, Edgar Friedenberg (1980, pp. 282, 283) has argued that:

> the argument that 'you have to do something about crime; you can't just let them get by with it' is false and misleading in itself, even if imprisonment were not the customary, and ineffective, sanction.

Why do you have to? Because violence to individuals and wilful misappropriation of property are something decent [people] cannot tolerate? They do tolerate it, in the form of highway accidents that could have been prevented by enforcement of existing legislation; industrial pollution that violates not only existing statutes but specific clean-up orders previously accepted by private corporations and the government itself. In both these cases, the number of victims, including fatalities, can be predicted quite accurately; and all the potential Hillside Stranglers and 44-calibre killers who might be at large … could not hope, collectively, to win even a bronze medal in competition with INCO[2] and its fellow industrial giants … The difficulty isn't that [we] couldn't bear the risks involved in closing [our] prisons or even abandoning the criminal code itself. It is, rather, that [we] couldn't bear the thought.

Both of these authors suggest ideas that seem unthinkable. One of the biggest obstacles to thinking such thoughts is found in the moral ideas, beliefs and judgements that surface when violent crime or other forms of serious harm occur. As discussed in Chapter 7, when such events happen there are often instant moral judgements made and commensurate legal responses taken – both of which are based on what is believed to be the right thing to do. However, our long experience with prisons, punishment and the delivery of pain illustrate that our instincts about how we must react when violent events occur, in actuality make us no safer and, indeed, often increase the likelihood of further violence (Gilligan, 2000; Kupers, 2006).

Moral ideas about what we think we ought or should do about crime and insecurity have dictated the solutions that we have employed to deal with them. Despite De Haan's suggestion that critical criminology (and mainstream criminology for that matter) has not engaged deeply enough with the moral dimensions of crime, morality is ever present in any criminological undertaking – empirical or theoretical – though there may be no explicit mention of the morality surrounding the questions examined. Quinney (2000, p. 210) has stated that 'whatever we do, our criminology is the advancement of one moral philosophy or another'. Whilst much inspiration can be found in Quinney's work and that of other critical scholars, the idea of embarking on a moral project, or more particularly a *moralising* one, is problematic. As I grappled with the problems considered in this book and the fact that most societies around the world have found it difficult to move beyond tried and failed solutions to problems of crime, criminal justice and security it seemed apparent that a lot of misdirection had been brought about by ideas of what we think we should do or by the idea that one person is good or another person is bad or that people should get what they deserve. Human beings seem to firmly hold on to these and certain other ideas about how we ought to handle difficult social problems. Such ideas are generally traceable to one moral framework or another or, indeed, to an ideological one (and the relationship between morality and ideology can be close, see Marx, 1975). However, our tendency as social beings to resort to moral arguments and judgements when looking for solutions to difficult and perennial human problems has often been a fruitless enterprise and, indeed, has prevented us from thinking our way through our problems. As a result we have tended to judge and moralise our way through them, often with disastrous and harmful results.

The foreclosure on thinking that moral judgements seem to generate leads to the question of whether there could be something beyond morality and if there is, how then are we to think about problems of crime and punishment? Richard Garner's (1994 and new edition, forthcoming) examinations of the merits of moral abolitionism may provide answers to these questions, or at least some further avenues for exploration. It is to Garner's work and questions of morality that this chapter now turns.

Beyond morality

Somewhat akin to the debate between positivism and social constructionism in the social sciences that concerns whether or not there are objective discoverable truths about social life, there is debate in moral philosophy about whether or not there is an objective morality. Moral realists argue that there is, whilst moral error theorists and other sceptics argue that there is not. I will not rehearse the details of the debate between these two broad positions or the many variations that have been put forward within them. On the moral realist position it is sufficient to say that it encompasses the widely held understanding and common belief that morality is real and not simply the invention of human beings. Such an idea coincides with religious or secular beliefs that set out the frameworks for particular moral positions and stipulate their virtues, values, moral rules and duties. Counter to this position is moral error theory. Put simply, moral error theorists argue that morality is a human-made myth (Mackie, 1977; Hinckfuss, 1987; Garner, 1994, 2010, 2011). For the purposes of embarking on new ways of thinking about social life and social problems it is worthwhile to consider the positions that moral error theory puts forward.

One of the starting points from which moral error theorists begin is to argue that persistent belief in morality may be dangerous and harmful, suggesting that morality may be responsible for more suffering than it prevents (Garner, 2010). Ian Hinckfuss (1987) has argued that so-called moral societies create a basis and intellectual framework for social and economic inequality, authoritarianism and elitism. Moral beliefs make it possible to designate certain individuals and groups as deserving and certain others as undeserving, and thereby enable the exploitation of the poor and the weak by the rich and the powerful (ibid., pp. 45–6). Further, moral ideas do not assist us in finding greater clarity when considering difficult issues. Instead, moral arguments often inflame conflict and make compromise more difficult. Relying on moral pronouncements that include 'shoulds' and 'oughts' seems to foreclose opportunities to think differently about the issues at hand, as Garner (2010, p. 219) argues:

> [M]orality is flexible enough to be available to support any choice anyone is likely to want to make, including the choice of government officials to suppress what they choose to call immorality. This throws a different light on the idea that the moral overlay is useful when we want to justify social and legal sanctions ... What good is morality if it can so readily be marshalled to defend the sanctions of a tyrant?

Unfairness and inequality can be preserved within moral frameworks, and misuses of power can be justified. In addition, moral beliefs and their tendency to foreclose communication and compromise can make global war possible (Garner, ibid., pp. 219–20). Moreover, and as a result of the tendency for moral arguments to close off discussions or produce stalemates, the persistence of moral beliefs has prevented us from thinking more carefully and sensibly about problems of crime and punishment.

Thinking about crime and punishment without morality?

Ideas about abandoning or even restricting morality may sound radical and unthinkable, but such ideas are useful as a way into imagining alternative ways of thinking about seemingly unsolvable social problems. Garner (1994, 2010, 2011, and forthcoming) provides some important insights on thinking beyond morality. He (2011, p. 3) suggests observing ourselves in the act of moral judgement.

> [N]otice what happens when the thought that someone is evil or deserves to suffer arises ... We can neutralise [these moral judgements] by displacing them with non-moral thoughts, such as the

thought that we could be biased, or mistaken about some detail, motive or prudential calculation. Or we could remind ourselves that we are conducting an experiment to see if we can back away from moralising without all Hell breaking loose.

Garner suggests that instead of moralising about the actions of others we could try expressing and communicating our attitudes, feelings and needs. We need not use moral language or beliefs to do so. Whilst these propositions may sound risky or foolhardy and some may suggest that the restriction or abandonment of morality could lead to anarchy, Garner suggests that we have no reason to believe that this would be so. He (2010, p. 222) argues:

> A world where the concept of moral rights has been abandoned is a long way from anarchy. Take away moral rights and there remain legal rights, civil rights, conventional rights, and countless entitlements and liberties people tend to give and demand … It is not hard to think of ways to encourage people to take the needs and interests of others more seriously. We could work harder at teaching and promoting communication skills, which would improve mutual understanding; and we could stop looking at compromise as if it were surrender.

But what about the problems of crime and punishment? Is it possible to think beyond morality when considering what we are to do when one human being harms another? Garner's work (2011, p. 5) touches on this question too.

> When moralists debate about punishment, every form of treatment has defenders. Some utilitarians support severe punishments in order to deter potential criminals. Kinder utilitarians say that mercy and rehabilitation have better consequences. Other moralists reject utilitarianism and say that criminals deserve to suffer or that it is our moral obligation to make sure that they do. … [Such arguments] are based on the flawed moralistic idea that it is sometimes morally right, or even morally required, for us to cause suffering to someone 'because it is merited by [the] wrong' that he or she has done … The metaphor at work here is justice balancing the scales … The objective scales of justice, not our anger or lust for revenge, are to determine how much someone must suffer to atone for some misdeed. There is much to argue about here, but fortunately the moral abolitionist is not saddled with the need to calculate how much any person, even the

most extreme offender, deserves to suffer. Apart from the stipulated penalties in the laws currently in force, any of which can be changed, nobody deserves to suffer for any reason whatever. It is this rejection of the idea of 'moral desert' that will finally make it possible to discuss remedies to crimes and incivilities without having to pander to moral ire and posturing.

Garner's moral abolitionist arguments provide a thought-provoking proposition. In particular, the suggestion of freeing ourselves from the moral imperative that suffering must be inflicted as retaliation to the initial harm caused offers a way into imagining alternative responses to crime. It also provides an indication of the type of thinking that may be required if we are to work towards the position suggested earlier – that is, the idea that we may want to consider paying closer attention to the coefficient of harm and human suffering that we are causing in the measures we take to improve our safety and security. Further, Garner's arguments also provide a means by which we might think differently about the purpose of the prison.

If punishment was not central to the experience of imprisonment, what then would be the purpose of the places we called prisons? Coming from a similar line of thought, Evgeny Pashukanis (1989, p. 177) has argued:

> Imagine for a moment that the court was really concerned only with considering ways in which the living conditions of the accused could be so changed that either he was improved, or society was protected from him – and the meaning of the term 'punishment' evaporates at once.

Our thinking about the problems of crime and harm can be transformed when moral imperatives are dispensed with or restricted only to a concern with harm and pain minimisation. This does not mean that there would not be a use for secure settings. As Gilligan (2000) has argued, when people are actively dangerous towards other people we may need to confine them for periods of time in locked facilities. However, he (ibid., pp. 767–8) states:

> [T]o punish people – that is, to deliberately cause them pain – above and beyond the degree that is unavoidable in the act of restraining them, only constitutes further violence (on our part), and only causes further violence (on the part of the 'criminals' we punish).

It could, therefore, be argued that our commitment to moral beliefs about the need for punishment prevents us from fully recognising the consequences of punishment and finding ways of imagining how we might learn to do without it.

Ending punishment

There is precedent in recent human history for the dispensation of punishment. South Africa's Truth and Reconciliation Commission is an alternative example of how serious conflict can be dealt with and deep human suffering responded to. The specific conditions under which the Commission operated and had to respond were quite distinct from the problems of interpersonal harm that occur between citizens, as in the case of violent crimes (e.g., murder, rape, serious assault). The system of apartheid, the curtailment and denial of the rights of South African people and the struggles, violence and suffering that persisted there for over 45 years amounted to a prolonged and sustained attack on humanity. According to Desmond Tutu (1999), the atrocities that occurred throughout this time were difficult to comprehend and required a special response. It may not be possible to completely replicate the response taken in South Africa outside of those specific conditions. However, there are some important ideas to consider within the South African experience.

In Tutu's (ibid., p. 33) considerations of the Truth and Reconciliation Commission he describes the methods and approaches that were taken in relation to the hearing of evidence. Facts were established on the basis of a balance of probability, rather than on that required in criminal court proceedings, that is, beyond all reasonable doubt. He argues that because a central part of the Commission's mandate was to restore the human and civil dignity of victims, the hearings allowed those who came to testify to tell their stories in their own words. Through taking this approach, the Commission found that there were different orders of truth that were not necessarily mutually exclusive. Tutu differentiates between forensic factual truth, which is verifiable, and the truth of experience, a 'social truth', which might be thought about as the social meaning of the event or events that took place. This social truth is established through interaction, discussion and debate (Tutu, 1999, p. 33, citing Boraine and Levy, 1995). Tutu (1999, p. 34) states:

> The main thrust of most of the work of the Commission concerned victims and survivors of gross violations of human rights – taking statements from them, investigating their accounts, giving a cross-section of them a chance to tell their stories publicly and drafting

recommendations for reparations and rehabilitation to place before the government.

Centralising the experience of victims, and creating a public space in which they could recount their stories, in their own words, and openly share their pain and suffering with the wider community, would be a useful starting point if we were to embark upon a radical rethinking of criminal justice processes. Adversarial models of criminal justice (in particular) are constrained in their ability to bring into the open the multiple truths and personal experiences of interpersonal harm and violence. Criminal court proceedings are so heavily bound into procedure, process and custom that they are, in effect, unconcerned with establishing the social truth of crime and victim experience and are poorly designed to offer a path forward towards a reconciliatory form of justice.

The second important idea to highlight, and which emerged from the experience of the Truth and Reconciliation Commission, is more controversial and has been the subject of much debate and criticism. Tutu (ibid., pp. 33–4) writes:

> Our country's negotiators opted for a 'third way' that avoided the two extremes of the Nuremberg trials and blanket amnesty (or national amnesia). This third way was the granting of amnesty to individuals in exchange for a full disclosure relating to the crime for which amnesty was being sought … There are still major issues which this third way raises such as, was this approach going to encourage people to think they could commit crimes, knowing that they would get amnesty? Is it ever enough for perpetrators merely to apologise and be humiliated through public exposure? What about justice?

Tutu (ibid., p. 47) goes on to ask: 'Can it ever be right for someone who has committed the most gruesome atrocities to be allowed to get off scot-free, simply by confessing what he or she has done?' As already discussed, a number of thinkers on punishment have considered versions of this very question with respect to street crime (see Friedenberg, 1980; Gilligan, 2000). It should be remembered that amnesty was offered in the context of South Africa to people who had committed politically motivated acts of violence in systematic ways over a long period of time. In large measure these were crimes of the state (though the situation was messier than that tidy phrase might imply). The harm that this involved had very different motivations and was of a different order to that of interpersonal violent crime that individual citizens sometimes perpetrate against other citizens. But, is it impossible for us to think about reacting to these types of harms in similar ways?

Reconciliatory justice?

If we think, once again, about the idea of a coefficient of harm – that somewhere, as human beings, we are accumulating a net total of human-made pain and suffering, then this would mean that each time we perpetrate or condone an act of human-made pain (for example, either in the violence people sometimes cause each other or in the form of violence we call punishment) we are, in effect, piling more suffering onto already unthinkable levels of accumulating harm. It is difficult to think about these complex issues without falling back on moral arguments and sentiments. Our well-worn patterns of thinking about such things steer us towards questions of justice and just deserts again. But what would a system of justice with restricted moral underpinnings look like? As Garner's work seems to imply, it might be more fundamentally concerned with communication, dialogue and debate between injured parties with the end goal of reaching greater mutual understanding. This is not a call for restorative justice *per se*. As Juan Tauri (2009) has argued, the words restorative justice have been co-opted by so many different interest groups, government policies and so-called justice processes that they have become almost meaningless (or, more accurately, they have come to mean different things to different people and organisations). Further, I do not wish to advocate that restoration is ever really possible after acts of serious violence or harm have taken place. There is no way to fully restore people's lives to how they were before a traumatic, violent event occurred. The best that can be achieved is becoming reconciled with, or resigned to, what has happened and finding a way of living with how one's life has been irreversibly changed. But what might a reconciliatory form of justice mean for criminal justice processes?

Firstly, it is questionable whether it is appropriate for only the state to own the processes by which we attempt to reconcile ourselves to harms caused. As human history has revealed, the state is just as capable as individuals, corporations or other powerful groups to perpetrate harm. Therefore a more cooperative and representative approach to justice or reconciliation might be more appropriate – one that is collectively owned by communities and run within them. Secondly, a key goal of reconciliatory processes might be to radically reorient our focus towards acknowledging the harm that has been caused by the act of violence or other larger-scale (state, corporate or environmental) harm that has taken place. Such an endeavour would need to provide space for dialogue, communication and debate and thereby would signal the importance of working towards collective and mutual understanding. There would necessarily need to be a mechanism in place for keeping both victims and perpetrators safe from further harm (to each other or at the hands of the state, corporations or other sources of violence). In the case of violent individuals, it may be necessary to restrain them for a period of time in a locked facility. But the simple act of removing a person from society either for their own safety or the safety of other social members (or even the security of the state) need not be a punitive enterprise. If places called prisons only existed for the interests of safety, imprisonment could be conceived much more humanely as an environment that is safe, humane and respectful and that above all does no further harm. The way we react to harms caused need not include expressing the moral imperatives of vengeance or even forgiveness. For example it might be possible to strive for a much more complex set of goals. The goals of criminal justice processes might instead be aimed at acknowledging and fully exposing the awfulness, pain and degradation of violent events. Such goals may facilitate collective understanding, meaning and social truth – from a variety of perspectives. This is as important for the perpetrators of harm as it is for the victims and for society at large. Likewise, it is also important for us all to understand more fully the processes that lead to violence. There is little space in existing criminal justice practice for us to fully comprehend the events that lead people (or states or corporations) to serious acts of harm. Furthermore current criminal justice arrangements offer little in the way of overcoming what has happened and forging a different future in the face of the harm perpetrated. Both perpetrators and victims need a way of being released from the harm that has been caused in order to start new beginnings. It is possible that nothing that went before can be restored, but a different future can be embarked upon that creates reasonable possibilities for healing or different ways of generating more positive practices or, at the very least, neutral outcomes for all parties.

These ideas are difficult to think about. Such goals for a new system of justice are somewhat lofty and do not come with an easy road on which to reach them. Despite the complexity of the solutions needed to resolve these issues there is much to be gained by thinking such thoughts and engaging in the debates that they will inevitably provoke.

If we are, indeed, moving towards a more globalised world then we are inevitably exposing ourselves to different cultures, beliefs, values, ways of thinking and traditions. In this context it seems unwise to set forth moral arguments that are rooted in one particular philosophy or another. As human history has illustrated – all too well – human beings have significant difficulty agreeing on what we believe in and a great deal of human suffering has been caused by defending moral, religious or other dogmatic beliefs. As Garner (2011, p. 5) has argued: 'If indeed a belief in morality is the next and final delusion to be overcome, it is never too early to start.' Restricting ourselves to only one moral imperative – the reduction of human-inflicted pain on earth (Christie, 2007) – may help to curtail the ongoing proliferation of ever more moralities, which, as we have seen, have only stood in the way of us thinking more carefully about actual solutions to our most difficult social problems. The belief in morality has also often prevented us from noticing and acknowledging the social, structural and economic inequalities inherent in political systems and has, therefore, served to perpetuate conditions that lead to greater human suffering and violence. As Gilligan (2000, p. 771) has stated:

> The problems of crime and violence can only be solved by reforming our social and economic system, and reformulating the cultural and moral values that have produced that system and are in turn reinforced by it. A good first step in that direction would be to renounce the quixotic illusion that revenge (punishment) can inhibit or prevent violence.

Conclusion

This book is not so much a call to action but a call to inaction – at least with respect to those forms of action that result in greater levels of human suffering. It has sought to provide a number of reasons why thinking more carefully and critically is important. The foregoing chapters have attempted to expose the problems associated with the use of imprisonment and punishment and with some of the methods that states use to pursue security and safety, as well as to draw attention to the inevitable difficulty that human beings have living peaceably together. It has sought to make clear that all of these problems are multidimensional and complicated further by other social forces, such as political decision-making, unequal distributions of power and wealth, individual contingency and plurality, as well as embedded moral, legal and ideological structures. Quinney (2000, p. 194) has stated that in criminology 'our underlying questions are these: how are we human beings to live? Who are we and of what are we capable? And how could things be different?'

This book has not provided any easy, overarching answers to Quinney's questions that we can apply, without fail, to resolve our most serious social problems. Those sorts of answers cannot be found. Nonetheless, societies have spent much time attempting to apply simple solutions (like prisons and harsh punishment) to extremely complex and difficult problems that have done little to contribute to our greater understanding. Likewise, states continue to pursue strategies of security that exclude individuals, divide social groups, undermine social well-being and promote intolerance and increasing individualism. Nothing promotes increased conflict better than more violence. By contrast, the best way we know of to diffuse conflict is through some form of mediation and the making of compromises and negotiation. On this Christie (2004, pp. 98–9) has argued:

> [A]trocities are general features of human history, part of our destiny. Many nations have been involved, as victims or as perpetrators, often as both ... We must find ways of both preventing and reacting to atrocities where we mobilise the common stock of knowledge on how to handle social conflicts ... But if the acts are fully, completely out of the usual? ... Can they be seen in a peace creating framework? Am I willing to negotiate with the Devil in Hell or with those seen as his brothers? Again, I am.

Our unfortunately vast experience of human suffering has illustrated that the most powerful weapon we have for diffusing hatred, intolerance, xenophobia and conflict is to build understanding. Joel Harvey (2011) has recently suggested that the goal of understanding other human beings is noticeably absent from much contemporary criminal justice policy, rhetoric and official practice. It is absent, too, from political decision-making about how to create safer and more secure societies and build greater social well-being. This book has not set out to provide a clear, practical first step towards how we get from our present circumstances to more universally humane, understanding, secure, inclusive and equal societies. However, it has provided some of the evidence and thinking we might use to begin to discuss what this first step might usefully be. While it is true that it is within the capacity of human beings to cause pain and suffering to one another, it is also within our capacity to empathise, cooperate and collaborate on finding solutions to difficult problems. Perhaps creating more opportunities for us to do so might be our first practical step.

Appendix: Research Methods and Reflections on Researching Maximum-Security Prisons

Brief research outline

This book has drawn on two related research projects. The initial study was a qualitative comparison of quality of prison life, order and legitimacy in two maximum-security prisons (Full Sutton and Whitemoor) in 2005. The subsequent study, which took place from 2007–09 was an extension of the first, but focused more heavily on prisoner experiences and included the other three long-term, maximum-security prisons (Frankland, Wakefield and Long Lartin). Both studies were concerned with gaining an in-depth understanding of long-term, maximum-security imprisonment from the various perspectives of those who are subjected to it. To develop a deeper understanding of life in maximum-security prisons the research included access to all of the long-term, maximum-security prisons in England. This was the first time a researcher had unrestricted and unlimited access to all of the long-term, maximum-security prisons in a single jurisdiction to carry out qualitative, ethnographic research. This research was different from most previous qualitative studies in this area because it included sustained and concentrated researcher exposure to a variety of different maximum-security prison environments. Such levels of access consequently allowed for the recognition of institution-specific peculiarities and provided the opportunity to draw out the broad patterns and commonalities between prison environments. In addition to the findings discussed in this volume, the research projects yielded a vast array of findings pertinent to organisational dynamics, the importance of institutional differences, the dynamics of prisoner societies, staff–prisoner relationships, and the problems of prison management (see Drake, 2006, 2009).

The prisons

At the time that the research took place (2005–09) and at the time of writing there were five long-term, maximum-security prisons in England: Frankland, Full Sutton, Long Lartin, Wakefield and Whitemoor. There are also three other prisons encompassed within the Directorate of High Security: Belmarsh, Manchester and Woodhill. These prisons, however, are local prisons and are part of the high-security estate due to their capacity to hold Category A prisoners on remand. They are not long-term prisons.

A brief summary of each of the prisons in which the research took place is provided below in order to provide some detail about each institution's location, capacity and speciality. I also have included characterisations of each prison from prisoners' perspectives. Before presenting these summaries, however, it is perhaps useful to define the four types of special units that maximum-security prisons sometimes encompass: vulnerable-prisoner units, dangerous and severe personality disordered units, close supervision centres and special security units.

Specialised units

Maximum-security prisons (and some lower category prisons) in England often manage separate wings or units and run separate regimes for vulnerable prisoners. Vulnerable or Rule 45 prisoners (Rule 49 for young offenders) are those who are segregated from the general prison population. In broad terms there are two groups of prisoners segregated under this rule:

- those who need or wish to be segregated for their own protection;
- those who are placed in segregation for the maintenance of good order and discipline (GOAD).

Prisoners who are on Rule 45 for GOAD are generally housed in segregation units for a period of time and are considered disruptive rather than vulnerable. Of those prisoners who fall under the first point above, there are several reasons certain prisoners might need or want to be segregated for their own protection, such as:

- if a prisoner's offence puts him at risk of attack from other prisoners (e.g., those who have committed sexual offences);
- if a prisoner has difficulty coping with prison life;
- if a prisoner has given intelligence information about another prisoner and he needs to be protected from retaliation;
- if a prisoner has been bullied by or is in debt to another prisoner;
- if a prisoner is trying to remove himself from illicit activities (such as drugs) within prison.

In the legal jurisdiction of England and Wales, many prisons operate vulnerable prisoner units (VPUs) for prisoners who are segregated for their own protection. VPUs serve to protect vulnerable prisoners whilst providing a regime and activities that are as close as possible to those that are offered to mainstream prisoners.

Dangerous and Severe Personality Disordered (DSPD) units house prisoners who have been diagnosed with a severe personality disorder and who, because of their disorder, are considered to pose a risk of serious offending. DSPD units are a joint initiative between the Prison Service and the National Health Service (NHS) (see Home Office, 1999).

Close Supervision Centres (CSC) are small units designed to house prisoners who are extremely disruptive. These units were established in 1987, based on recommendations of the Control Review Committee (Home Office, 1984), which argued that the removal of the most disruptive prisoners into smaller units would contribute to the overall order amongst the general population of maximum-security prisons (for a review of the treatment of disruptive prisoners in small units see Liebling, 2001).

Special Security Units (SSUs) were originally opened in 1965 for the purposes of housing prisoners who require the highest levels of security arrangements in the whole of the prison system (Sparks et al., 1996, p. 12; Bottoms and Hay, 1996; see also Walmsley, 1989).

HMP Frankland

Frankland is located in Durham and, at the time of the research, had the operational capacity to house 734 prisoners. Building works to expand the capacity at Frankland were underway during the research. The prison ran three regimes, one for the management of vulnerable prisoners, one for mainstream prisoners and one for prisoners located in the DSPD Unit, which at Frankland was called Westgate Unit. Broadly speaking, relationships between staff and prisoners in Frankland were amongst the least fractious across the dispersal system. In the most general terms, the overall atmosphere of Frankland, according to many prisoners, was 'reasonable, calm and generally safe'. However, as with all the dispersal prisons there were individual prisoners who experienced Frankland as a dangerous and unpredictable environment. Moreover, just prior to and just after the research there were some acts of extreme violence between prisoners at Frankland, perhaps suggesting that that atmosphere at Frankland was changing.

HMP Full Sutton

Full Sutton is located in the village of Full Sutton, 11 miles east of the City of York. At the time of the research it had the operational capacity to house 608 prisoners. The prison ran two regimes, one for the management of vulnerable prisoners (who made up 50 per cent of the population) and one for mainstream prisoners. The SSU at Full Sutton was reopened in the latter half of 2005 (though it was closed when the majority of this research took place) to house some of the prisoners charged in relation to the London bombings in July 2005. Full Sutton has had a troubled history of prisoner riots and other forms of collective prisoner disorder (Drake, 2006, 2008, 2009). This history seemed to have left a lasting legacy of contentious staff–prisoner relationships. During the research Full Sutton was characterised by prisoners as 'heavily controlled, inflexible, and unsafe'.

HMP Long Lartin

Long Lartin is located in Evesham, Worcestershire, and at the time of the research had the operational capacity to house 492 prisoners. Long Lartin was one of the original prisons included in the dispersal system, taking its first dispersal prisoners in 1973 (Home Office, 1984). The prison was undergoing building works to open two further residential wings at the time of the research. There were five residential wings at Long Lartin and a detainee unit. Just prior to the time of the research, Long Lartin re-roled one of its wings to cater for the needs of vulnerable prisoners. Some of Long Lartin's history has been captured in the previous research of Sparks, Bottoms and Hay in *Prisons and the Problem of Order* (1996). It was characterised throughout its early history as 'the only dispersal prison to have held fast throughout to the founding principles of a "liberal regime within a secure perimeter"' (Sparks et al., 1996, p. 105). However, this history was also marred by problems of safety between prisoners (Bottoms, 1999, p. 242). At the time of the research Long Lartin was difficult to broadly characterise. Certain areas of the prison were reported as safe by prisoners; others were seen as less so. Likewise, staff–prisoner relationships seemed to vary according to wing location. Although the research revealed that each prison included a vast mixture of different organisational cultures (often associated with particular wings, working groups or distinct areas), Long Lartin was perhaps the most differentiated in terms of both prisoner experiences and staff practices.

HMP Wakefield

Wakefield is located in Wakefield, West Yorkshire, and at the time of the research had the operational capacity to house 751 prisoners. The prison was operating as a main lifer prison with a particular focus on those who had committed sexual offences. As a result of this focus, the prisoner population at Wakefield primarily comprised vulnerable prisoners. Wakefield is the oldest prison in the dispersal system (a prison has been located on the Wakefield site since 1594). At the time of the research Wakefield was broadly characterised by prisoners as controlled (and many prisoners argued overcontrolled). The atmosphere between prisoners was viewed as reasonable and safe, but staff–prisoner relationships were viewed by many prisoners as strained by perceived overuses of authority on the part of staff.

HMP Whitemoor

Whitemoor is located in March, Cambridgeshire, and at the time of the research had the operational capacity to house 452 prisoners. The prison included two wings for mainstream prisoners, one wing for vulnerable prisoners and a wing designated as a DSPD Unit (since renamed The Fens Unit). Whitemoor also has a SSU, but at the time of this research it had been converted into a CSC. At the time of the research Whitemoor was broadly characterised by prisoners as orderly, relatively predictable and reasonably safe. However, staff–prisoner relationships were heavily constrained by the problem of security. Across the dispersal system Whitemoor presented the archetypical, starkest and most salient example of the problems of security.

The population

As discussed in Chapter 5, the population of maximum-security prisons in England is not strictly comprised of prisoners who require conditions of highest security. Many prisoners in dispersal prisons could, in theory, be allocated to a Category B establishment. The main criterion for being allocated to a dispersal prison is sentence length. Thus the population in dispersal prisons tends to primarily be made up of men serving life or long fixed-term sentences. Figure A.1 below shows the sentence lengths, in years, of the dispersal prisoner population at the time when the two research projects took place. All of the figures in this section are based on snapshots of the entire dispersal population, which was 2,900, at the time that the research projects took place.[1]

At the time of the research projects, around 60 per cent (1,725 out of 2,900) of the total population of dispersal prisoners were serving life or indeterminate sentences.[2] These sentences are represented in Figure A.1 as 99 years. All of the other sentence lengths in the figure are fixed terms. As Chapter 5 discussed, the definition of a life sentence in the United Kingdom does not, generally, mean life without the eligibility for parole. There are only about 30 men serving whole-life tariffs – without eligibility for parole (these men are included in the 99 lifers category in Figure A.1). However, ordinary lifers will generally serve a mandatory period of time inside prison (the usual starting point for a mandatory in-prison tariff for murder in England and Wales is 15 years, (see Appleton and Grøver, 2007, p. 602)). After completing this mandatory minimum tariff in prison, prisoners may apply for parole and release on life licence. If they are granted parole, the life-sentenced prisoner will be released from prison, but will remain on licence. Their licence will include certain restrictions and potential penalties that the lifer will be subjected to for the rest of his or her life. However, there is no guarantee that prisoners will be granted parole on their tariff expiry (see Padfield, 2002) and, as Chapter 5 illustrated, there can be much uncertainty and insecurity amongst prisoners concerning the question of whether they will ever be released.

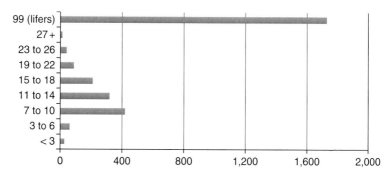

Figure A.1   Sentence lengths

In addition to sentence length the other main consideration made when allocating prisoners to a dispersal prison is their security categorisation. Indeed, across the prison system the security category of a prisoner and the particular prison establishment he or she will be sent to are determined based on a number of interrelated factors, including: length of sentence (as above), severity of offence, previous convictions, locality, and sex or age (i.e., there are specific establishments designated for women or for young people). In addition, a prisoner's behaviour whilst in prison can affect their security categorisation (usually prisoners work towards reducing their security category over the course of their sentence, although – rarely – security designations can be increased when a prisoner has been particularly disruptive within prison).

Figure A.2 shows the security categorisations of the prisoner population at the time of the respective research projects. Around 74 per cent (2,139 out of 2,900) were Category B prisoners and 23 per cent (663 out of 2,900) were designated as Category A. High-risk, Category A prisoners make up a special category who often occupy special security units in dispersals. However, not all high-risk prisoners will be in an SSU, though their movements within the prison will be more heavily monitored and controlled than the general population. They are often prisoners who have been designated as an escape risk. There were a relatively small number of prisoners allocated to this category at the time of the research projects (45 out of 2,900, i.e., about 1.5 per cent). (The remaining 1.5 per cent were unspecified, probably awaiting categorisation.)

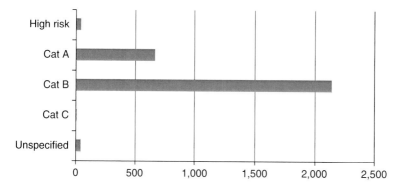

Figure A.2   Security categorisations

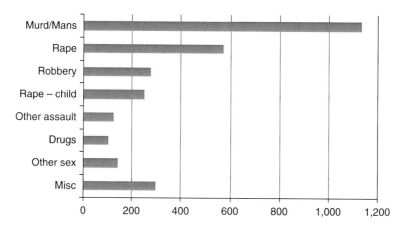

Figure A.3   Criminal convictions

Dispersal prisons have always housed the small proportion of prisoners who have been convicted of very serious crimes (e.g., terrorism, large-scale drug importation/exportation, espionage, etc.) or prolific violent crimes (e.g., serial or mass murder). This population is a tiny minority. Apart from the few prisoners who require the very highest conditions of security, the crimes for which prisoners in dispersals are convicted are not markedly different from those of prisoners serving in Category B establishments (e.g., HMCIP, 2001). Figure A.3 shows the criminal convictions for which dispersal prisoners were serving their sentences at the time of the research. I have created broader categories for some of the convictions because representing each category of conviction would have been unwieldy in graphic representation.

The category of 'murd/mans' in Figure A.3 stands for murder/manslaughter and includes murder, attempted murder, manslaughter and murder of a child. As is evident in the figure, this is the largest category and 39 per cent of the population in dispersals have been convicted of these types of crimes (1,134 out of 2,900). Rape is the second most common conviction for which dispersal prisoners were serving their sentences at the time of this research, accounting for 20 per cent of the dispersal prisoner population. The rape category includes sexual assault and buggery. Robbery includes, robbery, attempted robbery and conspiracy to rob. Rape of a child includes sexual assault of a person under 13 and buggery. The 'other assault' category includes grievous bodily harm (GBH), actual bodily harm (ABH), wounding and wounding with intent. The drugs category includes supply and importation of drugs. The 'other sex' category includes other sexual offences, including indecent assault of adults or children, trespassing with intent to commit a sexual offence and indecent photographing of children. The miscellaneous category includes a very wide range of convictions that were low in number amongst dispersal prisoners, including, for example, arson, burglary, terrorism, possession of a firearm, blackmail, kidnapping or false imprisonment (amongst a wide variety of other convictions).

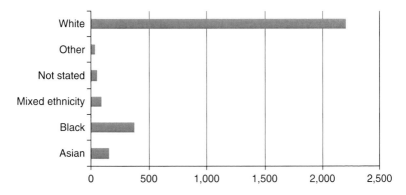

Figure A.4   Ethnic backgrounds

Finally, I also present a representation of the ethnic categories of prisoners in dispersal prisons. Again for the ease of graphic representation I have collapsed some of the categories.

As Figure A.4 reveals, most of the men in maximum-security prisons at the time of the research projects identified as white (2,203 out of 2,900 or 76 per cent), the vast majority of which identified as white British. The next largest category comprised black prisoners (372 out of 2,900 or around 13 per cent), the majority of whom identified as black British (though the next largest category identified as black Caribbean). The third largest category identified as Asian (149 out of 2,900 or around 5 per cent), which included men who identified also as Pakistani or Bangladeshi. Foreign nationals made up a small proportion of the dispersal prisoner population at the time of the research, but were not counted separately within the above figures.

Research methods

Both studies on which this book is based used similar methodological approaches. Indeed, the second study was, in essence, an extension of the first.

The second study did, however, include a small team of research assistants (see Drake, in preparation, for more detail). However, I carried out the majority of the ethnographic aspects of the research and all of the analysis myself. The descriptions of the research methods that follow, therefore, encompass both research projects.

A historically grounded account

The research designs of both studies sought to construct a historically grounded account of contemporary institutional relations and penal arrangements. Both studies aimed to situate current issues associated with prison life within both the contemporary and historical contexts of each prison and within wider penal policy formations. Studying an organisation's history can provide valuable cultural and contextual information about the inner workings of that organisation and about the nature of local realities and how cultural behaviour operates (Bowles, 1990; Gabriel, 1992, 1993). Historical context, meaningful events, organisational myth and folklore, and the stories people pass on to one another and the discourses or narratives they use inevitably shape the way people interpret their environment and their practices (Gabriel, 1993; Hall, 1997). Previous research on prisons has suggested that it is important to understand prisons as places and that the history of a particular prison can affect day-to-day prison life through organisational culture and historically established practices (Cohen and Taylor, 1972, pp. 112–5; Bottoms and Sparks 1997, p. 16). It was this recognition of the importance of grounding contemporary prison practice in wider penal sentiment and in historical organisational and institutional context that influenced the design of the research projects and provided the rationale for collecting historical as well as contemporary accounts.

The construction of meaning within organisations includes an interaction between discursive practices, shared interpretations of significant past events, and the way policies are implemented and put into practice (Schein, 2004, pp. 11–21). In order to capture such meanings and the sentiment of organisational and institutional context it was necessary to draw on numerous sources of information. Some academic literature was available on the history of dispersals (e.g., Sparks et al., 1996; Liebling, 2002) and detailed previous research had also been conducted in three out of five of these prisons (Sparks et al., 1996; Liebling, et al., 1997; Liebling and Price 1999). In addition, numerous existing Prison Service and Home Office policy documents and research studies were examined, including, commissioned reports (research, inquiry and evaluation), committee reports, Inspectorate reports, Independent Monitoring Board reviews, the Prison Service Journal and private papers from various governors. Finally, a considerable number of retrospective history interviews and informal conversations were undertaken as separate parts of both research studies.

Original materials were generated through 43 in-depth oral history interviews with both ordinary and key figures in the history of maximum-security prisons and within all of the institutions, including long-serving prison staff, former prison governors, civil servants, and senior managers in the Prison Service. These interviews were conducted separately from the interviews discussed below that were undertaken during the ethnographic phases of the research. In both research projects the history interviews began prior to entering each of the prisons and were not fully completed until after the ethnographic phases were finished. Participants were invited to take part in a history interview based on their length of service within the individual prison establishments or within the organisation. The semi-structured interview schedule included standard sets of questions as well as those tailored to the specifics of each institution. The interviews sought to capture individual work histories, shared (or divergent) interpretations of key past events and signifying moments either in individual prison establishments, within the wider organisation or the broader penal or political context.

An ethnographic approach

Both research studies used an ethnographic approach, where ethnography is defined as 'a research process in which the anthropologist closely observes, records, and engages in the daily life of another culture – an experience labelled as the fieldwork method – and then writes accounts of this culture emphasizing descriptive detail' (Marcus and Fischer, 1986, p. 18). The research included a cumulative total of 14 months of fieldwork. Between them, the two projects yielded over 450 hours of observation, over 350 typed pages of field notes, 105 in-depth, semi-structured interviews with prison staff (civilians, officers and governors) and 204[3] in-depth, semi-structured interviews with prisoners.

Observations were carried out in all areas of the prisons (e.g., the gym, chaplaincy, workshops, education, segregation units, healthcare and kitchens). Much of the research time was spent 'hanging around' on the landings with prisoners or in wing offices with discipline staff. Formal interviews were conducted in addition to observations and informal discussions.

Staff and managers were invited to participate in formal interviews on the basis of their position, location or function. Care was taken to include a cross section of staff from different areas of the prison and who served different functions (e.g., chaplains, nurses, psychologists, education or workshop staff). However, discipline staff (those who worked on the landings with direct contact with prisoners) made up the majority of those interviewed. Further, the majority of the staff interviewed were male (which was commensurate with the overall staff group) and most were white British (there were very few members of staff working in maximum-security prisons from other ethnic backgrounds). Staff were invited to participate in person (no one who was asked to participate refused) and consent forms were signed at the time of the interviews, each of which was arranged at a time and date that was chosen by each interviewee. Both staff and prisoner interviews were conducted in wing offices or association rooms on the landings. All of the interviews (except for three prisoners who refused to be tape-recorded) were recorded and fully transcribed.

Prisoners who participated in in-depth interviews were selected using snowball, opportunistic and purposeful sampling and included a representative sample according to the population demographics of each prison (based on ethnic composition, sentence lengths, age, offence type and security category). Prisoners were invited to take part in an interview using a three-step process. Firstly, they were asked face to face if they would like to take part in a formal interview. Secondly, if they agreed, in principle, to participate (very few refused) they were then given a letter explaining in greater detail what the study was about, provided with examples of the types of questions they might expect to be asked and were given a consent form for the research. These documents were provided well in advance of the interview (and indeed before an interview date and time had even been agreed) in order to provide prisoners with the time to more fully consider whether or not they wished to participate (no one who initially agreed to an interview withdrew, though three did refuse to be tape-recorded). Finally, several days after prisoners received the documents explaining the research, the example questions and the consent forms, they were approached and asked if they were still willing to participate (all were) and a time and date were then agreed upon for interview. These procedures for gaining consent were used in order to ensure prisoners were fully aware of the scope and purpose of the study and had an appropriate amount of time to think about whether or not they wanted to participate.

Both staff and prisoner interviews were concerned with in-prison experiences and not life histories. Staff interviews focused on working conditions, relationships (colleague, governor, prisoner), aspects of the work they found difficult or rewarding, attitudes towards prisoners, and working practices. These interviews ranged from 30 to 85 minutes in length, and, on average, lasted 60 minutes.

Prisoner interviews focused on experiences of imprisonment and provided prisoners with the opportunity to discuss their in-prison lives in whatever ways they chose. A semi-structured interview schedule was used that included questions on material conditions, relationships (prisoner, staff, governor, family), aspects of their experiences they found difficult or helpful, how they accessed social support and how they managed (i.e., coped with) their sentences. However, there was often little need to rely on the interview schedule because prisoners' self-directed discussions about prison life generally covered the range of issues that the interview schedule included. Prisoner interviews ranged from 45 to 180 minutes in length, and, on average, lasted 90 minutes.

The research and analysis followed a constructivist grounded theory approach, which included the simultaneous collection and analysis of data, comparative methods, in-field refinement of theoretical ideas, and focused methods of data-coding (see Glaser, 1978, 1992; Charmaz, 2000). These methods allowed for an inductive, data-led approach that was consistent with the overall ethnographic design of the research projects. Qualitative and grounded methods were used for both studies in order to take account of subjective and personalised assessments of experiences of imprisonment and punishment.

Qualitative data analysis

All of the formal interviews were taped and fully transcribed. The qualitative data (including field notes) were analysed by identifying overarching and subsidiary themes. Although the transcription of the interviews did not take place until after the fieldwork was completed, emergent themes and the beginnings of a coding system emerged during the research. Due to the time lag between the two research studies (which was two years) the findings from the first study were fully analysed, digested, reflected upon and written up (as a doctoral thesis) prior to beginning the second study. This sequence allowed aspects of the first study to inform the analysis of data from the second. Thus the second study was entered into with an existing coding framework available. Although it was not assumed that the coding system created in the first study would necessarily map onto the findings from the second, the broadest themes were shown to be relatively consistent between the two studies.

In addition to the above, further analyses were undertaken for the purposes of this book. This reanalysis was conducted in several iterations, each time seeking to draw out the essence of the experience of long-term imprisonment and the broadest and most constant themes that commonly emerged between the prisons. Distilling the research findings in this way brought into clearer focus the most salient and enduring findings from the research and formed the basis on which this book is presented and organised. In particular, the overarching importance of the concept of security became more and more apparent as the analyses progressed. Examining these findings in relation to other criminological considerations of security suggested that they may be indicative of wider processes and needed to be understood within wider social and political frameworks.

Measuring quality of prison life surveys

The first study, on which my doctoral thesis was based, included the collection of survey data from staff and prisoners. This data was collected for the purposes of attempting to quantify the qualitative experiences of prisoners and staff in the two prisons. (Similar survey data was not collected during the second research project, as will be discussed below). The survey used during the initial study was the Measuring Quality of Life (MQPL) survey, originally developed by Alison Liebling and Helen Arnold (see Liebling and Arnold, 2002, 2004).

The original staff and prisoner MQPL surveys were developed by Liebling and Arnold under the Home Office Research Development and Statistics Directorate's Innovative Research Grant Scheme. Developed in consultation with staff and prisoners, the MQPL surveys include dimensions related to what matters about prison life. Examples of some of these dimensions include, prisoner relationships, respect, humanity, staff–prisoner relationships, support, trust, fairness, order, safety, well-being, personal growth, family contact and decency. These dimensions are represented in specific survey statements. The format of the questionnaire presents participants with statements, such as 'I feel that I am treated with respect by staff in this prison', and they are asked to rate, on a five-point Likert scale, the extent to which they agree or disagree with the statements (the scale ranges from strongly agree to strongly disagree).

For the purposes of the first research project both staff and prisoner MQPL surveys were slightly modified to try to reflect some of the themes that emerged during the qualitative fieldwork in order to tailor the MQPL to the specificities of dispersal prisons (see Drake, 2006). Whilst the survey results revealed broad agreement with the overall findings of the qualitative research, they did not reveal the nuance of long-term prison experiences. In essence, the survey revealed low scores on prisoner quality of life in both dispersal prisons (with few significant differences), but the survey was too blunt an instrument with which to capture the specific ways that the environments of each prison contributed to those low assessments. However, because the MQPL survey revealed generally low scores across both prisons and between prisoner groups (main wing and vulnerable prisoners), the results may be interpreted to concur with the overall conclusion that prisoners' perceptions of their experiences of long-term, dispersal imprisonment were generally negative. This hypothesis seemed to hold up when their survey results were compared with other (lower security) prisons[4] (see Drake, 2006). Due to the lack of nuance revealed in the MQPL results in the first study and because the second study was concerned with focusing more heavily on the qualitative experiences of prisoners in the other three dispersal prisons, MQPL survey data was not collected during the second study (also, the Prison Service routinely collects this data in dispersals).

Reflections on researching maximum-security prisons

I conclude this Appendix with some final reflections on the challenges and difficulties of conducting research in men's maximum-security prisons. Access to all five men's maximum-security prisons in England provided a unique opportunity to explore these closed worlds. However, this access brought with it particular tensions. These final reflections on the research provide a more reflective account of the difficulties that I experienced in negotiating these prison worlds in order to understand the perspectives of prisoners and the realities of their criminal convictions.

Access, gatekeepers and 'doing your time'

Gaining access to undertake PhD research in high-security prisons was entirely facilitated by my PhD supervisor, Professor Alison Liebling. Her reputation within the Prison Service as a careful and sensitive researcher had been built up over numerous research projects and, as a result, she had a trusting relationship with Prison Service senior managers, which she (and they) graciously extended to her PhD students.

Findings from my PhD research facilitated my being asked to undertake the second research project in dispersals. The Whitemoor–Full Sutton research had revealed (among other findings) that prisoners experienced those two prisons as 'repressive' environments. In addition, my finding that the MQPL survey in its original format was perhaps too blunt an instrument to draw out the differences between dispersals corroborated findings from MQPL surveys carried out in dispersals by the Prison Service. My findings on the repressiveness experienced by prisoners coupled with the question of the utility of the MQPL survey in dispersals piqued the curiosity of Prison Service senior managers. I was subsequently asked, therefore, to undertake similar ethnographic work in the other three maximum-security prisons, focusing specifically on prisoner experiences, and with the intention of devising a qualitative measure of prisoner quality of life for use in dispersals that could be administered by the staff (further details of this project can be found in Drake, 2009, and see Drake, in preparation). This second research project, therefore, was greatly facilitated by coordination and support from senior managers in the Directorate of High Security and the continued guidance of Professor Liebling.

For both the PhD research and the subsequent dispersal study I was granted unrestricted access. I was given keys (though not at first, due to awaiting security clearance to carry keys, so I experienced both conducting the research with keys and without) and was not prevented from visiting any parts of any of the prisons. The question of keys often arises when prison researchers discuss their methods. Roy King (2000) has argued that although researchers differ on whether or not to carry keys, his stance has been never to do so. In his view (ibid., p. 305), 'the possession of keys is so symbolic of the difference between freedom and captivity that it would place the researcher too close to staff'. I did not have a position on whether or not to carry keys prior to undertaking the research, nor did I feel compromised by accepting them once they were offered. However, having experienced the research setting both with and without keys I came to the view that the experience of the research was vastly improved by the acquisition of keys. I was significantly hindered when not carrying keys and acquiring them subsequently allowed me access to areas and people that I might not have otherwise been able to reach. Without keys I was fully reliant on staff to collect me from the gate, accompany me around the prison and remain in close proximity to me as I spoke to prisoners. In many respects, a researcher is in the control of staff when they are without keys, which can result in being managed by them when they only allow the researcher to enter certain areas, but not others, or limit how much time is spent in particular places. The time I was able to spend with prisoners was short when I did not have keys. I also felt as though my presence in the prison was more burdensome to staff. I could not fade into the background if a member of staff felt they had to be responsible for me. In the security regime of maximum-security prisons, if one is without keys, one cannot be left in prisoner areas without staff accompaniment.

Prisoners' experiences are obviously frustrated by keylessness, and experiencing that sense of powerlessness or being in the power of those who hold keys was of value as a researcher. However, there are so many other ways in which prison researchers cannot fully appreciate the prisoner experience that refusing keys seemed like a tokenistic stance to take, which only added a further barrier between myself and prisoners because it ensured that I could not get access to them without the help of staff. As for King's concern about the symbolic power of carrying keys, I did not at any time feel too closely aligned with staff, nor did I think I was perceived by prisoners as being so. Indeed, I was rarely even mistaken for a member of civilian staff. My first appearances in each of the prisons usually resulted in immediate questions from prisoners about who I was because I was evidently not a member of the institution. In addition, at Whitemoor, for example, when I acquired keys (after a period of time operating without them) prisoners were pleased and relieved because it meant I could come to see them unescorted and unhindered by staff and could speak with them more freely (without officers hovering about).

There was only one recurring scenario when I felt disconcerted by the power of keys. At Full Sutton I frequently found myself in a position of being asked to unlock the gate for a particular prisoner who needed to access the laundry room (which was his job, but the laundry room was locked off from the landings and the laundry workers had to depend on officers to let them in and out of the laundry room at regular intervals throughout the day). On these occasions I felt uncomfortable about having keys and the division it highlighted between me and this particular prisoner (who was not one of my interviewees). However, I endeavoured to overcome this each day by explaining to this prisoner that the fact that I had keys did not mean that I had any authority or power over him or that I was, in any way, a part of 'the system' – to which, this prisoner always replied: 'I'm not bothered about all that, Miss. I just want to get this laundry done.' In some ways, his response suggested to me that the idea of keys having symbolic power is more salient and meaningful to researchers (and probably to staff) than it is to prisoners who see anyone who is not a prisoner as a literal outsider anyway.

With respect to my access within each prison, I was able to spend as much time in whatever areas I so chose and without having to arrange this in advance, though I often did so out of courtesy. Despite this level of formally agreed access, however, informal access and the negotiation of relationships with staff (in particular) and prisoners (to a lesser extent) needed to take place on an interactional level every day of the research in each one of the prisons. This was an exceptionally difficult aspect of both studies, which may have been complicated by the fact that these were men's maximum-security prisons and I am a woman. (This issue explicitly came up occasionally in relation to security concerns of the staff.) However, it seemed to me that the more pressing problem was that maximum-security thinking (as described in Chapter 4) created an environment of extreme suspicion and distrust that was difficult to overcome.

Due to the unusual access I had to each of the prisons and the rarity of sociological researchers in maximum-security prisons generally (though some of them are more researched than others), there was some level of suspicion (from both staff and prisoners) about what my true purposes were. On top of this, however, was the pervasiveness of general suspicion associated with security-thinking and the atmosphere that this created. Staff were not only suspicious of me and of prisoners, but often of each other. Although high levels of collegiality seemed to be enjoyed amongst staff groups across all five dispersals, all staff relationships seemed to have an edge to them. Small close-knit groups of staff could and did form small circles of trust, but the diameter of their circles did not extend out much beyond their close-knit group.

One of indications of the way trust was withdrawn or eroded in collegial relationships between staff was if a member of staff appeared to be too friendly with prisoners. As a researcher who needed to walk a fine line between staff and prisoners and not appear to be too friendly with either group for fear of stirring suspicion in the other, this was an exceptionally difficult task. Moreover, the division between staff and prisoners and the construction of prisoners as other meant that for me as a researcher, the prison staff were a more difficult group to negotiate with. That is, prisoners could understand why it was I needed to spend time with the staff – both for the sake of the research and because they could act as gatekeepers. However some staff seemed to have genuine difficulty understanding why I would want to speak to prisoners or why I would want to understand their perspectives and experiences. Despite the fact that I carried keys and had formal access, staff could still act as gatekeepers, and sometimes they did, particularly those who had difficulty understanding why I would want to interview, spend time with and have conversations with prisoners.

There were a number of ways staff could attempt to block access to prisoners. For example, they could avoid unlocking them (I did not have cell keys) or refuse to give access to an interview room when I had arranged a formal interview with someone. Such actions on the part of staff did not happen often, but I felt as though I had to work hard to avoid such eventualities and, therefore, tried to negotiate carefully with staff. I endeavoured to spend fairly even amounts of time with staff and with prisoners, which seemed to ensure that gatekeeping was kept to a minimum, though it remained a constant concern.

During the process of undertaking each of these research projects it seemed important that I was seen to be 'putting in time' (as King, 2000, has argued). In order to earn the respect of both staff and prisoners it was necessary to be visible and to spend a lot of time in the establishments. Although this was part of the ethnographic nature of the research, it also seemed to facilitate research relationships, contributed to rapport-building and allowed people to feel more comfortable about a researcher being present. Throughout both of the projects I spent long days (often 12-hour days and rarely less than eight hours) in the prisons and regularly spent five days a week in them (and on a few occasions six days a week). Methodologically, I wanted to ensure I spent enough time in each of the prisons to carry out similar types of observations, undertake comparable formal interviews and develop an understanding of staff and prisoner cultures in each institution. However it seemed that once I began entering the establishments it became important that I spend as much time in them as was practicable in order to build up enough trust, tolerance and familiarity to ease the research process and maintain momentum. Thus the periods of time I spent in each dispersal were intense and 'deep'. Whilst this was exceptionally difficult (as well as physically, emotionally and intellectually demanding and distressing) it resulted in my gaining a fuller and more nuanced understanding of each of the establishments and gave me the foundation on which to build the broader analyses on which this book is based.

Research with men convicted of serious acts of harm

In addition to my reflections above on the research process, it is also relevant for me to include within this Appendix some reflections on the experience of conducting in-depth research with people who have been responsible for committing very serious acts of harm against other people. I will not retreat too far back into autobiographical detail, but I feel a certain amount of personal context setting may be necessary in order to provide the frame of reference from which I began this research.

Just prior to undertaking my PhD I had completed a research-focused Master's degree in Canada (from where I originate). The research I undertook there was in the area of resettlement and explored the experiences of ex-prisoners returning to society after long-term imprisonment. Over-representation of First Nations peoples in the Canadian criminal justice system is a serious problem. At the time of conducting my research, in 2003, this was especially true in Saskatchewan (where I was researching resettlement). The adult Aboriginal incarceration rate was over 1,600 per 100,000, compared to 48 per 100,000 for adults who were non-Aboriginal (Correctional Service of Canada, 1999). Although my Master's research had included both Aboriginal and non-Aboriginal ex-prisoners my perceptions about those who become involved in the criminal justice system was significantly shaped by the fact that inequality, racism, marginalisation and structural barriers were the main factors that accounted for criminal involvement and resulted in uses of imprisonment (i.e., that individual pathology or rational choice had little to do with the reasons people become caught up in the criminal justice system). Furthermore, during the process of undertaking my Master's research I met and interviewed several men living in the community who had served long-term prison sentences for serious crimes and did not find them to be a different kind of human being. This was the moment when I began to think about the ordinariness of people who have committed serious acts of violence.

When I began considering the prospect of undertaking PhD research in English maximum-security prisons I wondered who I would encounter in these prisons. What were the factors that led people to prison in Britain? Would I finally confront those incorrigible criminals so often depicted in television, film and the popular press – people bereft of human capacity or perhaps men fully committed to a rational-choice approach to criminality? I did remain open-minded about this because I knew that I might meet people who had committed multiple acts of violence, including multiple acts of murder, and I wondered what that experience would be like. Would I encounter evil?

As Chapter 5 in this book attests, it is true that I did encounter several hundred men convicted of serious crimes. Some of them had engaged in prolific and persistent violence. There were a few men who had severe mental health problems[5] and were difficult company due to their unpredictability. However on no occasion did I encounter the villains that are so often depicted in representations of criminals in popular culture. I did not find evil. This was a troubling revelation. After the first few conversations and interviews with men who had committed serious acts of violence against other human beings I was struck by their ordinariness, their normality and especially their humanity. Although many of them alluded to quite difficult and damaging life experiences there was nothing in particular about them that suggested they were anything but normal human beings who had somehow ended up down a terrible and fateful path towards violence. And, indeed, many of them were likeable. The vast majority were not difficult company, no matter how many long hours I spent with them. There were occasions when I was present for violent outbursts from someone but this was invariably a result of a confluence of dynamic factors associated with the environment that they were in. I witnessed no incidents of random or unpredictable violence throughout these research projects. These were important experiences that I had to come to terms with. Perhaps it would have been less troubling if I had encountered terrible villains of a similar type to the fictional character Hannibal Lecter from the film *Silence of the Lambs*. It would, in many ways, have been easier when thinking about the proportionality of punishment if there had been a few examples of people who really were wicked or incorrigible or who displayed no human capacities. But the unpalatable truth that I came to confront was that those who we see fit to subject to the severe punishment that is maximum-security imprisonment are just as human and just as contradictory, complex and multilayered as the rest of us – as I hope their voices in Chapter 5 illustrated. I found no essentialisable villain who was a clear example of inhumanity. I found a good many people who had had damaging lives and had, in turn, inflicted further damage upon society, their own loved ones and random victims. Furthermore, there were only a relatively small number of men who seemed to be so out of their own control that I felt better knowing that they were currently encased by the state. That is, there were, of course, a small number of very troubled human beings living in maximum-security prisons who may have not been safe to cohabit in free society at the moment in time when I met them. However, even in relation to these cases I thought the meaninglessness of their existences was not a good measure of a civilised society and the punishment they were experiencing was surely contributing to their anger and violence.

The vast majority of the men I encountered during these two research projects seemed to me to be caught up in a prison system that offered them very little and was exacting much damage. This damage was inflicted in large measure by the fact that British prisons are fundamentally premised on a commitment to punishment, as discussed throughout this book. The problem of punishment was an issue I was confronted with during every moment of undertaking the research. It was a senseless infliction of pain. There was a troubling disjuncture between public perceptions of punishment and the superficial, surface-level way it is discussed in media and popular discourse and the actual lived reality of it. In addition, the subjective nature of assessments of punishment must also play a role in creating this disjuncture. One visit to a prison may give a person the impression that prison life does not look that painful. In a similar vein, even individual members of long-serving prison staff will often talk about how easy prison life is (and see Scott's (2008) work on strategies of denial amongst prison staff). These assessments do not, however, align with prisoners' perceptions, nor are they commensurate with my own ethnographically informed understanding of what the loss of liberty involves. Of course, not having been a prisoner I cannot possibly understand it in the same way as someone who is. None of us can. But knowing that even now as I write this Appendix, seven years after I first set foot in an English maximum-security prison, many of the men who I interviewed and whose words illustrate Chapter 5 are still occupying the same cells, walking the same grey landings and continuing to be cut off from any resemblance to normal social life all these years later, is testament to very harsh punishment.

It was against this context that I found the work of James Gilligan (cited extensively in Chapter 7) most helpful. It was reassuring and somewhat vindicating to find that someone with his extensive experience as a forensic psychiatrist, working with some of the most violent people in secure facilities in the United States, also saw the futility of punishment. Furthermore it was also reassuring to learn that he has successfully worked with people in ways that help make them 'safe' by overcoming the damage that has been caused to them as well as the damage they have caused to others, and that this was not achieved through punishment. His work stands as testament to the difficult, yet more hopeful solutions to violence we might pursue if it were to become possible to get over our desire to punish.

Notes

1 Demythologising the Prison and its Uses

1. The research methods used during the research on which this book draws are included in the Appendix.
2. There are no maximum-security women's prisons in England and Wales. Women who are categorised as high-security prisoners are housed amongst the general population (or sometimes in the segregation units) of women's prisons.
3. Although England and Wales form a single legal jurisdiction, all of the maximum-security prisons are geographically located in England.

3 Establishing Long-Term, Maximum-Security Imprisonment in England

1. The structure of a life sentence in England and Wales includes a minimum period of time to be spent in prison, after which the prisoner may be considered for parole. If a parole application is successful the prisoner will then be released from prison on 'life licence', which may include a range of conditions. He or she will remain on licence for the rest of their life and this licence can be revoked at any time.
2. Up until 1948, release under royal prerogative was generously exercised (Padfield, 2002, p. 16). Moreover, reprieves were fairly common both prior to and after the Homicide Act of 1957. Although, as stated in the text, 29 executions took place between 1957 and 1964, 48 prisoners had been sentenced to death for capital murder (Potter, 1993, p. 192). The apparent arbitrariness of the decision as to those who were put to death versus those who were reprieved of this punishment was one of the points on which the abolitionist movement gained ground (see Potter, 1993).
3. Prisoners in the English and Welsh prison system are divided into four security categories; likewise prison establishments are resourced and fortified on the basis of the category of prisoners they to hold (Home Office, 1966). The four security categories are as follows: Category A: those whose escape would be highly dangerous to the public, the police or to the security of the state; Category B: those prisoners for whom the very highest conditions of security are not necessary, but for whom escape must be made very difficult; Category C: prisoners who cannot be trusted in open conditions, but who do not have the ability or resources to make a determined escape attempt; Category D: prisoners who can be housed in open conditions (Home Office, 1966, p. 4, para. 15).
4. According to Appendix A in the Radzinowicz Report, the English witnesses included about 60 people, including prison governors, officers, civilian and medical staff, and prisoners.

5. These were Albany, Gartree, Hull, Parkhurst, Wakefield, Wormwood Scrubs (D-Wing) and, upon its completion, Long Lartin (Home Office, 1984).

6. Throughout this book the words 'dispersal' and 'maximum-security prison' will be used interchangeably when referring to English maximum-security prisons. High-security prisons in other countries will be identified as such and differentiated from English dispersals, as required.

7. Long Lartin, however, was already under construction as a Category C prison when it was upgraded and re-roled to become one of the new dispersal prisons (Home Office, 1984).

8. Four wings at Long Lartin, however, still remained without in-cell sanitation at the time of my research in Long Lartin, which was in 2008.

9. 'Slopping out' is a colloquial term referring to the need for prisoners to dispose of buckets of human waste (usually in the mornings after night-time or after other long periods of cellular confinement) when they are housed in cells without in-cell sanitation facilities.

10. The issue of food is not entirely unproblematic in dispersal prisons. Not all prisoners can afford to buy food nor have the skills to cook their own meals (most dispersal prisons include kitchen facilities for some prisoners to cook their own meals, though they are not large enough for all prisoners to do so). Many prisoners, therefore, rely on the prison for their meals. In these cases dispersal prisoners often have the same complaints about food as prisoners elsewhere in the system (e.g., insufficient or poor quality food).

11. As will be discussed, throughout the 1970s and 1980s the prisons in the dispersal system were troubled by problems of order. As a result, the extension of privileges to prisoners and the extent to which a liberal regime was implemented differed between establishments and waxed and waned in response to each serious incident or serious disturbance that took place within the dispersal system.

12. 'Grass' is a colloquial term for intelligence information.

4 A State of Security in Maximum-Security Prisons

1. Special Security Units are for prisoners who are such a high security risk that they cannot be held even in the most secure prisons without additional security precautions. They were first established in response to the high-profile prison escapes in the mid-1960s (Walmsley, 1989).

2. More recently, punishment and reform were used by a subsequent Home Secretary, Jack Straw, to describe what the purposes of prison ought to be. Straw was Justice Secretary at the time of making such comments (2007–10). This might be seen as evidence of a continuing discursive trajectory that began with Michael Howard's declarations that prisons should be decent but austere.

3. This was also, in part, facilitated by the introduction and implementation of the Incentives and Earned Privileges (IEP) policy, which occurred at the same time. This policy allocates prisoners to one of three privilege levels: basic, standard or enhanced. The types of privileges afforded to prisoners by the policy include, for example, television sets, more visits and slightly higher wage levels. Whilst the range of privileges are not generally viewed by prisoners as meaningful incentives, the IEP policy is intertwined with

prisoners' progression (or not) through the prison system, which makes it an important tool for encouraging prisoner compliance. This is especially true for life-sentenced prisoners who must complete a minimum tariff before being considered for release on life-licence. If their in-prison behaviour is not deemed to be acceptable they can be held beyond their tariff. For these prisoners an enhanced privilege status can be an important factor in the determination of whether they will be able to begin progression through the prison system, towards eventual release on licence.

5   Long-Term, Maximum-Security Punishment

1. The extent to which the brutality of prisons in some jurisdictions is intentional or not has been questioned by some scholars, especially in relation to the 'acceptance' of levels of prisoner-on-prisoner violence that can occur in some American prisons (White, 2008).
2. Marmott's work is primarily associated with the social determinants of health inequalities and he considers a vast range of factors (including crime) that come together to account for health and well-being (or lack thereof) in human societies.
3. MUFTI stands for Minimum Use of Force Tactical Intervention. MUFTI squads were, in effect, anti-riot teams. They are now called Control and Restraint (C and R) teams.
4. The quotation refers to the increased use of Control and Restraint teams in daily prison practice. For example, the reason a prisoner may need to be taken off a wing might be in response to a relatively contained outburst (i.e., a verbal altercation with another prisoner or member of staff; a fist fight between prisoners; or damage to prisoner or prison property). After such an event, prisoners are sometimes moved to the segregation unit to await an adjudication in which it will be decided whether the prisoner will receive a punishment for his actions and, if so, what this punishment will be (for example, reduced privileges; loss of employment; removal to another wing or prison establishment). As indicated, the move to the segregation unit after an event could be handled quite informally, allowing the prisoner to walk unrestrained, but accompanied by two officers. However, with the increased focus on security there seemed to be more routine use of Control and Restraint teams to move prisoners to the segregation unit. Previously, such teams would primarily be used as a last resort when there was concerted indiscipline amongst a group of prisoners or when an individual prisoner was behaving in particularly threatening ways. However, as part of the increased focus on the maintenance of security, Control and Restraint seemed to be increasingly called upon for pre-emptive purposes – at the first sign of discontent and seemingly as a symbolic expression of the power held by the prison authorities.
5. Alison Liebling has led the way in describing the nature and nuances of staff–prisoner relationships in English prisons (see Liebling and Price, 1999, 2001; Liebling and Arnold, 2004; Liebling et al., 2010). However, prison studies would also benefit considerably from a more comparative, and critical, approach that considers the distinctiveness of the English tradition of staff–prisoner engagement in contrast to models used elsewhere, which

are less interactive (many US prisons, for example), and the consequences and benefits to orderliness, quality of life, and safety that may be associated with differing custodial approaches.

6. The Dedicated Search Team is a team of prison officers who are specially trained in techniques of searching, surveillance and intelligence gathering.

7. 'Spin' is the colloquial term used for a cell search.

8. This prisoner felt he was not being treated fairly with regard to a transfer request he had made.

9. It should be noted that the definition of a life sentence in England and Wales is similar to many westernised countries and should not be confused with a whole life sentence or 'life without eligibility for parole' sentence (Appleton and Grøver, 2007). Those who are serving a life sentence in the United Kingdom will serve a mandatory period of time inside prison (the usual starting point for a mandatory 'in prison' tariff for murder in England and Wales is 15 years (ibid., p. 602)). After completing this mandatory minimum tariff, prisoners may apply for parole and release on life licence. If they are granted parole, the life-sentenced prisoner will be released from prison, but will remain on licence.

10. This figure was calculated separately from the figures on criminal convictions included in Figure A.3 in the Appendix. Figure A.3 includes a miscellaneous category that includes a very wide variety of offences that may or may not be violent (including burglary, blackmail, dangerous driving, arson, terrorism). The small numbers of each of these offences across the dispersal system made it impractical to present them all in a table or even in list form. The 10 per cent calculated here draws out convictions that did not explicitly include harm to a person.

11. It was difficult to decide whether or not to count robbery as a violent interpersonal crime or not. I have chosen to do so on the basis that during the research I enquired about the high numbers of robbery convictions (robbery, conspiracy to rob and attempted robbery accounted for 10 per cent of the total convictions of maximum-security prisoners at the time of the research) and what the details of these offences were. Staff and prisoners alike informed me that the majority of men in maximum-security prisons and convicted of robbery-related offences had used some form of weapon in the act of committing a robbery or had been repeatedly convicted of robbery. It was, anecdotally and perhaps culturally, agreed amongst staff and prisoners that the offence of robbery was quite a physically threatening crime and was often perceived amongst this population as a violent crime (even if no physical harm might come to a person in the course of a robbery).

6　Constituting Security in the Penal and the Social Realms

1. Data are presented in two separate tables because, according to the Ministry of Justice department that records these statistics, recording practices changed after 1999. As a consequence the data in Table 6.1 is not directly comparable to the data in Table 6.2. Further, the data included in these tables are drawn from the total number of assaults on staff and on prisoners and are not differentiated in terms of staff–prisoner, prisoner–prisoner or prisoner–staff assaults.

2. The Council of Europe *Sourcebook of Crime and Justice Statistics* (Aebi et al., 2006), which provides data on reported crime and prison statistics and includes national statistics data from different counties; International Crime Victims Surveys (ICVS); e.g., van Kesteren et al., 2000, European Social Surveys (ESS) (www.europeansocialsurvey.org, accessed 10 December 2011), and World Values Surveys (WVS) (www.worldvaluessurvey.org, accessed 10 December 2011) provided data on crime and social sentiments (fears, punitivity and trust); and the Organisation for Economic Cooperation and Development (OECD), Eurostat, the United Nations and the European Union System of Social Indicators provided the data for social and economic and political indicators.

8   Making the Unthinkable Thinkable

1. It may have been noted that the term 'neo-liberal' has escaped consideration in this book thus far. Whilst it can be useful to attribute tidy labels, such as 'neo-liberalism', to seemingly similar sets of political economic arrangements, I have avoided doing so because my concerns relating to the proliferation of ideologies of security extend beyond the confines of, and political arrangements within, nation states and, indeed, may manifest differently within different political regimes. I did not want to confuse the issue by conflating ideologies of security with ideas about neo-liberal rule. Further, the tendency to apply the term neo-liberal to essentially quite distinct political and economic arrangements between different countries seems to me to limit its explanatory potential, despite its relatively unproblematic acceptance and use within much social scientific theorising and criminological literature.
2. INCO is the International Nickel Company of Canada and has been a persistent source of pollution in Canada for many years. Friedenberg mentions it in this paper in 1980, but as recently as 2003 it was named as by far the worst mining polluter in Canada (PollutionWatch, 2003).

Appendix: Research Methods and Reflections on Researching Maximum-Security Prisons

1. The figures for the first research project were collected in 2005, and those for the second in 2008. As these figures were intended only to provide a snapshot and a general summary of the populations, the time lag between the collection of these figures was irrelevant.
2. At the time when the two research projects took place there was not, as yet, a large number of IPP prisoners in the dispersal system. (IPP prisoners are those who are serving indeterminate sentences for the protection of the public.) However, towards the end of the second project (late 2008) the numbers of IPP prisoners began to rise in dispersals. These sentences were introduced by the Criminal Justice Act 2003 and were initially intended for rapists and paedophiles, though they are also now frequently imposed for ordinary street crimes as well (Rose, 2007).
3. Research assistants were employed on the second project to assist with conducting prisoner interviews. However, the majority of the prisoner interviews

were conducted by the author (125 out of 204). All interview transcripts were analysed solely by the author.

4. In 2002 the Prison Service's Standards Audit Unit began to systematically carry out MQPL surveys in all of Her Majesty's prisons (Prison Service, 2004) due to its utility in differentiating between the less tangible aspects of prison environments. Further, Liebling and Arnold's development of the MQPL survey included an extensive programme of research that tested the tool. When compared to findings of Liebling and Arnold (2004) who tested and refined the MQPL survey through work in five different prisons, the Whitemoor and Full Sutton MQPL surveys yielded lower mean scores than other types of prisons. Thus it might be argued that the MQPL survey is a less powerful tool for determining differences between high-security prisons even though the measure is extremely adept at doing so in lower-security establishments.

5. These men probably should not have been housed in a prison but in a secure hospital. But in nearly all cases they had each spent time in a secure hospital but were subsequently returned to a dispersal (with no clear explanation given to me as to why this was).

References

Aas, K.F. (2004) 'From Narrative to Database: Technological Change and Penal Culture', *Punishment & Society*, 6, 4, 379–93.

Aebi, M.F., Aromaa, K., de Cavarlay, B.A., Barclay, G., Gruszczyñska, B., von Hofer, H., Hysi, V. Jehle, J.M., Killias, M., Smit, P. and Tavares, C. (2006) *The European Sourcebook of Crime and Justice Statistics – 2006* (The Hague: Boom Juridische uitgevers).

Aladjem, T. (1990) 'Revenge and Consent', unpublished manuscript on file with the *Indiana Law Journal*.

Agamben, G. (2005) *State of Exception* (London: University of Chicago Press).

Amnesty International USA (2008) *The Death Penalty and Deterrence*, http://www.amnestyusa.org/our-work/issues/death-penalty/us-death-penalty-facts/the-death-penalty-and-deterrence, date accessed 5 October 2011.

Appleton, C. and Grøver, B. (2007) 'The Pros and Cons of Life Without Parole', *British Journal of Criminology*, 47, 4, 597–615.

Aradau, C. (2004) 'The Perverse Politics of Four-Letter Words: Risk and Pity in the Securitisation of Human Trafficking', *Millennium Journal of International Studies*, 33, 2, 251–77.

Aradau, C. and van Munster, R. (2007) 'Governing Terrorism Through Risk: Taking Precautions, (Un) Knowing the Future', *European Journal of International Relations*, 13, 1, 89–115.

Aradau, C. and van Munster, R. (2009) 'Exceptionalism and the "War on Terror" Criminology Meets International Relations' *British Journal of Criminology*, 49, 5, 686–701.

Arendt, H. (1948) 'The Concentration Camps', *Partisan Review*, 15, 7, 743–63.

Arendt, H. (1958) *The Human Condition*, 2nd edn (London: University of Chicago Press).

Arendt, H. (1968) *The Origins of Totalitarianism*, new edn (London: Harcourt, Inc).

Arendt, H. (1971a) *The Life of the Mind*. (London: Harcourt, Inc.).

Arendt, H. (1971b) 'Thinking and Moral Considerations: A Lecture', *Social Research*, 38, 3, Autumn, 417–46.

Arendt, H. (1978) *The Jew as Pariah – Jewish Identity and Politics in the Modern Age* (New York: Grove Press).

Arendt, H. (2006) *Eichmann in Jerusalem: A Report on the Banality of Evil* (London: Penguin Books).

Austin, J. and Irwin, J. (2001) *It's About Time: America's Imprisonment Binge* (Belmont: Wadsworth).

Baker, E. and Roberts, J.V. (2005) 'Globalization and the New Punitiveness' in J. Pratt, D. Brown, M. Brown, S. Hallsworth and W. Morrison (eds) *The New Punitiveness: Trends, Theories, Perspectives* (Cullompton: Willan).

Bar-Tal, D. (1990) *Group Beliefs* (New York: Springer-Verlag).

Barker, V. (2009) *The Politics of Imprisonment: How the Democratic Process Shapes the Way American Punishes Offenders* (Oxford: Oxford University Press).

Bauman, Z. (1989) *Modernity and the Holocaust* (Cambridge: Polity Press).

Bauman, Z. (1991) *Modernity and Ambivalence* (Ithaca, NY: Cornell University Press).

Bauman, Z. (1997) *Postmodernity and its Discontents* (New York: New York University Press).

Bauman, Z. (2000a) *Liquid Modernity* (Cambridge: Polity).

Bauman, Z. (2000b) 'Social Uses of Law and Order' in D. Garland and R. Sparks (eds) *Criminology and Social Theory* (Oxford: Oxford University Press).

Bauman, Z (2006) *Liquid Fear* (Cambridge: Polity Press).

Bauman, Z. and Tester, K. (2001) *Conversations with Zygmunt Bauman* (Cambridge: Polity Press).

Beck, U. (1992) *Risk Society: Towards a New Modernity* (London: Sage).

Beck, U. (1995) *Ecological Politics in an Age of Risk* (Cambridge: Polity Press).

Beck, U. (1998) *World Risk Society* (Cambridge: Polity Press).

Beck, U. (2009) *World at Risk* (Cambridge: Polity Press).

Beckett, K. and Western, B. (2001) 'Governing Social Marginality: Welfare, Incarceration, and the Transformation of State Policy', *Punishment & Society*, 3, 1, 43–59.

Bondeson, U.V. (1989) *Prisoners in Prison Societies* (New Brunswick, NJ: Transaction Publishers).

Boraine, A. and Levy, J. (1995) *The Healing of a Nation?* (Cape Town: Justice in Transition).

Bottoms, A.E. (1983) 'Neglected Features of the Contemporary Penal System' in D. Garland and P. Young (eds) *The Power to Punish* (London: Heinemann).

Bottoms, A.E. (1995) 'The Philosophy and Politics of Punishment and Sentencing' in C. Clarkson and R. Morgan (eds) *The Politics of Sentencing Reform* (Oxford: Clarendon Press).

Bottoms, A.E. (1999) 'Interpersonal Violence and Social Order in Prisons' in M. Tonry and J. Petersilia (eds) *Prisons* (Crime and Justice A Review of Research, vol. 26) (London: University of Chicago Press).

Bottoms, A.E. and Sparks, R. (1997) 'How Order is Maintained' in A. Liebling (ed.) *Security, Justice and Order in Prison: Developing Perspectives* (University of Cambridge: Cropwood Conference Series).

Bowles, M.L. (1990) 'Recognizing Deep Structures in Organizations', *Organization Studies*, 11, 395–412.

Box, S. (1983) *Power, Crime and Mystification* (London: Tavistock).

Braswell, M.C., Montgomery, R.-H. and Lombardo, L.X. (1994) *Prison Violence in America* (Cincinnati: Anderson Publishing Company).

Brown, D. (2005) 'Continuity, Rupture or More of the "Volatile and Contradictory"? Glimpses of New South Wales' Penal Practice Behind and Through the Discursive' in J. Pratt, D. Brown, M. Brown, S. Hallsworth and W. Morrison (eds) *The New Punitiveness* (Cullompton: Willan).

Carlton, B. (2007) *Imprisoning Resistance: Life and Death in an Australian Supermax* (Sydney: Sydney Institute of Criminology Federation Press Series).

Carrabine, E. (2005) 'Prison Riots, Social Order and the Problem of Legitimacy', *British Journal of Criminology*, 45, 896–913.

Cavadino, M. and Dignan, J. (2002) *The Penal System: An Introduction*, 3rd edn (London: Sage).

Cavadino, M. and Dignan, J. (2006) 'Penal Policy and Political Economy', *Criminology and Criminal Justice*, 6, 4, 435–56.

Cayley, D. (1998) *The Expanding Prison: The Crisis in Crime and Punishment and the Search for Alternatives* (Toronto: House of Anansi Press).

Charmaz, K. (2000) 'Grounded Theory: Objectivist and Constructivist Methods' in N.K. Denzin and Y.-S. Lincoln (eds) *Handbook of Qualitative Research*, 2nd edn (London: Sage).

Christie, N. (1974) *Fangevokter ei konsentrasjonsleir* (Oslo: Pax).

Christie, N. (2000) *Crime Control as Industry: Towards Gulags, Western Style* (London: Routledge).

Christie, N. (2001) *Limits to Pain: The Role of Punishment in Penal Policy* (Eugene: Wipf and Stock Publishers).

Christie, N. (2004) *A Suitable Amount of Crime* (London: Routledge).

Clark, B. (1997) 'Are Custody, Control and Justice Compatible?' in A. Liebling (ed.) *Security, Justice and Order in Prison: Developing Perspectives* (University of Cambridge: Cropwood Conference Series).

Clarke, R.V. and Felson, M. (eds) (1993) *Routine Activity and Rational Choice. Advances in Criminological Theory*, vol. 5 (New Brunswick, NJ: Transaction Books).

Clear, T. and Cole, G. (1986) *American Corrections* (Monterey: Brooks/Cole).

Clemmer, D. (1940) *The Prison Community* (New York: Holt, Rinehart and Winston).

Cohen, S. (1985) *Visions of Social Control: Crime, Punishment and Classification* (Cambridge: Polity Press).

Cohen, S. and Taylor, L. (1972) *Psychological Survival: The Experience of Long-Term Imprisonment* (Harmondsworth: Penguin).

Coleman R. (2004) *Reclaiming the Streets: Surveillance, Social Control and the City* (Cullompton: Willan Publishing).

Coleman, R. (2009) 'Surveillance and Social Ordering' in D. Drake, J. Muncie and L. Westmarland (eds) *Criminal Justice: Local and Global* (Milton Keynes: Open University/Cullompton: Willan Publishing).

Correctional Service of Canada (1999) *Demographic Overview of Aboriginal Peoples in Canada and Aboriginal Offenders in Federal Corrections*, http://www.csc-scc.gc.ca/text/prgrm/abinit/know/10-eng.shtml, date accessed 3 October 2011.

Coyle, A. (1998) 'The Role of the Prison in New Britain', *Policy Studies*, 19, 3/4, 229–35.

Coyle, A. (2005) *Understanding Prisons: Key Issues in Policy and Practice* (Maidenhead: Open University Press).

Crawley, E. (2004) *Doing Prison Work: The Public and Private Lives of Prison Officers* (Cullompton: Willan Publishing).

Crewe, B. (2006) 'Prison Drug Dealing and the Ethnographic Lens', *The Howard Journal of Criminal Justice*, 45, 4, 347–68.

Crewe, B. (2009) *The Prisoner Society: Power, Adaptation and Social Life in an English Prison* (Oxford: Clarendon Press).

Davies, S. (2008) 'International Law and the State of Exception' in A. J. Bellamy, R. Bleiker, S.E. Davies and R. Devetak (eds) *Security and the War on Terror* (Abingdon: Routledge).

Debs, E.V. (1927) *Walls and Bars* (Illinois: Socialist Party).

de Beauvoir, S. (1946) 'Oeil pour Oeil' (*Les Temps Modernes*, 1, no. 5) in *Simone de Beauvoir: Philosophical Writings*, M.A Simons (ed.) (2004) (Chicago: University of Illinois Press).

De Giorgi, A. (2007) 'Rethinking the Political Economy of Punishment', *Criminal Justice Matters*, 70, 1, Winter, 17–18, http://www.informaworld.com/smpp/content~db=all~content=a791437444, date accessed 3 October 2011.

de Haan, W. (1987) 'Fuzzy Morals and Flakey Politics: The Coming Out of Critical Criminology', *Journal of Law and Society*, 14, 3, Autumn, 321–33.

de Toqueville, A. (1956) *Democracy in America* (New York: Mentor Books).

Dignan, J. (2005) *Understanding Victims and Restorative Justice* (Maidenhead: Open University Press).

Dilulio, J. (1987) *Governing Prisons: A Comparative Study of Correctional Management* (London: Collier Macmillan).

Downes, D.M. (1988) *Contrasts in Tolerance: Post-War Penal Policy in The Netherlands and England and Wales* (Oxford: Clarendon).

Downes, D. and Hansen, K. (2006) 'Welfare and Punishment in Comparative Context' in S. Armstrong and L. McAra (eds) *Perspectives on Punishment: The Contours of Control* (Oxford: Oxford University Press).

Downes, D. and Morgan, R. (2007) 'No Turning Back: The Politics of Law and Order into the Millennium' in M. Maguire, R. Morgan and R. Reiner (eds) *The Oxford Handbook of Criminology* (Oxford: Oxford University Press).

Drake, D. (2006) 'A Comparison of Quality of Life, Order and Legitimacy in Two Maximum-Security Prisons', unpublished PhD Thesis, University of Cambridge.

Drake, D. (2008) 'Staff and Order in Prisons' in J. Bennett, B. Crewe and A. Wahidin (eds) *Understanding Prison Staff* (Cullompton: Willan Publishing).

Drake, D. (2009) *Prisoner Experiences and Quality of Life in Dispersal Prisons* (Directorate of High Security, NOMS: unpublished internal research report).

Drake, D. (2011) 'The "Dangerous Other" in Maximum-Security Prisons', *Criminology and Criminal Justice*, 11, 4, September, 367–82.

Drake, D. (in preparation) 'Researching Prisoner Experiences with Prison Officers: An Action Research-Inspired Approach' (submitted to Action Research, published by Sage).

Durkheim, E. (1997) *The Division of Labor in Society* (New York: Free Press).

Ewald, F. (1999) 'The Return of the Crafty Genius: An Outline of a Philosophy of Precaution', *Connecticut Insurance Law Journal*, 6, 47–79.

Feeley, M. and Simon, J. (1992) 'The New Penology: Notes on the Emerging Strategy of Corrections and its Implications', *Criminology*, 30, 4, 449–74.

Felson, M. (2002) *Crime and Everyday Life* (London: Sage).

Fitzgerald, M. and Sim J. (1982) *British Prisons*, 2nd edn (Oxford: Blackwell).

Forum on Corrections (1992) *Violence and Suicide in Canadian Institutions: Some Recent Statistics*, 4, 3, http://www.csc-scc.gc.ca/text/pblct/forum/e043/e043b-eng.shtml, date accessed 3 October 2011.

Foucault, M. (1995) *Discipline and Punish: The Birth of the Prison*, 2nd edn (New York: Vintage Books).

Freedom of Information Act, Request/62512/09 Staff and Prisoner Assaults in Dispersals 1993–2009.

French, P. (2001) *The Virtues of Vengeance* (Lawrence: University Press of Kansas).

Friedenberg, E.Z. (1980) 'The Punishment Industry in Canada', *The Canadian Journal of Sociology*, 5, 3, Summer, 273–83.

Friestad, C. and Hansen, I.L.S. (2010) 'Gender Difference in Inmates' Anticipated Desistance', *European Journal of Criminology*, 7, 4, July, 285–98.

Furedi, F. (2002) *Culture of Fear: Risk Taking and the Morality of Low Expectation* (London: Continuum International Publishing Group).

Gabriel, Y. (1992) 'Heroes, Villains, Fools and Magic Wands: Computers in Organizational Folklore', *International Journal of Information Resource Management*, 3, 3–12.

Gabriel, Y. (1993) 'Organizational Nostalgia: Reflections on the "Golden Age"' in S. Fineman (ed.) *Emotion in Organizations* (London: Sage).

Garabedian, P. (1963) 'Social Roles and Process of Socialisation in the Prison Community', *Social Problems*, 11, 139–52.

Garland, D. (1996) 'The Limits of the Sovereign State: Strategies of Crime Control in Contemporary Society', *British Journal of Criminology*, 36, 4, 445–71.

Garland, D. (2001) *The Culture of Control: Crime and Social Order in Contemporary Society* (Oxford: Oxford University Press).

Garner, R. (1994) *Beyond Morality* (Philadelphia: Temple University Press).

Garner, R. (2010) 'Abolishing Morality' in R. Joyce and S. Kirchin (eds) *A World Without Values: Essays on John Mackie's Moral Error Theory* (Philosophical Studies Series, vol. 114) (London: Springer).

Garner, R. (2011) 'Morality: The Final Delusion?' *Philosophy Now*, Issue 82, January/February (digital subscription, date accessed 3 October, 2011).

Garner, R. (forthcoming) *Beyond Morality Beyond Morality*, http://beyondmorality.com/beyond-beyond-morality/, date accessed 3 October 2011.

Giddens, A. (1990) *The Consequences of Modernity* (Cambridge: Polity).

Giddens, A. (1991) *Modernity and Self-Identity Self and Society in the Late Modern Age* (Cambridge: Polity).

Gilligan, J. (2000) 'Punishment and Violence: Is the Criminal Law Based on One Huge Mistake?' *Social Research*, 67, 3, 745–72.

Gladstone Report (1895) *Report from the Departmental Committee on Prisons* C.7702 (London: HMSO).

Glaser, B.G. (1978) *Theoretical Sensitivity* (Mill Valley, CA: Sociology Press).

Glaser, B.G. (1992) *Basics of Grounded Theory Analysis: Emergence vs. Forcing* (Mill Valley, CA: Sociology Press).

Goffman, E. (1961) 'On the Characteristics of Total Institutions' in D. Cressey (ed.) *The Prison: Studies in Institutional Organization and Change* (New York: Holt, Rinehart and Winston).

Goodwin, B. (2007) *Using Political Ideas*, 5th edn (Chichester: John Wiley & Sons).

Goodstein, L. and Wright, K. (1989) 'Inmate Adjustment to Prison' in L. Goodstein and D. MacKenzie (eds) *The American Prison* (New York: Plenum).

Goold, B.J. and Lazarus, L. (eds) (2007) *Security and Human Rights* (Oxford: Hart Publishing).

Gorz, A. (1999) *Reclaiming Work* (Cambridge: Polity Press).

Green, D.A. (2008) *When Children Kill Children: Penal Populism and Political Culture* (Oxford: Clarendon).

Greenberg, D. (2001) 'Novus Ordo Saeclorun? A Commentary on Downes, and on Beckett and Western', *Punishment & Society*, 3, 81–93.

Greer, C. and Jewkes, Y. (2005) 'Extremes of Otherness: Media Images of Social Exclusion', *Social Justice*, 32, 1, 20–31.

Grusky, O. (1959) 'Organisational Goals and the Behaviour of Informal Leaders', *American Journal of Sociology*, 65, July, 59–67.

Guldberg, H. (2003) 'Challenging the Precautionary Principle', Spiked-Online, http://www.spiked-online.com/Printable/00000006DE2F.htm, date accessed 1 October 2003.

Hale, C. (1989) 'Economy, Punishment and Imprisonment', *Contemporary Crisis* 13, 327–49.

Hall, M. (2009) *Victims of Crime: Policy and Practice in Criminal Justice* (Cullompton: Willan Publishing).

Hall, S. (1980) *Drifting into a Law and Order Society* (London: The Cobden Trust).

Hall, S. (ed.) (1997) *Representation: Cultural Representations and Signifying Practices* (London: Sage/Milton Keynes: Open University Press).

Hallsworth, S. (2000) 'Rethinking the Punitive Turn: Economies of Excess and the Criminology of the Other', *Punishment & Society*, 2, 2, April, 145–60.

Hallsworth, S. and Lea, J. (2011) 'Reconstructing Leviathan: Emerging Contours of the Security State', *Theoretical Criminology*, 15, 2, 141–57.

Haney, C., Banks, W.C. and Zimbardo, P.G. (1973) 'Interpersonal Dynamics in a Simulated Prison', *International Journal of Criminology and Penology*, 1, 69–97.

Hannah-Moffat, K. (2005) 'Criminogenic Needs and the Transformative Risk Subject Hybridizations of Risk/Need in Penality', *Punishment & Society*, 7, 1, 29–51.

Hannah-Moffat, K. and Maurutto, P. (2003) *Youth Risk/Need Assessment: An Overview of Issues and Practices* (Ottawa: Department of Justice Canada).

Harvey, J. (2007) *Young Men in Prison: Surviving and Adapting to Life Inside* (Cullompton: Willan Publishing).

Harvey, J. (2011) 'Acknowledging and Understanding Complexity When Providing Therapy in Prisons', *European Journal of Psychotherapy and Counselling*, iFirst, 1–13, http://dx.doi.org/10.1080/13642537.2011.625204, date accessed 21 December 2011.

Harvey, J. and Smedley, K. (eds) (2010) *Psychological Therapy in Prisons and Other Secure Settings* (Cullompton: Willan Publishing).

Hegel, F. (1942) *Hegel's Philosophy of Right* (Oxford: Oxford University Press).

HM Chief Inspector of Prisons (1997) *Report of an Inspection of HM Prison Full Sutton: Part A Executive Summary* (London: HMSO).

HM Chief Inspector of Prisons (2001) *Report on an Announced Inspection of HM Prison Gartree 2–6 July* (London: HCIP).

HM Chief Inspector of Prisons (2002) *Report of an Unannounced Follow-Up Inspection of HM Prison Whitemoor 15–17 July* (London: HCIP).

Hillyard, P. and Tombs, S. (2007) 'From "Crime" to Social Harm', *Crime, Law and Social Change*, 48, 9–25.

Hinckfuss, I. (1987) *The Moral Society, its Structure and Effects* (Canberra: Australian National University). Available online, http://philosophy.ru/library/hinck/contents.html, date accessed 3 October 2011.

Hinds, L. (2005) 'Crime control in Western Countries, 1970 to 2000' in J. Pratt, D. Brown, M. Brown, S. Hallsworth and W. Morrison (eds) *The New Punitiveness: Trends, Theories, Perspectives* (Cullompton: Willan Publishing).

Hobbes, T. (2008) *Leviathan*, http://forgottenbooks.org, date accessed 21 December 2011.

Holmes, S. and Soothill, K. (2007) 'Dangerous Offenders and Dangerousness' in Y. Jewkes (ed.) *Handbook on Prisons* (Cullompton: Willan Publishing).

Home Office (1966) *Committee of Enquiry into Prison Escapes and Security* (Mountbatten Report) (London: HMSO).

Home Office (1968) *The Regime for Long-Term Prisoners in Conditions of Maximum Security* (Radzinowicz Report) (London: HMSO).

Home Office (1984) *Managing the Long-Term Prison System: The Report of the Control Review Committee* (London: HMSO).

Home Office (1990) *The Sentence of the Court: A Handbook for Courts on the Treatment of Offenders* (London: HMSO).

Home Office (1991) *Custody, Care and Justice: The Way Ahead for the Prison Service in England and Wales* (London: HMSO).

Home Office (1999) *Managing People with Severe Personality Disorder: Proposals for Development* (London: Department of Health).

Hope, T. and Sparks, R. (2000) *Crime, Risk and Insecurity: Law and Order in Everyday Life and Political Discourse* (London: Routledge).

Hsieh, C. and Pugh, M.D. (1993) 'Poverty, Income Inequality, and Violent Crime: A Meta-Analysis of Recent Aggregate Data Studies', *Criminal Justice Review*, 18, 2, 182–202.

Hudson, B. (1987) *Justice Through Punishment: A Critique of the 'Justice' Model of Corrections* (Basingstoke: Macmillan).

Hudson, B. (2003) *Justice in the Risk Society* (London: Sage).

Hudson, B. (2006) 'Beyond White Man's Justice: Race, Gender and Justice in Late Modernity', *Theoretical Criminology*, 10, 1, 29–47.

Huesmann, L.R. and Podolski, C.L. (2003) 'Punishment: A Psychological Perspective' in S. McConville (ed.) *The Use of Punishment* (Cullompton: Willan Publishing).

Ignatieff, M. (1978) *A Just Measure of Pain: The Penitentiary in the Industrial Revolution 1750–1850* (London: Macmillan Press).

Irwin, J. (1970) *The Felon* (Englewood Cliffs, CA: Prentice-Hall).

Irwin, J. and Cressey, D. (1962) 'Thieves, Convicts and the Inmate Culture', *Social Problems*, 10, 145–7.

Jacobs, J.B. (1977) *Stateville: The Penitentiary in Mass Society* (Chicago: University of Chicago Press).

Jefferson, A.M. (2005) 'Reforming Nigerian Prisons Rehabilitating a "Deviant" State', *British Journal of Criminology*, 45, 4, 487–503.

Jewkes, Y. (2002) *Captive Audience: Media, Masculinity and Power in Prisons* (Cullompton: Willan Publishing).

Jewkes, Y. (2004) *Media and Crime* (London: Sage).

Jewkes, Y. and Johnston, H. (2006) 'Prisons in Context' in Y. Jewkes and H. Johnston (eds) *Prison Readings: A Critical Introduction to Prisons and Imprisonment* (Cullompton: Willan Publishing).

Joffe, H. (1999) *Risk and 'the Other'* (Cambridge: Cambridge University Press).

Jones, R.S. and Schmid, T.J. (2000) *Doing Time: Prison Experience and Identity Among First-Time Inmates* (Stamford: Jai Press).

Karmen, A.J. (1992) 'Who's Against Victims' Rights? The Nature of the Opposition to Pro-Victim Initiatives in Criminal Justice', *Saint John's Journal of Legal Commentary*, 8, 157–75.

Kant, I. (1965) *Metaphysical Elements of Justice* (Indianapolis: Bobbs-Merrill).

Kendall, K. (2002) 'Time to Think Again About Cognitive-Behavioural Programmes' in P. Carlen (ed.) *Women and Punishment. The Struggle for Justice* (Cullompton: Willan Publishing).

King, A. (1975) 'Overload: Problems of Governing in the 1970s', *Political Studies*, 23, 284–96.

King, R.D. (1985) 'Control in Prisons' in M. Maguire, J. Vagg, and R. Morgan (eds) *Accountability and Prisons* (London: Tavistock).

King, R.D. (1995) 'Woodcock and After', *Prison Service Journal*, 102, 63–67.

King, R.D. (1999) 'The Rise and Rise of Supermax: An American Solution in Search of a Problem?' *Punishment & Society*, 1, 2, 163–86.

King, R.D. (2000), 'Doing Research in Prisons' in R.D. King and E. Wincup (eds) *Doing Research on Crime and Justice* (Oxford: Oxford University Press).

King, R.D. & Elliott, K. (1977) *Albany: Birth of a Prison* (London: Routledge & Kegan Paul).

King, R.D. & Morgan, R. (1980) *The Future of the Prison System* (Farnborough: Gower).

King, R.D. & Resodihardjo, S.L. (2010) 'To Max or Not to Max: Dealing with High Risk Prisoners in the Netherlands and England and Wales', *Punishment & Society*, 12, 1, 65–84.

King, R.D. and Wincup, E. (eds) (2000) *Doing Research on Crime and Justice* (Oxford: Oxford University Press).

Kropotkin, P. (1992) 'Law and Authority' in G. Woodcock (ed.) *Words of a Rebel* (New York: Black Rose Books).

Kruttschnitt, C. and Gartner, R. (2005) *Marking Time in the Golden State: Women's Imprisonment in California* (Cambridge: Cambridge University Press).

Kupers, T.A. (2006) 'How to Create Madness in Prison' in D. Jones (ed.) *Humane Prisons* (Oxford: Radcliffe Publishing).

Kury, H. (ed.) (2008) 'Fear of Crime – Punitivity', *New Developments in Theory and Research*, Crime and Crime Policy, 3, (Bochum: Universitätsverlag Brockmeyer).

Lacey, N. (2008) *The Prisoners' Dilemma: Political Economy and Punishment in Contemporary Democracies*, Hamlyn Lectures 2007 (Cambridge: Cambridge University Press).

Lacey, N. (2010) 'Differentiating Among Penal States', *The British Journal of Sociology*, 61, 4, 779–94.

Lappi-Seppälä, T. (2007) 'Penal Policy in Scandinavia' in M. Tonry (ed.) *Crime, Punishment and Politics in Comparative Perspective, Crime and Justice: A Review of Research*, 36, 217–96 (Chicago: Chicago University Press).

Lappi-Seppälä, T. (2008) 'Trust, Welfare and Political Culture: Explaining Difference in National Penal Policies' in M. Tonry (ed.) *Crime, Punishment and Politics in Comparative Perspective, Crime and Justice: A Review of Research*, 37, 313–87 (Chicago: Chicago University Press).

Lazarus, L. (2007) 'Mapping the Right to Security' in B.J. Goold and L. Lazarus (eds) *Security and Human Rights* (Oxford: Hart Publishing).

Learmont, J. (1995) *Review of Prison Service Security in England and Wales and the Escape from Parkhurst Prison on Tuesday 3rd January 1995*, Rep. No. Cm. 3020, (London: HMSO).

Lewis, D. (1997) *Hidden Agendas: Politics, Law and Disorder* (London: Hamish Hamilton).

Liebling, A. (1999) 'Doing Research in Prison: Breaking the Silence?' *Theoretical Criminology*, 3, 147–73.

Liebling, A. (2001) 'Policy and Practice in the Management of Disruptive Prisoners: Incentives and Earned Privileges, the Spurr Report and Close

Supervision Centres' in E. Clare and K. Bottomley (eds) *Evaluation of Close Supervision Centres* (Home Office Research Study 219).

Liebling, A. (2002) 'A "Liberal Regime Within A Secure Perimeter"?: Dispersal Prisons and Penal Practice in the Late Twentieth Century' in A.E. Bottoms & M. Tonry (eds) *Ideology, Crime and Criminal Justice* (Portland: Willan Publishing).

Liebling, A. and Arnold, H. (2002) *Measuring the Quality of Prison Life*. (London: Home Office), http://homeoffice.gov.uk/rds/pdfs2/r174.pdf, date accessed 3 October 2011.

Liebling, A. (assisted by Arnold, H.) (2004) *Prisons and their Moral Performance* (Oxford: Clarendon Press).

Liebling, A., Arnold, H. and Straub, C. (2011) *An Exploration of Staff–Prisoner Relationships at HMP Whitemoor: Twelve Years On* (London: Home Office).

Liebling, A., Muir, G., Rose, G. and Bottoms, A.E. (1997) *An Evaluation of Incentives and Earned Privileges: Final Report to the Prison Service* (Home Office, London: unpublished report).

Liebling, A. and Price, D. (1999) *An Exploration of Staff Prisoner Relationships at HMP Whitemoor Prison Service*, Research Report, No. 6, January (London: Prison Service).

Liebling, A. and Price, D. (2001) *The Prison Officer* (Leyhill: Prison Service and Waterside Press).

Liebling, A., Price, D. and Shefer, G. (2010) *The Prison Officer*, 2nd edn (Cullompton: Willan Publishing).

Loader, I. (2006) 'Fall of the "Platonic Guardians": Liberalism, Criminology and Political Responses to Crime in England and Wales', *British Journal of Criminology*, 46, 4, 561–86.

McCleary, R. (1992) *Dangerous Men: The Sociology of Parole* (Boulder: Lynne Rienner Publishers).

McCorkle, R.C., Miethe, T.D. and Drass, K.A. (1995) 'The Roots of Prison Violence: A Test of the Deprivation, Management, and "Not-So-Total" Institution Models', *Crime and Delinquency*, July, 41, 3, 317–31.

McGowen, R. (1995) 'Prison Reform in England, 1780–1865' in N. Morris and D.J. Rothman (eds) *The Oxford History of the Prison* (Oxford: Oxford University Press).

McLuhan, M. (1964) *Understanding Media: The Extensions of Man* (New York: McGraw Hill).

Mackie, J. (1977) *Ethics: Inventing Right and Wrong* (London: Penguin).

Mannheim, K. (1936) *Ideology and Utopia* (trans. E. Shils) (London: Routledge & Kegan Paul).

Mannheim, K. (1939) *The Dilemma of Penal Reform* (London: Allen and Unwin).

Marcus, G.E. and Fischer, M.M.J. (1986) *Anthropology as Cultural Critique: An Experimental Moment in the Human Sciences* (Chicago: University of Chicago Press).

Marmot, M. (2000) 'Inequalities in Health Causes and Policy Implications' in A.R. Tarlov and R.F. St Peter (eds) *The Society and Population Health Reader: A State and Community Perspective* (New York: The New Press).

Marmot, M. (2004) *Status Syndrome* (London: Bloomsbury Publishing).

Marmot, M.G., Ryff, C., Bumpass, L., Shipley, M.J. and Marks, N.F. (1997) 'Social Inequalities in Health: Next Questions and Converging Evidence', *Journal of Epidemiology and Community Health*, 32, 244–9.

Maruna, S., Matravers, A. and King, A. (2004) 'Disowning Our Shadow: A Psychoanalytic Approach to Understanding Punitive Public Attitudes', *Deviant Behavior*, 25, 277–99.

Marx, K. (1975) 'Contribution to the Critique of Hegel's Philosophy of Law: Introduction', *Karl Marx and Frederick Engels Collected Works*, vol. 3 (London: Lawrence and Wishart).

Mathiesen, T. (2000) *Prison On Trial*, 2nd edn (Winchester: Waterside Press).

Mathiesen, T. (2004) *Silently Silenced: Essays on the Creation of Acquiescence in Modern Society* (Winchester: Waterside Press).

Medlicott, D. (2001) *Surviving the Prison Place* (Aldershot: Ashgate).

Melossi, D. (2000) 'Changing Representations of the Criminal' in D. Garland and R. Sparks (eds) *Criminology and Social Theory* (Oxford: Clarendon Press).

Miers, D. (1978) *Responses to Victimisation* (Abingdon: Professional Books).

Millie, A., Jacobson, J. and Hough, M. (2003) 'Understanding the Growth in the Prison Population in England and Wales', *Criminal Justice*, 3, 4, 369–87.

Ministry of Justice (2011) *Prison Annual Performance Ratings 2010/2011* (London: National Offender Management Service), http://www.justice.gov.uk/downloads/publications/statistics-and-data/hmps/prisons-annual-performance-ratings2010-11.pdf, date accessed 7 October 2011.

Morgan, R. (1997) 'The Aims of Imprisonment Revisited' in A. Liebling (ed.) *Security, Justice and Order in Prison: Developing Perspectives* (University of Cambridge: Cropwood Conference Series).

Morris, T. and Morris, P. (1963) *Pentonville* (London: Routledge and Kegan Paul).

Newbold, G. (1989) *Punishment and Politics: The Maximum-Security Prison in New Zealand* (New York: Oxford University Press).

Nietzsche, F. (1969) *On the Genealogy of Morals and Ecce Homo* (New York: Vintage).

Nozick, R. (1981) *Philosophical Explanations* (Cambridge, MA: Harvard University Press).

Padfield, N. (2002) *Beyond the Tariff: Human Rights and the Release of Life-Sentenced Prisoners* (Cullompton: Willan Publishing).

Parliamentary All-Party Penal Affairs Group (1986) *Life-Sentence Prisoners* (Chichester: Barry Rose Publishers).

Pashukanis, E.B. (1989) *Law and Marxism: A General Theory* (London: Pluto Press).

Pelczynski, Z.A. (1971) *Hegel's Political Philosophy: Problems and Perspectives* (London: Cambridge University Press).

Peterson, A.W. (1961) 'The Prison Building Programme', *British Journal of Criminology*, 1, 4, 307–16.

Piacentini, L. (2004) *Surviving Russian Prisons: Punishment, Politics and Economy in Transition* (Cullompton: Willan Publishing).

Player, E. and Jenkins, M. (eds) (1994) *Prisons After Woolf: Reform Through Riot* (London: Routledge).

PollutionWatch (2003) 'PollutionWatch Fact Sheet', http://www.pollutionwatch.org/pressroom/factSheetData/PollutionWatch%20National%20Overview%202003%20-FINAL.pdf, date accessed 3 October 2011.

Potter, H. (1993) *Hanging in Judgment: Religion and the Death Penalty in England* (New York: Continuum).

Pratt, J. (1997) *Governing the Dangerous: Dangerousness, Law and Social Change* (Sydney: Federation Press).

Pratt, J. (2008a) 'Scandinavian Exceptionalism in an Era of Penal Excess Part I: The Nature of Roots of Scandinavian Exceptionalism', *British Journal of Criminology*, 48, 119–37.

Pratt, J. (2008b) 'Scandinavian Exceptionalism in an Era of Penal Excess Part II: Does Scandinavian Exceptionalism Have a Future?' *British Journal of Criminology*, 48, 275–92.

Pratt, J., Brown, D., Brown, M., Hallsworth, S. and Morrison, W. (eds) (2005) *The New Punitiveness* (Cullompton: Willan Publishing).

Price, D. (2000) 'The Origins and Durability of Security Categorisation: A Study of Penological Pragmatism or Spies, Dickie and Prison Security', *The British Criminology Conference Selected Proceedings*, 3, June.

Prison Service (2004) 'MQPL Survey Reveals Reality of Prison Life', *Prison Service News*, 14–15.

Quinney, R. (2000) *Bearing Witness to Crime and Social Justice* (Albany: State University of New York Press)

Reiman, J. and Leighton, P. (2010) *The Rich Get Richer and the Poor Get Prison: Ideology, Class and Criminal Justice*, 9th edn (London: Allyn & Bacon).

Richards, P. (1999) *Homicide Statistics, Research Paper 99/56* (House of Commons Library, Social and General Statistics Section), http://www.parliament.uk/commons/lib/research/rp99/rp99-056.pdf, date accessed 1 October 2011.

Roberts, J., Stalans, L., Indermaur, D. and Hough, M. (2003) *Penal Populism and Public Opinion: Lessons from Five Countries* (Oxford: Oxford University Press).

Rogers, C.R. (1957) 'The Necessary and Sufficient Conditions of Therapeutic Personality Change', *Journal of Consulting Psychology*, 21, 95–103.

Rogers, C.R. (1989) 'A Theory of Therapy, Personality, and Interpersonal Relationships as Developed in the Client-Centered Framework', reprinted in H. Kirschenbaum and V. Henderson (eds) *The Carl Rogers Reader* (Boston: Houghton Mifflin).

Rose, D. (2007) 'Locked Up to Make Us Feel Better', *New Statesman*, 19 March, http://www.newstatesman.com/politics/2007/03/risk-prison-sex-act-life, date accessed 1 October 2010.

Rose, N. (2000) 'Government and Control' in D. Garland and R. Sparks (eds) *Criminology and Social Theory* (Oxford: Clarendon Press).

Ross, J.I. and Richards, S.C. (2003) *Convict Criminology* (Belmont: Wadsworth).

Rowe, A. (2011) 'Narratives of Self and Identity in Women's Prisons: Stigma and the Struggle for Self-Definition in Penal Regimes', *Punishment and Society*, 13, 5, 571–91.

Rusche, G. and Kirchheimer, O. (1968) *Punishment and Social Structure* (New York: Russell & Russell).

Ryan, M. (2005) 'Engaging with Punitive Attitudes towards Crime and Punishment: Some Strategic Lessons from England and Wales' in J. Pratt, D. Brown, M. Brown, S. Hallsworth and W. Morrison (eds) *The New Punitiveness* (Cullompton: Willan Publishing).

Ryan, M. and Sim, J. (1998) 'Power, Punishment and Prisons in England and Wales 1975–1996' in R. Weiss, R. and N. South (eds) *Comparing Prison Systems* (Amsterdam: Gordon and Breech).

Sarat, A. (1997) 'Vengeance, Victims and the Identities of Law', *Social and Legal Studies*, 6, 2, 163–89.

Scraton, P., Sim, J. and Skidmore, P. (1991) *Prisons Under Protest* (Milton Keynes: Open University Press).

Schein, E.H. (2004) *Organizational Culture and Leadership*, 3rd edn (San Francisco: John Wiley & Sons).

Scott, D. (2008) 'Creating Ghosts in the Penal Machine: Prison Officer Occupational Morality and the Techniques of Denial' in J. Bennett, B. Crewe and A. Wahidin (eds) Understanding Prison Staff (Cullompton: Willan Publishing).

Shalev, S. (2009) *Supermax: Controlling Risk Through Solitary Confinement* (Cullompton: Willan Publishing).

Shaw, S. (1995) 'For Gladstone, read Woodcock and Learmont' in S. McConville, L. Blom-Cooper, Lord Allen of Abbeydale, P. Cavadino and S. Shaw (eds) *Gladstone at 100: Essays on the Past and Future of the Prison System* (London: Prison Reform Trust).

Sieh, E.W. (1989) 'Less Eligibility: The Upper Limits of Penal Policy', *Criminal Justice Policy Review*, 3, 2, 159–83.

Silberman, M. (1995) *World of Violence: Corrections in America* (Belmont: Wadsworth).

Sim, J. (1994) 'Reforming the Penal Wasteland? A Critical Review of the Woolf Report' in E. Player and M. Jenkins (eds) *Prisons After Woolf: Reform through Riot* (London: Routledge).

Sim, J. (2009) *Punishment and Prisons: Power and the Carceral State* (London: Sage).

Simon, J. (2007) *Governing Through Crime: How the War on Crime Transformed American Democracy and Created a Culture of Fear* (Oxford: Oxford University Press).

Simon, J. (2010) 'Do These Prisons Make Me Look Fat?: Moderating the USA's Consumption of Punishment', *Theoretical Criminology*, 14, 3, 257–72.

Singer, L.R. (1991) 'A Non-punitive Paradigm of Probation Practice: Some Sobering Thoughts', *The British Journal of Social Work*, 21, 6, 611–26.

Snacken, S. (2007) 'Penal Policy and Practice in Belgium' in M. Tonry (ed.) *Crime, Punishment and Politics in Comparative Perspective, Crime and Justice, A Review of Research*, 36 (Chicago: University of Chicago Press).

Snacken, S. (2010) 'Resisting Punitiveness in Europe?' *Theoretical Criminology*, 14, 3, 273–92.

Snacken, S., Beyens, K. and Tubex, H. (1995) 'Changing Prison Populations in Western Countries: Fate or Policy?' *European Journal of Crime, Criminal Law and Criminal Justice*, 1, 18–53.

Sparks, R. (2000) 'Risk and Blame in Criminal Justice Controversies: British Penal Coverage and Official Discourse on Prison Security (1993–6)' in M. Brown and J. Pratt (eds) *Dangerous Offenders: Punishment and Social Order* (London: Routledge).

Sparks, R. and Bottoms, A.E. (1995) 'Legitimacy and Order in Prisons', *British Journal of Sociology*, 46, 45–62.

Sparks, R., Bottoms, A.E. and Hay, W. (1996) *Prisons and the Problem of Order* (Oxford: Clarendon Press).

Sutton, J.R. (2000) 'Imprisonment and Social Classification in Five Common-Law Democracies, 1955–1985', *The American Journal of Sociology*, 106, 2, 350–86.

Sykes, G. (1958) *The Society of Captives: A Study of a Maximum Security Prison* (Princeton: Princeton University Press).

Tauri, J. (2009) 'An Indigenous Perspective on the Standardisation of Restorative Justice in New Zealand and Canada', *Indigenous Policy Journal*, 1, 3, 315–39.

Terry, C.M. (2003) Overcoming Prison and Addiction (Belmont: Wadsworth).

Thomas, J.E. (1972) *The English Prison Officer Since 1850: A Study in Conflict* (London: Routledge and Kegan Paul).

Tittle, C.R. (1972) *Society of Subordinates – Inmate Organisation in a Narcotic Hospital* (Bloomington: Indiana University Press).

Toch, H. and Adams, K. (1989) *Coping: Maladaptation in Prisons* (Piscataway: Transaction Publishers).

Tombs, S. and Whyte, D. (eds) (2003a) *Unmasking the Crimes of the Powerful: Scrutinising States and Corporations* (New York: Peter Lang Publishing).

Tombs, S. and Whyte, D. (2003b) 'Unmasking the Crimes of the Powerful', *Critical Criminology*, 11, 3, 217–36.

Travis, A. (2008) 'Jack Straw Puts Victims First and Says Punishment is Main Point of Prison', the *Guardian*, 27 October, http://www.guardian.co.uk/society/2008/oct/27/prisonsandprobation-justice, date accessed 12 December 2011.

Tutu, D. (1999) *No Future without Forgiveness* (London: Rider Books).

Useem, B. and Kimball, P. (1989) *States of Siege: US Prison Riots, 1971–1986* (Oxford: Oxford University Press).

van Kesteren, J., Mayhew, P. and Nieuwbeerta, P. (2000) *Criminal Victimisation in Seventeen Industrialised Countries: Key Findings from the 2000 International Crime Victims Survey* (The Hague: Netherlands Ministry of Justice).

Valier, C. (2004) *Crime and Punishment in Contemporary Culture* (Abingdon: Routledge).

Vlastos, G. (1991) *Socrates: Ironist and Moral Philosopher* (Ithaca NY: Cornell University Press).

Wacquant, L. (1999) '"Suitable Enemies": Foreigners and Immigrants in the Prisons of Europe', *Punishment & Society*, 1–2, 215–23.

Wacquant, L. (2001) 'The Penalisation of Poverty and the Rise of Neo-Liberalism', *European Journal on Criminal Policy and Research*, 9, 401–12.

Wacquant, L. (2002) 'The Curious Eclipse of Prison Ethnography in the Age of Mass Incarceration', *Ethnography*, 3, 4, 371–97.

Wacquant, L. (2005) 'The Great Penal Leap Backward: Incarceration in America from Nixon to Clinton' in J. Pratt, D. Brown, M. Brown, S. Hallsworth and W. Morrison (eds) *The New Punitiveness: Trends, Theories, Perspectives* (Cullompton: Willan Publishing).

Wacquant, L. (2006) 'The "Scholarly Myths" of the New Law and Order Doxa', *Socialist Register*, 42, 93–115.

Wacquant, L, (2008) *Urban Outcasts: A Comparative Sociology of Advanced Marginality* (Cambridge: Polity Press).

Wacquant, L. (2009) *Punishing the Poor: The Neoliberal Government of Social Insecurity* (Durham: Duke University Press).

Waldram, J. (2009a) '"It's Just You and Satan, Hanging Out at a Pre-School": Notions of Evil and the Rehabilitation of Sex Offenders', *Anthropology and Humanism*, 34, 2, 219–34.

Waldram, J. (2009b) 'Challenges of Prison Ethnography', *Anthropology News*, 50, 1, January, 4–5.

Walklate S. (2005) 'Imagining the Victim of Crime', *Social Justice*, 32, 1, 89–100.

Waklate, S. (2007) *Imagining the Victim of Crime* (Maidenhead: Open University Press).

Walklate, S. (2009) 'Are We All Victims Now? Crime, Justice and Suffering', *British Journal of Community Justice*, 7, 2, 5–16.

Walklate, S. (2011) 'Reframing Criminal Victimisation: Finding a Place for Vulnerability and Resilience', *Theoretical Criminology*, 15, 2, 179–94.

Walmsley, R. (1989) *Special Security Units* (London: HMSO).

Walmsley, R. (2000) *World Prison Population List*, 2nd edn (London: International Centre for Prison Studies).

Walmsley, R. (2011) *World Prison Population List*, 9th edn (London: International Centre for Prison Studies).

Welch, M. (1995) 'A Sociopolitical Approach to the Reproduction of Violence in Canadian Prisons' in J.I. Ross (ed.) *Violence in Canada: Socio-political Perspectives* (Toronto: Oxford University Press).

Wheatley, P. (2005) 'Perrie Lectures: Managerialism in the Prison Service', *Prison Service Journal*, September, 33–34.

White, A.A. (2008) 'The Concept of "Less Eligibility" and the Social Function of Prison Violence in Class Society', *Buffalo Law Review*, 56, 737–820.

Williams, B. (2005) *Victims of Crime and Community Justice* (London: Jessica Kingsley).

Wilson, T.P. (1968) 'Patterns of Management and Adaptations to Organisational Roles: A Study of Prison Inmates', *American Journal of Sociology*, 74, 146–57.

Woolf, L.J. (1991). *Prison Disturbances* (Cm. 1456) (London: HMSO).

Woodcock, J. (1994) *Report of the Enquiry into the Escape of Six Prisoners from the Special Security Unit at Whitemoor Prison, Cambridgeshire, on Friday 9th September 1994* (Cm. 2741) (London: HMSO).

Young, J. (2002) 'Critical Criminology in the Twenty-First Century: Critique, Irony and the Always Unfinished' in K. Carrington and R. Hogg (eds) *Critical Criminology: Issues, Debates, Challenges* (Cullompton: Willan Publishing).

Young, P. (1987) 'The Concept of Social Control and its Relevance to the Prisons Debate' in A.E. Bottoms and R. Light (eds) *Problems of Long-Term Imprisonment* (Aldershot: Gower).

Young, W. and Brown, M. (1993) 'Cross-National Comparisons of Imprisonment' in M. Tonry (ed.) *Crime and Justice: A Review of Research* (Chicago: University of Chicago Press).

Young-Bruehl, E. (2006) *Why Arendt Matters* (London: Yale University Press).

Zaibert, L. (2005) 'Prolegomenon to a Theory of Punishment', *Law, Culture and the Humanities*, 1, 2, 221–46.

Zaibert, L. (2006) 'Punishment and Revenge', *Law and Philosophy*, 25, 81–118.

Zedner, L. (2003) 'Too Much Security?' *International Journal of the Sociology of Law*, 31, 155–84.

Zedner, L. (2004) *Criminal Justice* (Oxford: Clarendon Law Series).

Zedner, L. (2005) 'Security Liberty in the Face of Terror: Reflections from Criminal Justice', *Journal of Law and Society*, 32, 4, 507–33.

Zedner, L. (2009) *Security* (London: Routledge).

Index

215